Triumphs o
in R

Stephen,
with every good wish,
Walter

# Triumphs of the Spirit in Russia

## DONALD NICHOLL

DARTON · LONGMAN + TODD

For our children,
Mary, Margaret, Pat, Richard and Hilary,
in gratitude

First published in 1997 by
Darton, Longman and Todd Ltd
1 Spencer Court
140–142 Wandsworth High Street
London SW18 4JJ

ISBN 0–232–52191–3

A catalogue record for this book is available
from the British Library

Thanks are due to Quartet Books for permission to quote from
*The Brothers Karamazov* by Fyodor Dostoevsky, translated by
Richard Pevear and Larissa Volokhonsky (1990).

Phototypeset by Intype London Ltd
Printed and bound in Great Britain by
Page Bros, Norwich

# Contents

# Acknowledgements

I would like to express my appreciation to the following for their help in bringing this book to completion: my literary executor, Professor Adrian Hastings; my editor, David Moloney; Bishop Kallistos Ware for kindly agreeing to write the Foreword; the Revd Jonathan Goodall, Cecily Bennett, Bishop Basil Osborne, Wendy Robinson, Jim Forest, Professor Colin Richmond and Dr Frank Field; and last, but by no means least, my wife Dorothy, for her constant secretarial help and sage advice.

# Foreword

There is a Jewish saying, 'I learned the Torah from all the limbs of my teacher.' Donald Nicholl is exactly that kind of teacher. Although only on five occasions have I heard him speak, each separate occasion stands out in my memory as a *Kairos*, a moment of disclosure. And I can recall not only what he said but the way in which he said it: his voice, face and gestures, his total presence.

All of us ask ourselves, from time to time, what we would have wished to do if our life had worked out differently. For myself I answer: I wish that in my early years I could have studied under Donald. For he is a teacher who does much more than simply provide information. What he communicates – through personal contact and through friendship – is *scientia cordis*, the wisdom of the heart.

As his guiding principle in this present book Donald has taken a statement by Father Pavel Florensky which he himself quotes: 'One showing is worth a thousand theories.' Instead of offering an abstract, systematic account of Russian Orthodox spirituality, Donald sets before us – with striking vividness and originality – the specific testimony of particular persons, the witness that they have given through their life and, in many instances, through their death as martyrs. As he observes, theories and doctrines are not, in the end, the most helpful means of shaping human beings to confront ultimate issues; but living 'models' and symbols *are*, whether in the form of icons or of biographies, especially when these are set in the context of the Divine Liturgy.

The 'triumphs' of which Donald speaks in this book are very far from being 'triumphalistic' in any aggressive sense. They are triumphs of gentleness and Kenotic generosity – but triumphs which at the same time exemplify the truth of Dostoevsky's affirmation: 'Loving humility is a terrible force:

it is the strongest of all things, and there is nothing else like it.'

Three *leitmotifs* give unity to this book: compassion, freedom, resurrection.

First of all, *compassion*. In Dostoevsky's words, cited by Donald: 'The one thing in the world is spontaneous compassion. As for justice, that is a secondary matter.' It is compassion that animates the Russian sense of *sobornost* or 'togetherness'; and it was compassion that, during the Soviet era, made the persecuted believers stronger than their totalitarian oppressors. Secondly, *freedom*. What Dostoevsky proclaims, as indeed do all the witnesses included here, is precisely 'the religion of spiritual freedom'.

Thirdly and finally, *resurrection*. The source of Saint Seraphim's uniqueness, as Donald points out, was exactly his faith in Christ's resurrection: 'Seraphim, more than anyone known to history, embraced the truth that Christ has abolished death.' Equally it is Christ's resurrection that gives meaning to the strange yet challenging vision of the 'common task' which inspired Fyodorov.

Donald called Saint Seraphim 'an infinitely daring man'. Donald himself, in his thought and work, has also been a daring man. May he transmit something of Saint Seraphim's and his own boldness to all who read these pages.

BISHOP KALLISTOS OF DIOKLEIA

# Introduction

Almost from the very beginning of the recorded history of the Russian lands and peoples Russia has represented an enigma to the peoples of western Europe and even to those of the neighbouring regions of central Europe, for both of whom it has almost always seemed impossible to enter into meaningful relations with the people who dwelt eastwards of the great forests stretching south from the Baltic Sea towards the Black Sea. That world has usually been a closed world, as much so in the twentieth century as in the intervening centuries following the conversion to Christianity in A.D. 988 and the beginning of historical records.

Apart from the sheer facts of geographical distance and dissimilar patterns of trade, the main factor accounting for the separation between these two worlds can be traced back to the moment when the Emperor Constantine established a second 'New' Rome and named it Constantinople. From that moment onwards the peoples under the sway of these great centres of power, Rome and Constantinople, moved steadily apart and elaborated two very distinctive and different cultures.

In general terms one may say that the culture that emerged in western Europe centred on Rome bore the marks of the late Roman Empire. Most influential was the Latin language, which had been shaped as an instrument of government: adapted both to clarifying legal concepts whether in civic or ecclesiastical thinking and to establishing strong institutions for the enforcement of law throughout the cities of the empire, as well as for guaranteeing the orderly transmission of power from one generation to the next.

The mental disposition of Roman tradition and the Latin language was absorbed, inevitably, by the Latin Church, to use a term employed by Christians of the East. During the Middle Ages the popes in Rome, for instance, adopted the title *pontifex maximus* from the Roman emperors and established an extremely centralized ecclesiastical system, which enabled them to make appointments in bishoprics as far apart as Ireland in the north-west and Sicily in the south. At the same time the very need of the popes and secular rulers for men who could service the various institutions through which they governed, and who could defend their separate interests when they clashed, meant that the rulers had to train those men in skills that on occasion could even be turned against the rulers themselves.

In respect of such training the most characteristic institution of the Latin Middle Ages was the university, and the outstanding achievement of the university itself was the scholastic method of disputation. According to that method the only way one may prove victorious in a dispute, whether in law, in theology or natural science, is to propose one's opponent's case at its strongest and then disprove it. As a result any historian who studies the Middle Ages in depth is left with the impression that the whole of educated western Europe from the level of the parish, the town councils and the local law courts up through the diocesan courts to the royal and papal curia was engaged in constant debate about truth and justice, whether in civil or criminal law, natural or heavenly law.

And contrary to the impression conveyed in present-day popular education, it was precisely as a result of this disputatious habit of mind inherited from the Middle Ages that Europe gave birth to the Renaissance, the Reformation, the Enlightenment and the French Revolution. Indeed, all spheres of western European culture have been permeated by it to this day, as was strikingly shown by some remarks made recently by John Tavener, the contemporary composer, who joined the Orthodox Church a few years ago. He was asked in a radio interview whether, now that he had become Orthodox, he would try to introduce western musical modes into the Orthodox tradition. In reply he said, 'Oh no! no! You see, Russian liturgical music is a kind of icon in sound and it is wholly serene. That is what an icon is – serene. But all western music is argumentative.' In those words he was echoing a statement made by one of the leading practitioners and expositors of Russian icon painting, Leonid Uspensky, when he said, very firmly, 'This art is not intended to reflect the problems of life but to answer them.'

Faced with those confident statements of Tavener and Uspensky the archetypal disputatious westerner may in response, as if by second nature, point to what happened in the nineteenth century when such 'problems of life', the 'accursed questions' as they became known in Russia, impinged so insistently upon the awareness of a highly sensitive person such as Dostoevsky. For as his wife, Anna Grigoryevna, tells us, when in August 1867 he went to look at the painting *The Body of Christ* by Hans Holbein the Younger, he stood in front of the picture for ages transfixed; eyes accustomed to the serenity of icons now riveted upon a realistic painting. It is difficult not to believe that his experience of transfixion before that representation of *The Body of Christ*, which is starkly realistic and offers no hint of resurrection, is reflected in the words of Prince Myshkin, the hero of Dostoevsksy's novel *The Idiot*. When Rogozhin presents Myshkin with a copy of Holbein's painting the prince says, 'That painting is enough to destroy a man's faith.'

It would obviously be impossible in a short introduction such as this to enter into a judgement on the implications of the words of Tavener, Uspensky and Dostoevsky; but, at least, in a book such as the present one intended for the general reader, it is appropriate to refer to some of the issues raised by their remarks since those issues are ever present in the background to the story of Russian spirituality.

In the course of the endless debates between westerners and Slavophiles that raged back and forth among educated Russians during the nineteenth century, the Slavophiles, in a defiant riposte to their opponents who spoke of Russia being backward, coined the phrase 'the advantages of backwardness'. They did so in order to point to the wounds the human spirit had suffered as a consequence of the Renaissance, the Reformation, the Enlightenment and the Revolution, all movements whose beneficence no self-respecting educated westerner was allowed to question.

The Renaissance, for example, said the Slavophiles, is held

up for admiration by a chorus chanting a litany of artists' names, such as Raphael and Michaelangelo among others, ignoring the fact that the Renaissance was not primarily motivated by artists but by rulers who wished to establish their power in the form of a nation state. Hence the first texts from the classical world that they sought after were Cicero's *De republica* and Vegetius' *De re militari*, because such rulers were mainly interested in a powerful nation state supported by an efficient army for both external and internal use. Moreover, the natural science that was generated by the Renaissance was driven in the first place by the desire for weapons of war, whence the enthusiasm for the mechanical inventions that would guarantee victory in warfare. Scientific thinking has been dominated since the Renaissance by the enormous success of such mechanical inventions. And since it is characteristic of machines that they work by means of the pressure of one part upon another the parts have to remain separate if the machine is to work properly. Consequently, overwhelmed by the success of the machines, thinkers propagated the philosophical notion that the universe is just a great machine in which the parts, including each human being, can only have external relations with any other and cannot really enter into the life of another and share it.

Even in the realm of art a critique of European painting issuing from the Renaissance was mounted which denied that the much vaunted rules of natural perspective were the only acceptable ones. For naturalistic perspective can no more claim to be the only perspective any more than the Euclidean geometry on which it is based can claim to be the only valid geometry. Indeed, those naturalistic rules are actually far from natural since, according to them, all the psycho-physiological processes in the observer are to be excluded from the act of seeing – the eye is meant to look at the object presented as if the eye were an optical lens. There is no room for accompanying feelings or memories, such as are evoked by icons, for instance: the process is a purely external, mechanical one, having nothing in common with the *human act of seeing*.

Every word in such a critique of the Renaissance could be applied to the reign and work of the ruler of Russia who most clearly thought of himself as in line with the Renaissance of western Europe, namely Peter the Great. Nor is it any wonder that the city which Peter had built on the bodies of thousands of enforced labourers, his window on the West, St Petersburg, should have symbolized for Dostoevsky everything that is recti-linear, Euclidian, a vast parade ground, inorganic, unable to enter into the life of those who dwelt in the Russian land, an emotionally cold invention.

Though Dostoevsky was not, in the strict sense, a Slavophile, nevertheless the same tone as in his remarks about St Peters-burg and its 'Renaissance' founder is heard again and again in the Slavophile criticism of those other movements that were only now beginning to bear upon traditional Russia; that is, the Reformation, the Enlightenment and the Revolution. When the Slavophile Konstantin Aksakov, for example, made a tour of England he was appalled to discover how far the Reformation had drained the life out of English churches. The code of dress and the stiff manners in church, the class-based nature of the congregation, with the lower orders hardly being represented, all led to a dead atmosphere and total lack of warmth. As for the impression made by Continental Prot-estantism on many Russians it was scornfully expressed by Vasily Rozanov when he wrote, 'In their churches they don't actually worship. They have a lecture followed by a concert.'

Indeed, even though Tolstoy and Dostoevsky were such different personalities from widely differing backgrounds, their independent reactions when they found themselves confronted by the real consequences of the French Revolution, as opposed to the slogans *Liberté, Égalité, Fraternité*, were remarkably similar. Tolstoy first visited western Europe in 1857; Dosto-evsky did so four years later. Tolstoy's reaction is best shown in an incident that occurred when he was staying in the posh Schweizerhof hotel on the shores of Lake Lucerne and a small Tyrolian street-singer entertained the overdressed and overfed clientele of the hotel. After the singer had finished the rich guests failed to put anything in the singer's proffered cap. The young Russian *barin* was scandalized, and then himself caused a scandal by inviting the singer to join him in the hotel and share a bottle of Moët champagne. What had enraged Tolstoy

was the lack of brotherhood shown on that occasion, a lack
of brotherhood in the European bourgeoisie which he continued to deplore since they had merely appropriated the noble
words *Liberté, Égalité, Fraternité* in support of their own class
interests.

Four years later Dostoevsky was independently to make the
same observations: '*Liberté, Égalité, Fraternité*: excellent. What
is *liberté*? What freedom? Equal freedom for all to do anything
one wants within the limits of the law. When can a man do
anything he wants? When he has a million. Does freedom give
everyone a million? No. What is a man without a million? A
man without a million is not a man who does anything he
wants, but a man with whom anything is done that anyone
wants. And what follows? What follows is that besides freedom
there is also equality, in fact equality before the law. There is
only one thing to be said about this equality before the law –
that the way in which it is now applied enables, indeed forces,
every Frenchman to consider it as a personal insult. What,
then, remains of the formula? Fraternity, brotherhood. Now
this is a most curious concept and, it must be admitted, constitutes the principal stumbling block in the West. . . . It was,
however, found to be absent in French and in western nature
generally; what was found to exist instead was the principle
of individuality, the principle of isolation, of intensified self-
preservation, of self-seeking, of self-determination within one's
own personality or self, of a contrast between this self and the
whole of nature as well as the rest of humanity. And this
contrast was considered as an independent and separate principle completely equal in value to all that existed apart from
itself.'

Of course, the unmistakable note of exaggeration in those
words of Dostoevsky, like those of many other Russians who
criticized the West, is itself a sign that these highly intelligent
men were uncomfortably aware of the disadvantages accruing
to Russia on account of Russian history having taken so
different a course in the preceding millenium from that of the
rest of Europe. A glance at some of those disadvantages is
essential if we are to understand the advantages they claimed
as a counterweight.

The clue to much of Russia's history is to be found in the earliest chronicle, *The Tale of Bygone Years*, where we are told that in the year A.D. 859 the people of Novgorod, tired of intertribal warfare, addressed the Viking Rurik in the following words: 'Our land is great and rich, but there is no order in it. Come to rule and reign over us.' Truly the land is indeed great, extending for thousands upon thousands of miles, much of it without the sort of physical boundaries such as mountains and sea that provide natural security to many European nations. But that very extensiveness has been at the root of Russia's troubled existence: because of its lack of natural guarantees of security the people of Russia have throughout the centuries called for strong men who will, like Rurik, impose a man-made order.

However, that task of inspiring order has virtually always proved beyond the capacity of anyone called upon to carry it out. As a result there has been unceasing internal strife when one after another has failed and rivals for power have intrigued and fought against one another. Thus for long periods the fate of rulers was in the hands of *boyarin* who were supposed to administer the country but more often behaved like war lords. And when the country was attacked by Germans, Poles, Swedes and Tatars, and by the French Revolutionary Army under Napoleon in 1812, each of them putting the land to fire and the sword, there were nearly always some princes or *boyarin* prepared to help the invading power.

The resulting unstable, arbitrary, haphazard character of Russian life was accentuated by the brute reality of the climate, which produces periods of abundant rainfall and rich harvest suddenly followed by periods of drought and famine – hence the word *rasputitsa* to denote the season when sudden changes in the climate make the roads impassable. Not surprisingly these sudden, seemingly contrary swings of fortune have been reflected in the Russian temperament whereby after a man has committed some crime, for example, he may either 'burn down a church or set off wandering as a penitential pilgrim. No one could predict which.'

All the factors cited above inevitably affected the history of the Church in Russia and the special quality of Russian spirituality. For just as secular rulers in Russia were hampered by lack of stable institutions to serve them, likewise the Church had no structures comparable, for instance, to the Vatican or to the great European ecclesiastical establishments in Canterbury, Paris or Cologne, by means of which administrative and juridical skills could be developed and transmitted from generation to generation so as to produce habits of order and control over Church life throughout the whole of a country, and churchmen enabled to be influential in every area of secular life. Above all, through the lack of universities no great schools of theology were developed as at Oxford or Salamanca, for example, where for centuries the theologians formed the dominant intellectual group in the university. So when the first university, that of Moscow, was founded in 1755, no one even suggested establishing a faculty of theology. And when more universities were set up during the nineteenth century there was no place for a faculty of theology. The ministers of the Church in Russia had to be trained in seminaries or monasteries, a marginalized group of people with their own distinctive speech, dress and manners whose families were given to intermarriage.

Yet it was precisely at this point that those Russians who had become aware of the advantages of the West but had not been blinded by them came into their own and pointed to the advantages of backwardness. Inevitably, they were at first a small group of people, many of them landowners, occasionally princes or highly placed functionaries, soldiers or members of priestly families who had left the seminaries. What they did, briefly, was to examine the accepted direction of western thought as it had shaped the Renaissance, the Reformation and the Enlightenment and to conclude that these movements had also brought about such a narrowing of the western mind and the western heart that as human beings the westerners had become shrunken: they had sat so long on their own, in their studies, that they had lost the capacity for addressing the questions – those life and death question – that human beings are constantly asking themselves.

The crux of the matter was put succinctly by Dostoevsky on one occasion when he was speaking to an educated group about the need to learn from the peasantry. One of the group asked him, quizzically, what on earth could one learn from the peasantry? Dostoevsky answered, 'How to live and how to die.' Nor was he the only one of the great writers to give that answer for Tolstoy was for ever urging the same. And even the sceptical westerner Turgenev was full of admiration for the seemingly calm manner in which the peasants died: 'almost as if carrying out a familiar ritual', he said.

Nor are grounds for turning to the peasantry difficult to discern. After all, the peasants in their millions had for a thousand years been facing the most intractable mystery of human experience, that of suffering. Moreover, they had faced that ultimate mystery not as isolated individuals but as members of a community with a tradition of how to do so. 'To do anything in common is good, even dying,' was one of their proverbs; and it surely points to the origin of the Russian peasants capacity for spontaneous sympathy – that *zhalost*, pity, which led them to describe convicts, for example, as *neschastii*, unfortunates. It also helps to explain the seemingly mysterious way in which they managed their cooperation in working the land without any formal structure, a customary practice known as the *mir*, which so intrigued Karl Marx as a possible road to communism.

But the rich mixture of wisdom that was to be found in the treasury of the Russian peasantry would have been impossible without the leaven of the Spirit introduced by the saints who gave the Russian Church its shape and special ethos. In that sense it may well have been an advantage that Russian Christianity was not so dominated as was western Christianity by academic theology: an imbalance which has contributed to the fact that the very word academic now seems to signify a lack of reality. Theories and doctrines are not, after all, the most helpful means of shaping human beings to confront the issues of life and death. But models are: whether in the form of icons or biographies of the saints, especially when these are set in the context of a liturgy where the chorus of human voices raises the spirit of the worshipper. And all those advantages the Russian tradition of spirituality provided in abundance, whether through the glorious liturgy of resurrection at Easter or through the biographies of saints in one of the most popular of all compilations, the *Acts of the Martyrs*.

Among those icons and biographies none were more cherished than those of the saints Boris and Gleb who in 1015, independently of one another, offered no resistance to their brother Sviatopolk when he came to kill them so that he could be sole ruler of the land. Boris and Gleb were venerated as *strastotpertsi*, passion-bearers, who 'emptied' themselves in imitation of Christ's emptying himself on the cross. Alongside Saints Boris and Gleb stood Saint Sergius, whose prayers the people believed to have won the day for the Russian army at the battle of Kulikovo in 1381 against the marauding Tatars. Then there was Saint Nicolas of Pskov, the holy fool who in 1570 outfaced Ivan the Terrible when he was threatening the city of Novgorod with fire and the sword.

Of all this vast treasury of Russian spirituality scarcely anything was known in the West, not even in Church circles, until 1922. In that year Lenin precipitated a great exodus from Russia of intellectuals – Berdyaev, for instance, and Bulgakov, Shestov and scores of others – many of whom had become believers and whose writings were soon to become world famous as presenting the West with liberatingly refreshing alternative ways of addressing ultimate issues. They would not have been in a position to do that so effectively had they not absorbed the wisdom of the *starets*, the supramoralist, the great novelist, and the holy folk presented in the following pages.

# 1

# The *starets*: Saint Seraphim

The life of Saint Seraphim, and the wondrous incidents in his life recorded by those who witnessed them, together present the deepest challenge imaginable to our common-sense view of the world. And though it is easy for us nowadays to assume that it is only we of the twentieth century, with our sophisticated minds, who find it difficult to accept those incidents to be true, that is not the case. In Seraphim's own day – in educated circles and even within the Church – a profound scepticism prevailed concerning the sort of amazing stories being retailed about Seraphim. To take but one instance: the Metropolitan of St Petersburg, himself named Seraphim (who died in 1848), managed to prevent the publication of the first *Life* of Seraphim for some years on the grounds that the miraculous stories contained in it would be a snare and temptation to the faithful.

Indeed, Seraphim himself anticipated how difficult it would be for people to accept the stories as true, and he explained the cause of that scepticism: 'There is nothing incomprehensible here. The failure to understand comes about because we have wandered far from the spacious vision of the early Christians. Under the pretext of education we have reached such darkness of ignorance that now we find inconceivable what the ancients saw so clearly that even in ordinary conversation the notion of God's appearance did not seem strange to them. Men saw God and the grace of his Holy Spirit, not in sleep or in a dream, or in the excitement of a disordered imagination, but truly, in the light of day.'

Yet it is quite understandable that people should doubt the witness of other people to extraordinary happenings since with the passage of the years we human beings can even come to doubt the reality of extraordinary events in which we ourselves have taken part. Take, for example, what Elie Wiesel, the

famous Holocaust survivor, said one day to a friend. Wiesel
had been complaining that people have forgotten about the
Holocaust and are behaving as though it was not a reality. To
which his friend responded, 'Elie! Do you believe it happened?' Wiesel was taken aback by his friend's question and
then slowly replied, 'No! I who was there – I do not believe
it happened.' A similar doubt afflicted one of Seraphim's closest
friends, Nicholas Motovilov, who had written accounts of
Seraphim's deeds during the *starets'* lifetime. After Seraphim's
death Motovilov wanted to deepen his knowledge of the saint's
early years and so journeyed to Seraphim's native city of Kursk
in order to do so. He tells us that as he was sitting in his
carriage on the way back from Kursk he was thinking about
events in the life of Seraphim when he suddenly felt that such
things could not have happened. But then he remembered that
he had, of course, written them down soon after he had
witnessed them. So when he got back and checked his notes
he confirmed that the events had occurred 'not in sleep or in
a dream, or in the excitement of a disordered imagination but
truly, in the light of day'.

The fact is that many people can testify to the way in which
the veil between this world and an other world is very thin in
certain places or in the presence of certain people. Often the
places are those where, in the poet's words, 'prayer has been
valid', such as the island of Iona, permeated by the spirit of
Saint Columcille, or the cell of the fourteenth-century English
mystic Dame Julian in Norwich. Concerning the latter we
have a testimony from our own day to an incident that matches
many of the stories told of Seraphim. This happened in the
early summer of 1974 when there came to Julian's cell a blind
man, assisted by his companion. His blindness was due to his
cruel treatment at the hands of Japanese soldiers in a prison
camp during the Second World War. As he and his companion
knelt silently in the cell Julian herself appeared, bringing with
her the Japanese soldier responsible for the blind man's suffering. The dead man had come to seek forgiveness of his
wartime victim, who had himself been unable to overcome
the bitterness felt against his captor. What then took place
none can tell, only that the blind man was heard to speak to

his visitor in Japanese. Then, released from his resentment in the reconciliation which followed, he lapsed into an ecstacy of joy. The two next made their way to the All Hallows' Convent next door, where they were given tea by one of the sisters. In her presence, during the tea, the vision was repeated and the blind man poured out his heart in great animation once more in Japanese. The vision was for him only, and not for his companions, who saw nothing – though, in any case, the fact of his blindness indicates that we are not speaking of the ordinary channels of seeing. Understanding now the reason for his journey and knowing that reconciliation had been effected, the blind man left in great happiness.[1]

Nor is Seraphim's gift of *prozorlivost* without parallel in our own day. I myself, for example, remember vividly a certain Brother Bill coming to our apartment, his eyes still open with wonder. Bill was a seeker who had travelled the world and had met many gurus from various traditions but had lately been spending some months in a desert monastery. One day he managed to arrange a visit to an aged monk named Serafim. Now in his eighties, Serafim had spent the previous sixty years or more in the very same remote monastery which he had never left during all that time. He was not learned, and he scarcely knew anything about the modern world. 'But', said Brother Bill to me, his eyes wide with astonishment, 'he opened me up and read me like a book. He knows me far better than I know myself.' Yet that was the first time Bill had spoken with Serafim.

Truly 'there are more things in heaven and earth than are dreamt of in our philosophies'. And whatever may have been the limitations in the outlook of the citizens of Seraphim's native Kursk they did at least accept the truth of those words by Shakespeare, as the many churches within its boundaries testified at the time in 1758 that a third child was born to the Mashnins. The father was named Isidore and the mother Agatha. The child (later to become Seraphim) was baptized Prokhor, the name of a disciple of Saint John the Evangelist.

Situated at the confluence of the rivers Kur and Tuskara, the city in which Prokhor spent his youth was one of Russia's outposts, which over the years had withstood attacks from the

Crimean Tatars on one side and from Polish forces on the other. Consequently the 8,000 souls who made up the population of the city in 1758 were the descendants of soldiers, Cossaks, gunners, coachmen and clergy. But by this period they had achieved fame throughout Russia for their skill as merchants and traders in St Petersburg, Nizhny-Novgorod, Moscow, Kiev and distant Siberia. Moreover Kursk citizens took a leading part in projects to establish Russian settlements in Alaska and Northern California.

Isidore Mashnin was himself a brick-maker and builder who came to prominence in Kursk as a result of the fire which in 1751 destroyed one of the old wooden churches of the city, the church dedicated to Saint Sergius. The following year the city authorities decided to build a much more imposing church dedicated again to Saint Sergius with the Kazan icon of the Mother of God and subsequently known as the Kazan cathedral. The erection of this cathedral, based upon a plan designed by the famous architect Bartholomew Rastrelli, was entrusted to Isidore Mashnin in 1752, and was to be the overriding concern for the Mashnin family until it was consecrated in 1778. Sadly Isidore himself died in 1760 but his wife Agatha – a splendid woman, revered throughout Kursk for her warm heart, her care for the poor and her generosity to orphan girls needing a dowry – took upon herself the task of overseeing the completion of the cathedral. It was while his mother was busy superintending the work on the bell-tower one day, with the seven-year-old Prokhor alongside her, that the first dramatic occurrence recorded about him took place. He fell from the height of the tower. And yet, miraculously in the eyes of the witnesses, he suffered no harm. It was enough to lead the local *iurodivi* – 'fool for Christ' – to remark that it showed Prokhor to be 'one of God's elect'. The memory of that *iurodivi* seems to have remained with Prokhor all his life and to have influenced him deeply.

His miraculous preservation at his fall from the tower was the first of many occasions, according to Seraphim, that he was saved by the intervention of the Mother of God. She was to intervene again two years later, on the tenth Friday after Easter 1767, when Prokhor had been confined to his bed for some time due to a mysterious sickness which the doctors seemed unable to cure. Prokhor had already told his mother that the Mother of God had appeared to him and had assured him that he would be healed. Then on the Friday in question a religious procession bearing the icon of the Mother of God known as 'the Sign' was processing along the road close to the Mashnin's house when a heavy shower of rain fell and the procession sought shelter in the Mashnin's courtyard. Agatha took advantage of this to carry Prokhor from his bed and present him before the icon. Within a few days Prokhor was completely well again.

With such a family background it is not surprising that young Prokhor soon became the leader of a small group of young men of the city who came together regularly in order to study the scriptures and lives of the saints, and who were themselves moved to consider becoming monks. In order to discern their vocation five of them, Prokhor among them, set out one day to walk the three hundred miles to Kiev and there seek advice from a holy monk named Dorothei. The upshot was that all of them eventually did become monks. Three of them, including Prokhor, followed Dorothei's advice to go to the monastery of Sarov.

When considering the significance of the choice of Sarov we need to bear in mind the harsh attacks to which the Russian Church had been subjected throughout the eighteenth century. The State had virtually taken over the Church and had wreaked havoc, especially on monastic life, impoverishing the monasteries, arresting and torturing abbots and rendering orderly monasticism almost impossible in the Russian land. But when the persecution eased, the current of genuine monasticism began to flow once more in certain establishments, inspired in many cases by the revival of a mysticism derived from the Desert Fathers. One such monastery was established at a place remote from prying government officials in the great lumber forest of Sarov, on a hill below which the rivers Sarov and Satis meet, a place some forty miles south of Nizhny-Novgorod but at the northern edge of the province of Tambov. For centuries a stronghold of the Tatar invaders, in the early eighteenth century the site had attracted a number of hermits. Eventually a monastery grew up there which became notable for a form of communal life more closely regulated than was usual in Russia, a regularity in any case necessitated by the need to boost the monastery's income by felling the surrounding timber, and floating it down river.

When Prokhor went to Sarov it was not in the company of the other two young hopefuls who had earlier accompanied him to Kiev. Instead he waited until 22 October 1778, for on that day the Kazan cathedral was consecrated. Thereby was completed the life's work of the Mashnin family, and in particular of his mother. It was she who now placed around Prokhor's neck a copper cross which he was henceforth to wear every day of his life. At his death it was laid upon his breast. And when his relics, once stolen by the Bolsheviks in 1927, were discovered in 1990 the cross served as a guarantee of their authenticity.

## 1778–93: towards the priesthood

It is not difficult for us to picture the young man who arrived at Sarov on the eve of the Feast of the Entry into the Temple of the most Holy Mother of God on 20 November 1778. He was five feet ten inches tall, broad shouldered, strongly built, his hair thick and light brown, as were his bushy eyebrows, though both hair and eyebrows were to turn white in later life. His nose was finely shaped and people remarked how deep was his voice when he spoke. But what, above all, caught an observer's attention were his strikingly light blue eyes.

No less clear is the personality which shines out of the evidence we have for the following fifteen years as he passed through the stages of the monastic novitiate and on to the diaconate and, in September 1793, the priesthood. To begin with, he was clearly an excellent worker, as befitted a Mashnin, and could turn his hand to anything, serving not only as a sacristan, watchman and baker but especially as a carpenter. In this latter capacity he was to make an altar table from cypress for the chapel allocated to the sick and senile members of the community. And already we hear from him a note which was to characterize his actions throughout the whole of his life, the note of cheerfulness born of courage. Whenever the other novices, for instance, fell into grumbling and dejection as they were working he would always try to cheer them up by whistling or singing something to lift their spirits. 'There's nothing so blocks the Spirit', he said time and again, 'as gloom and despondency and downheartedness.' And on a later occasion when he was a hermit and he came upon two monks exchanging gloomy words he stamped his foot and exclaimed, 'There is no place here for depression, for Christ has subdued all things; he has raised up Adam; he has set Eve free and slain death.'

The source of such courage and cheerfulness, undoubtedly, was the rigorous manner in which he was faithful in his observance of the monastic rule. Not only was he among the first into choir but he would also stand alone before the icons, both in the church and in his cell, for many hours in silent prayer. Indeed his rigorous observance may well have been responsible for the illness which affected him, as it did so many Russian monks, through standing for so many hours at the liturgy, the illness known as dropsy. For three years Prokhor was ill, much to the distress of the monastery's abbot, Pakhomius, himself a native of Kursk and a man filled with affection for his attractive novice. The young man had lain on his pallet in his cell for eighteen months and Pakhomius was on the point of doing what monks only did in desperate circumstances, that is to send for a doctor. At this point Prokhor said to Pakhomius, 'I surrender myself, reverend father, to the true doctor of both soul and body, our Lord Jesus Christ and his most Pure Mother. If your love considers it appropriate, provide me with spiritual medicine.' Pakhomius assented. The liturgy was celebrated for his healing. And Prokhor began to recover. Many, many years later he revealed to a trusted friend what had happened. After receiving the eucharist, he said, 'there appeared to me in ineffable light the most Holy Mother of God with the Apostle John the Theologian and Peter. Pointing towards me the Sovereign Lady said, "Here is one of us!" She then placed her right hand on my forehead. And with her left hand she touched me with the sceptre she was holding. In that place, on my right thigh, a hole appeared. Out of it the water flowed. That is how the Queen of Heaven healed lowly Seraphim.'

In his desire to thank God for his healing he asked and received permission to go on foot throughout the country, in the company of his old novice-master, Joseph, to beg alms for the monastery and, in particular, for the money to build a little chapel over the cell in which he had suffered so much, and where he had received a heavenly visitation. The journey that the young monk and his elder undertook led them to his native city of Kursk where he had the joy of finding his mother still among the living and his older brother Alexis established as a family man, prosperous enough to make a substantial donation for the chapel at Sarov.

We shall never understand the Russia of those days, and the young monk from Sarov especially, unless by way of our imagination we envisage those pilgrims tramping day after day across the Russian land and meeting people of all ranks as they did so; because it was precisely that experience that enabled a monk to embrace in his prayers and his counsel the needs and sufferings of his fellows. As Prokhor was to say years later when someone quoted the judgement that a hermit, by withdrawing from society – or even from the society of monks – is behaving like a Pharisee: 'It is not our business to judge others.' He went on to explain that withdrawal from society enables a person to take upon himself the task of resisting the forces of evil, yet even the monk in his monastery is confronting evil forces in the form merely of doves, whereas the hermit faces them in the shape of lions and leopards.

By the time of the next journey Prokhor is recorded to have made he had been received fully into the monastic order and had been ordained deacon, receiving in the process a new name by which he was to be known in future, the name Seraphim (which was pronounced Serakhvim in the Kursk dialect). In Hebrew, *seraphim* means 'flaming ones', a most appropriate description for someone who was subsequently to radiate so much warmth and light.

It was in the early June of 1789 that Abbot Pakhomius took Seraphim with him to officiate at the burial of a rich ben-

efactor of their monastery. On their return journey they
stopped at a place which was to play a central part in the life
and destiny of Seraphim, the village of Diveyevo, situated some
eight miles from the monastery of Sarov.

Diveyevo in the mid-eighteenth century seems to have been
a turbulent place. The countryside was scarred by early
industrialization since settlements of miners had been introduced in order to extract iron. The miners were as rough as
their work and their wives often had to go labouring in the
fields of the local peasants to the neglect of their children.
Into this unpromising situation had come the widow of a
colonel, a wealthy landowner in her own right, who had
decided, on becoming a widow, to devote her life to serving
God and her neighbours. Agatha Semenova Melgunova, as she
was called, was advised by one of the elders at Kiev to seek
direction at the monastery of Sarov. Consequently she was on
her way there one day when she stopped to rest at the village
of Diveyevo. Sitting down near the old village church she fell
into a light sleep in which the Mother of God appeared and
told her that this was the place where she was to settle
and begin her monastic life. When she later told her story to
the elders Ephrem and Pakhomius at Sarov they confirmed
her in her intention. So she returned home, sold all her
properties, and began to live a monastic form of life under the
name of Alexandra.

Under the influence of this highly intelligent and well-
educated woman the situation in Diveyevo and the surrounding district began to be transformed. To begin with she
arranged for a new church to be built in the village, a stone
one, to replace the ancient, rickety wooden one. In the church
she placed a copy of the famous miracle-working Kazan icon
of the Virgin, which she herself went to obtain. Then she
established herself and her daughter in a building adjacent to
the church which soon became a focus for helping the needy
of every sort in the neighbourhood, a place where even the
local landowners and clergy would come in search of counsel.
Then slowly peasant girls gathered around her. Cells were
added to Alexandra's own cell and a little monastic community
formed – not yet a canonically recognized community, let it

be said, but one which enjoyed the approval, friendship and guidance of the Sarov elders. There were many mutual exchanges of gifts between the monastery at Sarov and Mother Alexandra's sisters, who made clothing for the monks and did their mending for them.

Sadly, however, when in early June 1789 Abbot Pakhomius and the deacon Seraphim called in upon the little community of sisters in Diveyevo they found Mother Alexandra lying in bed near to death's door. But they were in time to anoint her with the unction for the dying and to hear her last wishes. These were that they should take charge of three small bags containing some 40,000 roubles, all that remained of her previous fortune, and use the money for the sustenance of her little community of 'orphans' as she described the simple, unlettered sisters to whom she had been a mother. 'Dear mother', replied Abbot Pakhomius, 'I ask nothing better than to do your will . . . but I am old and God alone knows how long I may still live. But Deacon Seraphim here is young and will live long enough to see your community grow and prosper.' That is how Seraphim came to receive the charge that was eventually to prove the crown of his vocation. And though he immediately and ever afterwards remained conscious of his charge, nevertheless it was nearly thirty years before he was called upon to live the implications of it to the full.

Two days after this encounter in Diveyevo Abbot Pakhomius, Isaiah and Seraphim were called back there on 13 June to celebrate a requiem mass for Mother Alexandra who now lay in her coffin surrounded by her orphans. Surprisingly, Seraphim did not stay on after the funeral for the customary meal with the sisters. Instead, despite a violent rainstorm which continued for several hours he made his way along the eight miles to Sarov on foot and alone. The likely explanation is that the young man was conscious of the traditional warning to monks regarding women. 'Flee from those painted crows as from a fire. Often they transform a warrior of the king into a slave of Satan. The virtuous ones are as much to be avoided as the others . . . the heart of a monk is always weakened through commune with the feminine sex.' How utterly an older Seraphim was to gainsay such fears!

## 1793–1822: the vocation ripens

For the next few years Seraphim seems to have followed smoothly the path laid out for the monk to progress in the spiritual life along the monastic highway. We know, for instance, that he journeyed to Tambov, the seat of the bishop of the diocese, for there on 2 September 1793 he was ordained a priest and accorded the rank of *hieromonk* (a priest-monk). And there were already indications that the community of Sarov monks was beginning to see him as a person of unusual spiritual stature, like his older friends Pakhomius, Joseph and Isaiah – something of a *starets* in fact. But he himself was yearning to take a further, more dangerous step along the path of the spirit. He wanted to go alone into the forest, as a hermit, to outface the forces of evil in single combat, relying not on any earthly comradeship or human ingenuity but solely on the Spirit of God infusing his own heart.

An appropriate moment to do so arrived in 1794 when his friend and mentor Abbot Pakhomius died on 6 November, and was succeeded as abbot by Isaiah. It says much about the straitened situation of the Church in Russia that Seraphim had to receive official permission to become a hermit – as well as having to renew the permit each year – on the grounds that hermitages, like monasteries, were under government surveillance. The formal authorization ran: 'The bearer of this licence, the priest-monk of the Sarov desert, is retired to separate quarters within the desert by reason of his incapacity for communal life, his sickness and his zeal, and after prolonged probation in the community; and is retired within the desert solely for the peace of his mind in God, and subject to the prescribed rule according to the statutes of the Fathers; and let no one hinder him from dwelling there.'

The term desert was, of course, derived from the pattern of the Desert Fathers of Egypt but in this case it referred to the great forest which stretches some thirty miles from Sarov to Temniki. It was into that forest that Seraphim entered on the 21 November 1794, exactly sixteen years to the day since he entered the monastery as a novice. He knew full well that he did not know entirely what he was letting himself in for since he himself warned that there are two vocations that no one should try to follow without a very special, very distinct call from God: one is the life of a hermit and the other is that of a *iurodivi*. For both of these vocations, he insisted, one needs an extremely strong mind and body, because otherwise the attempt will end in disaster, like a man (St Matthew, 12: 43–5) who sweeps his house and clears it of an evil spirit that 'passes through waterless places seeking rest, but finds none, so he returns to the house he came from bringing seven other spirits even more evil than himself. They settle in there, and the last state of the man is worse than the first.'

The risky undertaking on which Seraphim was about to embark is known in the Russian tradition as a *podvig*. That is to say, the determination to surrender oneself utterly to God, not retaining any earth-bound attachment but to be set upon arriving at a condition of total surrender, no matter what terrors of mind and body one has to face and endure on the way. The place Seraphim chose as the arena for his battle with the forces of evil was a little hut situated on a wooded hillock overlooking the river Sarovka, some three and a half miles distant from the monastery buildings, further away than the huts of other hermits who also belonged to Sarov. The hut contained an icon in one corner, a stove in another, and in the middle a stump of a tree to serve as a chair. That was all. And it was here that a *podvig* was accomplished as astounding as any in all the two thousand years of Christian history.

Though we obviously cannot know much about even the externals of Seraphim's *podvig* the essence of what took place is beyond doubt. It is that for a thousand days and a thousand nights Seraphim stood in continuous prayer, doing so by day on a rock in the clearing round his hut and by night standing on a rock which he had manoeuvered into his hut. At night he slept no more than two or three hours and he ate next to nothing, at one period living on a plant which the local peasants used to feed on in times of famine. Named *snit* it seems to have been a kind of sorrel, and Seraphim used to gather it and dry it against the winter. Concerning the form of his prayer during this period we cannot be confident of knowing much, only that the source was the Jesus prayer which Dorothei of Kiev had urged him to practice some thirty years previously. Accordingly we can be confident that after those thirty years of practice the words *Bozhe, milostiv budu mne greshnomy* (God be merciful to me a sinner, or, more usually, Jesus, be merciful to me, a sinner) had become second nature to his lips and then in his mind until finally, by the grace of God, it had descended into his heart so that the prayer continued to flow through his whole being, no matter what he might otherwise be doing.

Almost the only account Seraphim was ever prepared to give concerning those days and nights ran, 'The hermit, tempted by the spirit of darkness, is like dead leaves chased by the wind, like clouds driven by the storm; the demon of the desert blows down on the hermit about mid-day and sows restless worries in him, and disturbing desires as well. These temptations can only be overcome by prayer.' And since we can hardly avoid imagining the scene of such a great *podvig* we are right to pay heed to an inspired passage from the pen of a woman who during the 1930s herself knew suffering at a concentration camp in the great forest of Temniki where she came to feel the presence of Seraphim:

Entering deeper into the realm of silence, Seraphim completely stemmed the flow of words within him. Not only the spoken words; even the flow of words that well up in the mind.

His prayer ceased to be a logical sequence of words. The name of Jesus, the essence of the constant prayer, ceased to be a word; it became the direction of his soul in its flight Godward.

When it reached the limits of the notion of speech, he entered a realm more perfectly still than any other. In this realm his mind was trained to hear the primordial word.

When the ebb set in, and human life was once more set out before his mind's eye as a concrete network of ordinary facts, the fabric of particular human lives appeared before him with its particular design; the pattern that every one of these lives should follow was obvious to him. Men's mistakes – intentional and unintentional, in the present, past, and

future – stood out as clearly discernible blotches and tangles.
They disfigured the particular pattern of divine purpose.[2]

After the ebb had set in the pattern of Seraphim's own life
now becomes perceptible to us. In a break with monastic
tradition he did not always wear the black cloak of the monk
but instead he usually wore a white smock favoured by peasants; and for footwear he adopted the peasant *lapti* made of
birch bark. He would rise soon after midnight from the sack
of stones on which he slept, using a log for his pillow. He
would immediately begin to pray the prayers in the monastic
rule (attributed to the father of Eastern monks, Saint Pacho-
mius of Egypt) until day dawned. Then he would go to work,
either cutting timber or cultivating his vegetable garden. If, in
the course of doing so he was bitten by mosquitoes or gnats
he would never kill them because they also were the work of
the creator. And every minute of the day the current of the
Jesus prayer flowed throughout his being. But not only was
his time suffused with the Spirit of God, so also was the space
he had established in the forest, which he transformed into
the holy land of Jesus. One spot, for instance, he named
Nazareth, for there he would go to read the gospel story of
the annunciation. There was also a cave named Bethlehem
where he celebrated the incarnation. Another place was his
Mount Tabor and yet another the Garden of Gethsemane,
while in every place there flowed the current of resurrection;
for Seraphim was constantly bursting out into the singing of
Easter hymns.

However, on 12 September 1804 the peace of this holy land
was shattered. For on that day, as Seraphim was busy chopping
wood, three men approached him. They came from the neighbouring village of Kremenek and demanded money from him,
thinking that the people who came to visit him must be paying
him for some service. But when Seraphim said, 'I don't take
anything from anyone' the robbers attacked him. And though
the powerful Seraphim, still holding his axe, might well have
defended himself, he chose not to do so but laid his axe aside.
Whereupon one of the robbers struck Seraphim on the head
with the axe and the other robbers trampled him and beat

him unconscious. They then tied him up and left him, as they thought, for dead. Going into Seraphim's hut they found nothing except two or three potatoes.

Yet Seraphim was not dead. He regained consciousness and managed to wriggle out of his bonds, then set off slowly, dragging himself towards the monastery. At this point a monk walking on the path came across him and ran to alert the abbot to what had happened. When Seraphim had been transported back to his cell in the monastery no one imagined that he could possibly survive. But feeling that they nevertheless ought to do something the monks sent for doctors to come from Arzamas. When the doctors arrived they diagnosed the patient to be suffering from a fractured skull, broken chest and ribs, to say nothing of innumerable wounds. In their wisdom the doctors proposed to bleed the patient. In his wisdom Abbot Isaiah disagreed. Seraphim in the meantime entered into a gentle slumber.

During the course of this light sleep Seraphim again received a visitation from the Virgin, accompanied this time by the apostles Peter and John. Once more the Virgin assured Seraphim that he belonged in their company, and then she departed along with her attendants. When he opened his eyes Seraphim was in a state of bliss, a state which, according to those gathered around him, lasted for four hours. After declining the help of the doctors Seraphim went quiet and then, to everyone's astonishment, he stood up, took a few steps around his cell and, for the first time in eight days, took a little food – a portion of sauerkraut and some bread. In spite of this miraculous healing, however, it was five months before Abbot Isaiah would permit him to return to his 'distant desert', for Seraphim was no longer the strapping man he had been. His hair had now turned completely white, his whole body was bent and in pain, and as he walked he had to lean upon a stick or his axe. And, as a consequence, he now came back to the monastery less frequently than before, a fact which may have contributed to a crisis that was now to shape the rest of his life.

We cannot know precisely what events within the monastery led to the crisis but we do know that it was precipitated in

1806 by the resignation of Seraphim's friend, Abbot Isaiah, on account of his prolonged illness. As his successor the monks elected Seraphim. But he refused the office, just as in 1796 he had similarly declined to become abbot of the monastery at Alativ and, later, the monastery of Krasnolobodsk. Such an office was not within his vocation. But the man who was elected, Niphont, the treasurer, was such a different person from Seraphim that the monastery itself became a different place, a place where Seraphim was made to feel an alien.

In temperament Niphont and Seraphim were at opposite poles, as can even be seen from the pictures we have of them. Niphont stands glorying in the splendour of his abbatial robes, wearing around his neck the crosses devised to show off his elevated place in the hierarchy and holding in his right hand the crozier reflecting the same status. By contrast Seraphim's picture shows us a bent old peasant pilgrim wearing the cross of copper given to him by his mother, and in his glance there is a touch of the *iurodivi*. This temperamental division between Seraphim and Niphont and its effects on the monastery were glossed over by the monks in the story of Seraphim right up until 1903 so that his canonization in that year should not cast shame upon the monastery of Sarov for having persecuted Seraphim. 'Abbot Niphont was strict. He disliked *batiouchka* Seraphim, and he liked us still less', said one of the nuns from Diveyevo. And her words, in a nutshell, not only elucidate the story of the last twenty-five years of Seraphim's life but also suggest that he should more properly be entitled not Saint Seraphim of Sarov but Saint Seraphim of Diveyevo.

It will be remembered that Seraphim had been entreated by Mother Alexandra of Diveyevo and Abbot Pakhomius to take care of her 'little orphans', the sisters, when she died. For some dozen years after her death, however, there is little evidence that Seraphim took much active interest in the affairs of Diveyevo, partly because the mutual help already established between Diveyevo and Sarov seems to have continued in a routine fashion, and partly out of prudence. The path from Diveyevo to his distant hermitage, for instance, ran northwards through Sarov, straight past the monastery gatehouse, so that the wagging tongues that are so frequently the bane of religious houses would soon have been spreading malicious gossip about the hermit's relations with the sisters. Indeed, Seraphim had very deliberately chopped down a number of trees and stacked them across the path to his hermitage in order, at least for a time, to distance the sisters from any other contact with him than the spiritual.

It is not difficult, of course, to understand why the Sarov monks, and Abbot Niphont in particular, should have been exasperated by Seraphim. After all, Seraphim rarely wore the *klobouk*, the hood that was an essential sign of a monk. Instead he was often seen bareheaded and almost indistinguishable from a peasant. Whereas Niphont was the head of a large establishment that was rapidly becoming a centre of pilgrimage for which substantial buildings were required, which could only be paid for by aggressive exploitation of the forest such as Niphont carried out on the grand scale. The idiosyncratic life style of a hermit could be a constant source of disorder and an occasion of scandal that would harm the reputation of the monastery.

There was an occasion, for instance, when a serf girl ran away from a nobleman's estate, clothed herself as a nun, and led a vagrant's life. When she was arrested she claimed that Seraphim had given her permission to do so. What was worse, the governor-general of Moscow became involved because his mother-in-law owned lands nearby, and he went into a rage about the incident. Certainly he was mollified by Seraphim's patient, gentle denial of the girl's story. But the publicity was something a busy and dignified administrator such as Abbot Niphont could well do without.

Among similarly undesirable events were the investigations of Seraphim's behaviour that led two bishops of Tambov, Bishop Jonas in 1821 and Bishop Arseny in 1832, to come to Sarov. On each of these occasions what had prompted the bishop's inquest had been suspicion of Seraphim's relations with the nuns of Diveyevo. And in both cases not only did the bishops dispel any suspicions attaching to Seraphim but each of them left Sarov convinced of the holiness of the calumniated hermit.

In any case, by the time of these visitations Seraphim was

no longer the constrained young priest who in 1794 had
refused to stay on at the funeral meal of Mother Alexandra.
Now he really could exercise the freedom of the children of
God. Commenting on the accusations he said with a smile –
impish, one imagines – 'For my own part I am not in the
least scandalized at scandalizing everyone', and then went on
to say that the greater fault lies with those who take scandal
rather than those who are said to give it. And on one occasion
when Abbot Niphont stopped Seraphim in the monastery
court and told him that his relations with the sisters could not
go on Seraphim bowed to the ground and answered him
quietly: 'You are a pastor; do not let yourself be influenced by
false witnesses; do not listen to what is told to you out of
spite. Life eternal is our aim in all things, so do not block the
way to it by pettiness. You are a pastor; let your words be
worthy of what you proclaim.' The man who could speak so
freely to his superior was all of a piece with the man who
one day, while working in the fields raking in the hay, took
Sister Praskovya Miliukova into his arms to let her down from
the rick she had set up – not an embrace advisable for the
average, struggling monk.

Obviously, however, it was no longer possible for Seraphim
to continue as though nothing had changed as a result of the
monastic crisis of 1807. His refusal to accept the abbacy
allowed Niphont and his supporters to take charge of the
monastery.

It is clear, for instance, that the principal reason Seraphim
had been chosen to succeed Isaiah as abbot was because, as
one aged monk said in later years, 'all the monks were his
disciples at that time'. But now that Niphont was in charge
Seraphim decided that it would be for the good of the community that he should cease to be the *starets* for any of the
Sarov monks. And in order not to be a cause of discord among
the brethren he would once more plunge into the deepest
silence. Therefore, that silence was a *podvig* not only for Seraphim personally but also on behalf of the community. He was
in no doubt that he would now be the object of calumny and
harassment. But, as he once said when explaining why he did
not wear iron chains next to his skin in the manner of many

ascetics, 'If anyone offends us either by word or by deed and we bear the injury in gospel fashion that is our hair shirt and that is our chains.'

What the gospel required of him in 1807, so Seraphim decided, was to go to a nearer hermit hut in the forest, no more than one and three-quarter miles from the monastery, and to live there without speaking to anyone, indeed without any human contact at all. He did not come out of the hut, for instance, if anyone arrived to speak with him. Should anyone approach when he was working in the forest he would throw himself face down on to the ground and lie there until the visitor went away. He even stopped going to the monastery on Sundays or feast days. Instead, one of the brothers used to bring him some food once a week, even in winter when the path was under deep snow. On arriving at the hut the brother would knock on the door and say aloud the Jesus prayer, at which the *starets* would answer 'Amen', and open the door into the porch where there was a small tray on which Seraphim would place a piece of bread or cabbage to indicate what he would like the next time. The brother would then return to the monastery having heard no other sound of the *starets* nor caught sight of him.

Not unnaturally questioners throughout Seraphim's life expressed their puzzlement at each of his several periods of long silence and Seraphim's answer was always the same: above all one should adorn oneself with silence, since Saint Ambrose of Milan said that he had seen many people saved by silence but not one through constant talking. Silence is the mystery of the world to come whereas words are implements of this world. Silence brings a person nearer to God and makes of him a sort of angel on earth. The fruit of silence, among other spiritual gifts, is peace of soul. As Saint Gregory [Nazianzen] the Theologian says, 'It is excellent to theologize in God's service. But best of all is when a person purifies himself for God's sake.'

Yet Seraphim's behaviour remained a rock of offence to Abbot Niphont and his confidants in the monastery. So in May 1810 they faced Seraphim with a choice: either come to the monastery on Sundays and feast days to take communion, or, if the condition of your legs does not allow you to do so, then come to stay in the monastery. This message was entrusted to the monk who took Seraphim his food. The first time he heard the message Seraphim made no answer. The second time he silently accompanied the monk back into the monastery. Seraphim did not, however, allow the change to interrupt his increasing communion with God. He went straight to his old cell, which was completely bare apart from an icon and its lampstand and a stump of wood to sit upon. He was to sleep either sitting against the wall or in the coffin he himself had made which stood in the porch entrance. And for the next few years he took on the status of a recluse.

The only occasions when he emerged from his cell were on Sundays and feast days when he did so in order to take communion. This he did always in silence and with bowed head. But such already was his fame that pilgrims and visitors to the monastery would line the route of his passage to and from the church, themselves standing in reverence as Seraphim limped past them. Yet they might often hear his voice and receive the word of God from him because in his cell he continued his long established practice of reading the whole of the New Testament throughout each week; and he did so in a loud voice which all who gathered outside his cell could hear. Moreover, not only did he read the Scriptures he also spoke commentaries on the sacred text, full of spiritual wisdom which both monks and lay folk imbibed.

Inevitably over the course of the years, with more and more of the faithful, high-born as well as simple, coming just to be near Seraphim, he eventually began to relax his rule of not speaking and he assumed once more his role of *starets*, not only on behalf of the visitors from outside the monastery but also on behalf of the monks. According to Seraphim's own words the relaxation began towards the end of 1813 or beginning of 1814. But the first specific incident recorded of this new phase took place a week after the feast of the Assumption, 1815. On that day there came to Sarov the governor of Tambov, Alexander Bezobrazov, accompanied by his wife. They approached Seraphim's cell to seek his counsel. The door was opened. They entered and said to Seraphim what was upon their hearts.

He himself stood in silent prayer facing the icon before turning to the governor and his wife and dismissing them with his silent blessing.

One senses that throughout these years of silent witness on Seraphim's part something of tremendous significance for himself and for millions of others was ripening. What that was emerged into the light some seven years later with the appearance of a desperately sick young man at the *starets'* cell door. From his own behaviour on that day in 1822 one can see that Seraphim himself could feel swelling up a tremendously significant wave for the future: it was a flow of healing that God was pouring into the world through him. The man who was to be the first beneficiary of that flow, Mikhail Vasilievich Manturov, was the landowner of Nucha, an estate in the province of Nizhny–Novgorod, some 27 miles from Sarov. Born in 1796 he had chosen a military career that led him to serve for a number of years in the Baltic provinces where he married a Lutheran woman, Anna Ernst. But a severe, mysterious illness curtailed his military career and he returned with Anna to live on his estate where his beautiful, intelligent and lively sister Helen also lived. When Manturov was brought to Seraphim's cell door, the monk, George, guestmaster of Sarov, witnessed what happened.

He tells us that Seraphim approached Manturov and affectionately asked him, 'What ails you? Why have you come to see poor old Seraphim?' Manturov then gave him an account of his illness and of how doctors had confessed themselves unable to do anything for him. Then, falling down before Seraphim, Manturov begged the *starets* to heal him. Seraphim solemnly and lovingly asked him three times, 'Do you have faith in God?' And three times, with lively conviction, Manturov confessed before the *starets* his unconditional faith. Then the *starets* spoke the following words of encouragement to the sick man, 'My joy [such was Seraphim's customary way of addressing people both in life and in his post-death appearances] if you truly believe then you must believe that everything is possible for a believer through faith in God. And since you do indeed believe then God will heal you. And I, poor Seraphim, will help.'

At this point the *starets* left the sick man sitting in the porch and went to pray in his cell. When he emerged again he was carrying the holy oils. He signalled to Mikhail Vasilievich to uncover his legs and pronounced the following sentence, ¦By virtue of the grace bestowed on me by God I cure you, the first of such healings.' Then the *starets* applied the oils to the sick man's legs and, going back into his cell, brought with him a heap of blessed bread which he stuffed into the sick man's tunic and told him to walk to the monastery. At first Mikhail Vasilievich was frightened when he heard the *starets*' order, because he had no control over his legs. But then, out of obedience to the *starets*, he made an effort to walk and discovered that he could stand firmly on his two feet in spite of the weight of the bread. In a burst of delight he threw himself down before the feet of the *starets* and began in ecstasy to pour out words of thanks to him. But the *starets* pulled him up and spoke severely to him, 'Do you really imagine that bestowing life and death is the work of Seraphim? What are you thinking of, man? This is the work of God alone who forms the will of those who fear him and listens to their prayers.' Then the *starets*, with great emphasis, added, 'Give thanks to the Lord almighty and to his most Holy Mother.' This Manturov did, and returned home completely cured.

With hindsight it is not difficult to see that the healing of Manturov marked the beginning of an outpouring of the Spirit as powerful and fresh as that which inspired Saint Francis of Assisi and his followers. And in order to trace that movement of the Spirit, of which Seraphim was the chosen initiator, it is convenient to try to describe it under three headings. First, we must consider the external events of this crucial decade. Secondly, a number of incidents in Seraphim's life need to be related which reveal what was going on beneath the surface of the events. And, thirdly, we need to reflect on what appears to be the special spirit in Seraphim's response to these incidents, a spirit which has particular significance for Russia, but also for all who are searching for the pearl of great price.

## Events from 1822

The first arena where the healing power of the Spirit most clearly manifested itself was in the immediate physical presence of Seraphim, whether that be his cell in the monastery or his hermit's hut less than two miles into the forest. It was to this near hermitage that Seraphim now began to retreat more and more often. Usually he would set out before dawn to hobble there, leaning on his axe or a stick, and would return late in the evening. He did so partly to escape the stifling atmosphere of the monastery, both physical and spiritual, and partly so that he might more freely receive those from all over Russia, of every rank, who came either in search of his counsel or simply to be in his presence.

For some his mere presence, silent or even sleeping, was enough, as for the student who tramped many miles to Sarov, burdened with doubt and sorrow. The student asked for Seraphim at the monastery but was informed that the *starets* was at his forest hermitage. It was a warm day, and when the student arrived at the clearing around the hermitage Seraphim was nowhere to be seen until the student noticed him, apparently asleep, in the long grass. For a long time the young man simply gazed at the sleeping *starets*. And as he did so his doubt and sorrow were lifted, so much so that he even refrained from disturbing the old man but simply turned round to take the long journey home.

Thousands of other pilgrims also found consolation and strength simply in Seraphim's presence during this last decade of his life. Often they were peasants. The peasant Vorotilov, for instance, comes to ask Seraphim to pray for his desperately sick wife to be healed. Another's workhorse is missing, whether lost or stolen, and he trusts in Seraphim's second sight to find it for him. Yet another comes to plead the cause of a friend who had died in a drunken stupor; and though strictly speaking it was forbidden to pray for such unfortunates yet Seraphim does so. Again, in 1831, a regiment is passing en route from the Caucasus to Poland and the commander, a devotee of Seraphim's, comes to ask his prayers for his soldiers.

Not that Seraphim fell into the trap of treating prayer as

magic. On 14 September 1824, for instance, Princess Kolontshakov visited him to ask his blessing and his prayers for her brother serving in the Caucasus having received no news about him for a long period. But even before she could voice her concern Seraphim received her with the words, 'You must not be sad. In every family there is sorrow.' Three months later she was informed that her brother had fallen in battle.

Yet it is fitting that the liveliest account of a meeting with Seraphim should be a memory of childhood. In the *Moscow Journal* for 1903 N. Aksakov, sister of the celebrated philosopher Konstantin Aksakov, related the following encounter: Having arrived at the monastery of Sarov the Aksakov family were told that the *starets* was in the forest. 'I very much doubt whether you have much chance of seeing him', said Abbot Niphont, 'at least not unless he hears the voices of your children. Take them with you and send them on ahead!' There were about twenty children at Sarov that day who had come with their parents. Everyone took the abbot's advice and they set out for the forest.

It became darker and darker, and more and more dense. We were afraid. Luckily a ray of sunshine shone through the branches, and with it our courage revived. Then we ran towards a glade bathed in sunlight; we saw there, beside a fir tree, a little hunch-backed old man deftly hacking at the tall undergrowth around the base of a tree. When he heard us coming he cocked his ear and darted into the thicket. Then, breathless, he looked at us and hid again in the undergrowth. We lost sight of him. Then all twenty of us children called to him in chorus: 'Father Seraphim, Father Seraphim!' At the sound of our voices he could hide himself no longer and his white head appeared above the greenery. Finger on lips, he seemed to be imploring us not to give him away to the grown-ups. He came towards us and sat down on the ground, motioning us to come and join him. Our little Liz was the first to run into his arms, burying her rosy face on his shoulder. 'O my treasures, O my treasures', the *starets* kept on saying, tenderly folding each to his heart in turn. Then, when he had to go and meet the crowd, we stayed and watched, lying on the grass. On the way back little Liz said, 'You know, Father Seraphim only looks like an old man, but he's really a child like us.'[3]

Yet it was as though Seraphim sensed from the beginning that the continuation of his work required some more stable base than was provided by the waves of enthusiasm which brought to Sarov thousands from all corners of Russia. And, by the grace of God and the special intervention of the Mother of God, he found such a base in Diveyevo, where he was to nurture a community of sisters. In that work he was blessed with three worthy collaborators in addition to the sisters themselves: Mikhail Manturov, the priest Vasily Sadovski and Nicholas Motovilov. There, however, he also had to face a malign enemy in the person of Ivan Tikhonovich Tostocheyev.

How far in advance Seraphim could clearly see what lay in store for the sisters at Diveyevo it is impossible to say, but there is no doubt that he saw the need for changes there since he had become a confidant of a good number of the sisters in the period after 1815. In particular he did not think that the superior of Diveyevo, Ksenya Mitchailovna Kotcheoulova, was an appropriate person for that office. An illiterate widow, she had entered into Diveyevo in 1796 along with her daughter Irina and had been elected superior. She was described by Seraphim as 'a spiritual scourge' on account of the asceticism that she imposed on the sisters in the form of too much work and not enough food and rest. He objected especially to her insistence that they should all follow the same very long ritual of prayers observed by the monks of Sarov. And though he always treated her with respect he did tell her plainly to stop behaving towards the sisters like a severe father but instead to be a tender mother. But since she took little notice of his advice he realized that God was pointing him in another direction.

He almost certainly did not see the goal towards which he was being pointed, but he had at least heard the direction when Mikhail Manturov paid him a further visit in 1823. This second visit of 'Mishenka' (the affectionate form of his name which Seraphim now used) was prompted by a moment of compunction in Manturov's heart. For back in his Nucha estate he had grown accustomed to his good health and become slightly forgetful, perhaps, of what he owed to Seraphim, and to God. So, mindful once more of what he owed to the *starets*, he made his way again to Sarov to be greeted by Seraphim with the words, 'My joy! So we have promised now to give thanks to God.' It was by second sight that the *starets* knew what had prompted Manturov. And by that same inspiration he now told Manturov how to give thanks: 'Now, my joy, give all that you possess to God and take upon yourself voluntary poverty.'

For a moment or two Manturov was stunned: the good life which God had restored to him, he was now taking away again. But Seraphim assured him, 'God will not abandon you. You will never be rich but you will never lack for daily bread.' And so it happened that on Seraphim's instructions Manturov gave his serfs their freedom and sold his estate. The proceeds of that sale he was to keep for the time being with a view to some later, undisclosed plan of Seraphim's; but a portion of the money was to be used to buy forty acres of land in Diveyevo where Manturov and his wife were to live in voluntary poverty. Seraphim also told Manturov to drive stakes into the ground over a specified area in Diveyevo, for that was the place designated by the Mother of God for a church to be erected.

What all this was building up to became much clearer when, to quote the words of one of Seraphim's friends,

in the year 1825, on the feast day of Saint Clement, bishop of Rome, and Saint Peter of Alexandria [25 November], the Mother of God appeared to the holy *starets* after he had returned to his hut in the woods. She ordered him to divide the Diveyevo community and showed him a new place for a church. A little time previously a landowner had presented the adjacent land to Father Seraphim without being asked, but of his own accord, for charitable purposes. The money for the building of the church was that which Mikhail Manturov had retained.

The significance of this last sentence becomes obvious when we learn what Seraphim said to someone who brought an offer of money with which to build the church, 'Remember once and for all that not every sort of money is acceptable to the Lord and his Holy Mother. Not everything that people wish to give me is going to enter into my convent. There are plenty of people only too ready to give, but the Queen of Heaven does not accept every such offer. Some money is the fruit of wrong-doing, tears and blood. We have no need of such money.'

Also, significantly, the Diveyevo community, now numbering fifty, was to be divided. Why? Because Seraphim had realized that in spite of the worthiness of Mother Ksenya and of those she had gathered around her, the community was too rigid and inflexible to be able to nourish sisters so sensitive to the Spirit as he hoped for. Admittedly many of the sisters had been accepted into the community on his recommendation, and for many he had remained their *starets*. But among them were widows, and he maintained that widows, having been used to running households, developed masterful habits and hardly understood how to live with gentler, delicate virgins. And already he had discerned a small group of the latter whom he regarded as the nucleus of the new community desired by the Mother of God. Out of the fifty sisters living in Diveyevo in 1825 there were eight upon whom he wished to establish that community.

However, not for nothing was Seraphim the child of a builders' family and himself a carpenter. He was endowed with great, practical common sense and realized that if his new community were to be genuinely free and independent then they needed a source of income to guarantee it. That is why he directed the chosen sisters to help him set about building a mill for grinding corn; and they spent the whole of the year 1826 getting the materials ready. He himself felled trees and sawed them up, planeing the beams and joists while all the sisters were given jobs to do as well. For instance, one of them, Ksenya Ilinichna, was entrusted with the task of purchasing the two millstones, one of which had to be brought from Arzamas. And so by the summer of 1827 the mill was in working order. As one of the sisters was later to report: 'When the mill was built it became our home and we slept there until

autumn on the two great millstones. They also served for our
choir and it was on them, also, that we learned to sing and
recite the Psalter. We still had to go back to the refectory of
our former community for our meals, which was a grief to
us. That was why in the following year Father Seraphim
told us to bake our own bread, which we used to bring him
to taste.' Seraphim also provided them with oil and wine and
candles out of the money given to him by pilgrims, in addition
to the vegetables grown in his own garden.

When religious groups become engaged in such building
enterprises they are notorious for losing the vision of the one
thing necessary (which is not a building or a piece of property)
but Seraphim never allowed the sisters to fall into that trap. At
every turn he listened for direction from God. So it was that
when Mikhail Manturov came to see him one day Seraphim
told him: 'My joy, our poor community does not yet have a
church, and the Holy Virgin wants one built, consecrated to
the nativity of her Son, our Lord Jesus Christ.' Moreover, in
his desire to emphasize the spiritual significance of the event
he insisted that the work of building the church should begin
on the feast of the Transfiguration (1827), just as it was to
be on the feast of the Transfiguration 1829 that the church was
consecrated by Archimandrite Joachim of Nizhny–Novgorod.

The visitation that the Mother of God had made on 25
November 1825 contained another instruction from her. She
herself made a circuit of the area around the site of the mill,
an area of some eight acres, and ordered that a deep ditch
should be dug along the path she had traced. Seraphim told
the nuns it was to be ten feet across and ten feet in depth.
Not unnaturally the sisters were reluctant to undertake such
arduous physical work; but they were galvanized out of their
reluctance by a vision of the bent-backed Seraphim himself
setting to work on it. They worked away with pick and shovel
for several years; and on the spoil thrown inwards they had,
by the time of Seraphim's death in 1833, also planted thorn
bushes.

There were several considerations that may have prompted
Seraphim to give the ditch around the 'mill community' the
rather fortress-like pattern that it received. To begin with,

the population around Diveyevo contained many rough, unruly characters; and then again, the sisters were naive virgins who needed their sense of danger to be quickened. But the main reason, probably, was to ensure that the community of the mill should have a firm sense of identity that would enable them to withstand the threat to that treasury of the Spirit which Seraphim had lodged with them. Because by this time Seraphim, in virtue of his spiritual insight, had clearly discerned a malign force approaching Diveyevo.

The malign force in question had materialized in the form of a postulant who came to the monastery of Sarov in the year 1820. A native of Tambov, born in 1801, his name was Ivan Tikhonovich Tostocheyev, though he was often referred to as 'the Tambov painter' because he was a skilful painter. Indeed, he was in his own way a clever man: too clever for his own good and completely out of his depth when trying to ingratiate himself with Seraphim. Seraphim, with the penetration of a fool for Christ, saw through Ivan Tikhonovich (Josaphat, as he was called in the monastery) whereas many others were blind to his real character. And though Seraphim never denounced Ivan by name he was constantly telling stories about the Antichrist, or performing puzzling actions, the significance of which only became apparent as Ivan tried to take over and destroy Seraphim's legacy during the course of the next thirty years.

Already, however, providence had put in place the very man destined by his firm, modest character to withstand the assault on Seraphim's work unleashed by Ivan after the *starets'* death. That man, Vasily Sadovsky, had been born in the same year as Ivan Tikhonovich, and soon after his ordination in 1824 or 1825 had come to Diveyevo as assistant to the parish priest, whose daughter he married. From the time of Vasily's first visit to Seraphim in 1825 we learn that Seraphim entrusted him with the care of the Diveyevo sisters, who were not entitled to a regular chaplain since they had no canonical status but were simply a group of the faithful who followed the daily services and encouraged others to do so. It is a sign of Seraphim's freedom from conventional habits of thought that in the following year he sought the advice of this young priest regarding the names of the little band of sisters who were to constitute the nucleus of the community of the mill. And it was similarly a sign of Vasily's maturity that he should have declined to offer any such advice. Nonetheless Vasily was to be the chief confidant of Seraphim during the last years of the *starets'* life, as well as being the leader in the trio who withstood the wiles of Ivan Tikhonovich. The other two were Mikhail Manturov, of whom we have already spoken, and Nicholas Motovilov who came upon the scene on 5 September 1831.

Nicholas Alexandrovich Motovilov was born in 1809 into a powerful landed family that owned estates in the provinces of Simbirsk and Nizhny–Novgorod. A sensitive, temperamental but highly intelligent young man, he had studied law at the university of Kazan and then returned to his estates where he was entrusted with a role in the elections of the nobility. He received the civil rank of state counsellor, was a judge in the tribunal of conscience of the province and inspector of schools in the district of Khorsun, a distance of two hundred miles from Sarov. Unfortunately he was afflicted with rheumatism and various other ailments so painful that he could not walk. He sought help from the famous surgeon Fuchs and from Hanemann, the founder of homeopathy, as well as from mineral baths, but all to no good; so he finally determined to turn to Seraphim in Sarov.

He arrived at Seraphim's nearer cell in the forest, carried there by four of his servants holding his limbs, a fifth supporting his head. They found Seraphim standing under a great fir tree surrounded by a crowd of supplicants. Eventually Motovilov was able to ask the *starets* to cure him only to receive the same answer as Manturov received: 'I am not a doctor.' But then Seraphim went through the same questions with Motovilov as he had done previously with Manturov. He asked the sick man whether he truly believed in our Lord Jesus Christ made man and in his most Holy Mother, and so forth. Motovilov answered, 'I believe with all my heart: indeed, without this faith I would not have had myself transported here.' To which Seraphim replied, 'Very well, you are already healed.' When Motovilov demurred Seraphim briskly stood him up, gave him a push and said, 'you can walk perfectly well without my help, because the Lord has healed you. Go on!'

There is, indeed, a certain briskness in all the recorded dealings of Seraphim with Motovilov which suggests that Seraphim was aware of the psychosomatic origin of much of his illness and had decided that a brisk manner was the most appropriate for such a one. At the same time he did not allow his awareness to obscure the fact that Motovilov was an unusually gifted person who would thrive on responsibility: so much so that there is an element of sacramental ordination in Seraphim's action when bestowing responsibility for his little community upon Motovilov. One day, accordingly, Seraphim summoned Motovilov to come to him and then explained to his young confidant in great detail how the community of the mill was to be nurtured and to flourish in future, explaining to Motovilov that it was the Mother of God herself who had appointed him to be the foster-father of the community during future years. Then the *starets* sent for two sisters to come, Evdokiya Efremovna and Irina Semenovna. He took each of the sisters' right hands and placed each into one of Motovilov's hands. Then 'he ordered them not only to tell him [Motivilov] in detail everything that the Mother of God had laid down [but] that all the sisters should conceal nothing from him. Because it has pleased the Mother of God that Nicolas should be named the foster-father of the community.' And turning to Motovilov he said, 'The day will come when only you and Mishenka [Manturov] will be witnesses of everything that has taken place in Diveyevo during the time of poor Seraphim and to bear witness that all the buildings themselves, erected during his time, have been his work under the mandate and guidance of the Queen of Heaven. Not even the smallest stone has been placed there by my own volition.'

From that moment onwards, until his death in 1879, Motovilov proved faithful to his charge. For by the time of Seraphim's death the number of sisters in the community of the mill had risen to sixty-three while there were one hundred and thirteen living in the Kazan community (so called on account of the famous icon of Kazan which had been installed by the foundress, Mother Alexandra). And by 1879 the two communities had happily become reunited as a canonically-recognized convent of some eight hundred sisters.

## Things beneath the surface

If we are to penetrate to the source of such astonishing fertility of religious life we need now to consider a few out of the hundreds of incidents involving Seraphim which, in one way or another, all point us towards that same source, the person of the *starets* himself. It may well be that an incident enshrined in a painting most dear in the popular devotion to Seraphim is as illuminating as any other. It happened that in 1844 a sister called Matrona Plechtcheeva came into a room where another sister, Euthyme Vassilieva, was painting a portrait of Seraphim, and Matrona spontaneously suggested that the painter should represent the *starets* giving bread to a bear. The subsequent painting, so frequently copied since, enshrines a story about which Matrona had remained silent for many years at the behest of Seraphim himself.

The story goes that at a time when Matrona was finding religious life very difficult she had decided to leave Diveyevo without saying a word to anyone. However, so she says,

> doubtless Father Seraphim [through his gift of clairvoyance] *saw* my temptation, because he sent me a brisk message to come and see him. To do as he said I went to him on the third day of Saint Peter's Lent, once I had served the sisters' meal. I was in tears all the way. [From Diveyevo to Sarov is all of seven miles.] Once I reached his cell in Sarov I said the usual prayer. [Russian monks do not knock on the door, they say a prayer out loud.] The *starets* replied 'Amen', came to open the door and greeted me like a loving father. Then taking me by both hands he led me into the cell. After which he said, 'Well, my joy! I have been expecting you all day!' I was crying as I answered, '*Batiouchka*, you know what my job is. I couldn't come any sooner. As soon as I had served the sisters their meal I set off to see you that same minute and I have been crying all along the road.' Father Seraphim dried my eyes with his handkerchief and said,

'*Matouchka*, your tears falling to the ground are not lost.'
Then he took me over to the icon of the celestial Queen of
Tenderness, saying, 'Come, *matouchka*, to kiss the Queen
of the heavens and she will console you.' I kissed the icon
and felt such joy in my soul that I was completely restored.
Then Father Seraphim said to me: 'So for the present,
*matouchka*, go to the monastery guesthouse and tomorrow
come and find me in the distant hermitage. [This was situated over three miles away in a wild forest; which meant
that Seraphim was giving her a day off work.] But I objected,
'*Batiouchka*, the distant hermitage! I would be scared to go
there alone.' Father Seraphim answered, 'Go on, *matouchka*,
and keep saying the *Kyrie eleison*, in Russian', and he sang
the *Kyrie* several times. 'When you get up don't go to matins.
Instead make fifty prostrations and then set off.' I did as
Father Seraphim had ordered; after getting up I made the
fifty prostrations and set off, singing the *Kyrie eleison* all
the way. And thanks to that not only did I not feel any fear
but my heart was filled with great happiness, because of
Father Seraphim's prayers.

But as I drew near to the hermitage I suddenly caught a
glimpse of Father Seraphim sitting on a stump near his cell
and there in front of him was a horribly enormous bear. In
my fright I fainted to the ground, crying, '*Batiouchka*! I'll
die!' When he heard my voice Father Seraphim tapped the
bear and motioned to him to go away. And the bear straight-
away loped off into the depths of the forest as if he had
understood like any rational creature. As for me, watching
all that, I kept on trembling with terror. Even when Father
Seraphim came over to me, saying, 'Don't be frightened,
don't be scared', I still kept on crying, 'I'll die!' Then the
*starets* answered me, 'No, *matouchka*, you are not going to
die. Death for you is a long way off. Here is a joy.' After
which he led me towards the stump where he had been
sitting and, after saying a prayer, he made me sit down and
then sat down himself. We had scarcely had the time to seat
ourselves before that same bear came out of the depths of
the forest, approached Father Seraphim and settled at his
feet. Finding myself before such a fearsome wild beast I was
absolutely terrified and could not stop trembling. But later,
seeing that Father Seraphim had no fear whatsoever but
treated the bear as if it were a gentle lamb, and that with

his own hands he was feeding it some bread which he had brought in a sack, little by little my faith brought me back to life. What was particularly wonderful was the appearance of the face of my great spiritual father; it was as radiant as that of an angel, and full of joy.

Eventually, when I had become completely calm and the *starets* had got the bear to eat almost all the bread, he gave me what was left and told me myself to feed the bear. But I answered, 'I'm frightened, *batiouchka*, that he'll eat my hand as well.' Father Seraphim looked at me, smiled and said, 'No, *matouchka*, believe me, he won't eat your hand.' So I took the bread he gave me and I gave it to the bear down to the very last morsel, and with such a feeling of consolation that I would have liked to have been able to go on feeding it more because that savage beast was also gentle towards me, thanks to the prayers of Father Seraphim.

Seeing that I was now at ease Father Seraphim said to me, 'You remember, *matouchka*, how Saint Jerome on the banks of the Jordan had a lion at his service. Well, poor Seraphim has a bear at his service. So you see, *matouchka*, that the wild beasts obey us, yet you are discouraged. What reason is there to be discouraged? Look! If I had brought some scissors with me I would have given it a monastic tonsure.' Then in my innocence I said '*Batiouchka*, what if the sisters were to see the bear? They would die of fright.' But he replied: 'No, *matouchka*, the sisters will not see him.' 'But suppose somebody else does and kills him? Poor beast!' The *starets* replied, 'No! They will not kill him. Apart from yourself no one will see him.' Then I began to think how I was going to tell the sisters the story of this terrifying miracle but Father Seraphim read my thoughts and answered, 'No, *matouchka*, don't tell this to anyone until at least eleven years after my death. At the right moment the will of God will reveal to you to whom you must recount it.'

Some time after 1844, soon after Sister Matrona had told the story to Sister Euthyme, the hunting of bears in the forest of Sarov was forbidden in honour of Seraphim. The prohibition was maintained up to the time of the Revolution of 1917, and no attacks by bears were ever reported.

There were, in fact, a number of other people who witnessed Seraphim communing with a bear, two of whom assure us that not only bears but also wolves, hares and foxes, lizards and all sorts of reptiles used to gather around his hermitage waiting for him to feed them. So the predilection of the simple folk of Russia for the painting of Seraphim with the bear should not be dismissed as just an instance of popular sentimentality any more than it is wise to be sceptical about Saint Francis of Assisi and the wolf of Gubbio, or about the prophet Isaiah's vision of the wolf lying down with the lamb and the leopard with the kid. All these are glimpses of what it will be like in the new heaven and the new earth, that time foreseen by Dante when the human heart will be moved no longer by fear and hatred but by the love that moves the sun and the other stars and, indeed, the whole of creation.

In these last years Seraphim was actually living in the new heaven and the new earth foreseen by Isaiah, so much so that he was able to bring good things from the new heaven and the new earth to comfort those who did not yet dare to live where he lived. For instance, he was constantly in his later years presenting little items of food to those visiting his hermitage; and they, just as regularly, would report that his gifts tasted 'paradisal'. That was the term used by Sister Praskova Ivanovna. And some words of Vasily Sadovsky explain why that term is justified.

Soon after the feast of Mary's Assumption [of 1830] I visited Father Seraphim. He was alone in his cell. He began to speak about the lives of the saints who during their life time have been granted different graces, including visions, and had even shared in appearances of the Queen of Heaven. Unexpectedly he asked me, 'Have you a handkerchief?' I handed him one. He spread it out and placed some small biscuits in it, of a whiteness I had never seen before. 'I have had a visit from a queen, and that is what was left over.' He said that so merrily and cheerfully, and his face had a transfigured expression such as I could never describe. Then he knotted the handkerchief, gave it to me and said, 'Go home, father, taste a biscuit, and give some to your wife and when you go to the "orphans" (the sisters at the mill) give each of them three biscuits.'

At that time Vasily did not understand who Seraphim was

referring to as a queen, but later he was to learn from the *starets* himself that it was the Queen of Heaven. No wonder the biscuits tasted so good, as did the raspberries that Seraphim gave him on another occasion, or the onion which Seraphim gave to Natalia Evgrafova, so sweet and yet so bitter, prophetic of the bitter sweet life she was to experience. After all, these gifts were gifts from heaven.

Never for one minute did Seraphim forget that for none of his great gifts could he take the credit – the gift of what the Russians call *prozorlivost,* for instance, which may be translated as insight, or second sight, or clairvoyance, and of which there are scores of examples in his life. One very detailed example of his *prozorlivost* is given by a beneficiary, a certain cavalry officer named Karatayev. Put briefly, Ivan Karatayev was passing near Sarov in 1830 when he felt drawn to consult Seraphim. But, at the same time, he was scared to do so because of his sins, and especially on account of his negative attitude towards icons: he could not accept that icons, the work of the sinful hands of a man, might be a source of blessing and be worthy of reverence. However, the pull of Seraphim's attraction overcame his reluctance and he found himself outside Seraphim's cell as one of a great crowd. Immediately Seraphim glanced at Karatayev and made a gesture to him to come into his cell. 'There Father Seraphim blessed me with the copper cross which hung over his breast, kissed me and then began to confess me, he himself recounting my sins as if he had himself been present when they were being committed. At the end of this consoling confession he said to me . . . all that we need is to stay constantly vigilant in spirit and to remember that although we are sinners nevertheless we are all under the loving protection of our Saviour without whose will not one hair of our head falls.'

If we are puzzled as to how such insight into another human being is possible, we are granted the explanation in an account by Anthony, a priest-monk from the monastery of Vissoko-gorsk. One day Anthony was present in Seraphim's cell when the latter was holding a conversation with a merchant from Vladimir whom Seraphim had never seen before but whose soul he read as if it were an open book. Once the merchant had left, Anthony immediately asked Seraphim in amazement how he managed to penetrate into the most intimate depths of another's conscience without even asking questions or waiting for confidences. Seraphim answered, 'That man came to me, like all the others, and like yourself, seeing in me a servant of God. And I, unworthy Seraphim, that is how I see myself – a poor servant of God, and whatever God transmits to his servant that is what I pass on. The very first thought that comes to mind is, in my eyes, sent by God, and I speak without knowing what is going on in the soul of the person before me, but believing firmly that it is the will of God and for the good of that person. Occasionally I have responded trusting in my own reasoning, thinking that the answer was easy. In all such cases it has led to mistakes. Just as iron is submitted to the smith, so I submit to the will of God. I do what he wishes. I have no will of my own.' But Anthony persisted, maintaining that Seraphim could see the soul of a person just as clearly as you can see a face in the mirror, on account of his own purity of spirit. At this the *starets* put his right hand over the monk's mouth and said, 'No, my joy! You mustn't speak like that. The human heart is open to God alone and when one comes near to it one finds oneself on the brink of an abyss.'

It was precisely by virtue of his obedience to the will of God that Seraphim was able to behave with what Saint Paul terms 'the glorious freedom of the children of God', often in a manner that those around him found disconcerting. Some were disconcerted, for instance, by the way he presented bread and wine to pilgrims which could be mistaken for the sacred species; others were scandalized when he gave permission to Sister Praskovya Semenova to undertake 'foolishness for Christ', as he also did for Pelagia Ivanova, much to the consternation of her husband. Then there was the occasion when a woman addicted to drink was brought along to Seraphim by her son who never stopped calling attention to his mother's vice. Thereupon Seraphim stuck out his hand and squeezed the man's mouth to keep it shut. After which the *starets* turned towards the mother and said, 'open your mouth' and he proceeded to breathe three times into the woman's open mouth. The woman was cleansed of her vice.

Sometimes, moreover, he could be surprisingly severe, as, for example, when some nuns from a neighbouring monastery were visiting him in his hermitage and they turned their noses up at the potatoes he was offering them because they had not been peeled. They would not eat them, as the Diveyevo nuns used to do. So without more ado the holy man drove the offending nuns away. However, there is one instance of Seraphim's confidence in his ability to respond to the will of God being taken to an extreme that even now remains shocking. The story of it centres round Helen Manturov whom we have already mentioned, the sister of Mikhail Manturov, the beneficiary of Seraphim's first healing.

Helen, the fun-loving sister of Mishenka, was betrothed to marry at the age of seventeen in 1822. But not long afterwards, influenced by her brother's healing through the prayers of Seraphim, she broke off the engagement and joined the community of sisters at Diveyevo. Cultured, intelligent and a forceful personality, she was the one who was asked by Seraphim to become superior of the little group of sisters who in 1825 formed the community of the mill. She declined the office because she felt called to pursue a more strictly contemplative life. Yet, at the same time, her personal attractiveness meant that she was effectively the source of inspiration to the other sisters. Also she wanted to be free to look after her old chamber maid, Ustina, who had decided to join her mistress in the convent but who was now suffering from tuberculosis. So Helen and Ustina shared a small cell somewhat apart from the other sisters.

By the spring of 1832, however, the tenor of Helen's life had changed. Ustina, whom she had nursed faithfully to the end, had died. And Helen's brother, Mikhail, was far away in the province of Simbirsk. He had gone there in 1830 with Seraphim's is blessing at the request of General Kuprianov. The general was even then setting out for the Turkish campaign and needed a responsible person to take charge of his estates and of the peasantry during his absence. Manturov and his wife had proved a blessing to the peasants whom they had helped in every way but, unfortunately, the district where they lived suffered from an unhealthy climate as a result of which Manturov fell gravely ill with malaria.

As soon as the news of Manturov's severe illness reached Sarov, Seraphim sent for Helen. When she arrived, accompanied by Ksenya Vasilievna, the following extraordinary conversation took place:

'You have always obeyed me, my joy. Well now I want to give you an "obedience". Are you ready to carry it out?'

'I always obey you, *batioushka*.'

'Then look, my joy. The time has come for Mikhail Vasilievich to die. He is ill and bound to die. But he is needed for the convent and for the Diveyevo orphans. So this is the obedience for you: die in the place of Mikhail Vasilievich.'

After saying that Seraphim kept Helen beside him for a long time speaking to her about the unending happiness of the future life. All her life, however, Helen had harboured a great fear of death, and she suddenly cried out,

'*Batioushka*, I am frightened of dying.'

'My joy', replied Seraphim, 'why should we fear death? For us it will be nothing but eternal joy.'

Nevertheless as Helen was leaving the cell after taking her leave of Seraphim she fainted into the arms of Ksenya. Within a few days she was indeed dead.

This episode inevitably raises the question of whether any human being may claim to decide who should live and who should die. In explanation of Seraphim's extreme demand it may perhaps be agreed that he was aware, through his clairvoyance, that Helen was already mortally ill. She had been infected through nursing the consumptive Ustina, and by transforming her death into an obedience from her beloved *starets* he actually made dying easier for Helen. And it is true that she who had so feared death did, in fact, die a peaceful and joyful death, enlightened by heavenly visions.

Even so the only possible justification for Seraphim's action is that he had by this time of his life responded totally to the promise of God spoken of in the first chapter of Saint Peter's second letter: 'God has bestowed on us human beings the capacity to become partakers in the very being of God.' And there is overwhelming evidence in his life that Seraphim had indeed responded with the whole of his being to the promise of God and become such a partaker in the very being of God. He had, therefore, in Saint Peter's words, 'escaped the corruption and lust which has infected the world'. The evidence to show that such a transformation of the young Prokhor Mashnin of Kursk had indeed taken place is to be found in the reports of so many independent witnesses to those occasions when Seraphim was transfigured in a manner which indelibly recalls the accounts in the gospels of the transfiguration of Jesus.

Most of these instances of transfiguration take place during Seraphim's later years, at a time when he is himself aware that he will soon be departing this life. On one occasion, for instance, he was speaking with Sister Praskovya Ivanovna (a most reliable witness) when he began to recite for her the joys that wait us in heaven, and in the course of his account he himself was transfigured. 'Father Seraphim had gone silent', she tells us. 'He bowed his head and placed his hand over his breast. His face was shining so brightly that it was impossible to gaze upon him.' A similar happening is reported by Mother Efremovna on the feast of the Annunciation, 25 March 1831. The subject of eternal life was also on Seraphim's mind when in 1830 the young widow Anne Eropkin came to Sarov on pilgrimage. She tells us what joy filled her when Seraphim said to her some amazing words about the kingdom of God. 'I could not', she says, 'repeat either the Father's actual words or the impression they made on me; I shall only say that the expression on his face seemed so extraordinary; a light shone from within, illuminating his features, his whole being seemed enfolded in the grace of the Holy Spirit and raised him above the earth. . . . It was as though he himself was actually living all this at that very moment, partaking of this bliss and enabling me to live it with him.'

However, by far the most detailed description of a moment of the transfiguration of Seraphim comes from the pen of Nicolas Motovilov.

One of the most striking documents in all Christian writing,

the *Conversation with Motovilov* or *Conversation on the Holy Spirit*
constitutes for later generations the high point in the *starets'*
life the point at which his life and his teaching become fused.
As a result anyone who wishes to understand his life or
teaching needs to study the *Conversation*. It is the point at
which life and teaching are revealed as inseparable, indistinguishable, each needing the light of the other if it is to be
comprehended. Such being the case, Motovilov's own account
must always be given precedence over the words of any commentator.

It was a grey day [one Thursday in November 1831], and
the ground was covered with a thick layer of snow. Great
flakes were still falling when Father Seraphim began talking
to me in the glade close by his near hermitage on the banks
of Sarovka. He seated me on a recently-felled tree-trunk
and sat down opposite me.

Seraphim then said he had been shown that Motovilov had
always wanted to know what is the true goal of the Christian
life. He continued, 'Prayer, fasting, works of mercy – all this
is very good but it represents only the means, not the end of
the Christian life. The true end is the acquisition of the Holy
Spirit.' But Motovilov continued to be puzzled by Seraphim's
explanations and finally said, in some exasperation,

'Father, you keep on saying that the grace of the Holy Spirit
is the goal of the Christian life, but how or where can I see
such a grace? Good works are visible, but can the Holy
Spirit be seen? How can I know whether or not he is in
me?' . . .
'God-loving one', replied Seraphim, 'I've already told you
that it's very easy. . . . What more do you want?'
'How I long to understand completely!'
Then Father Seraphim gripped me firmly by the shoulders
and said,
'My friend, both of us, at this moment are in the Holy
Spirit, you and I. Why won't you look at me?'
'I can't look at you, Father, because the light flashing from
your eyes and face is brighter than the sun and I'm dazzled!'
'Don't be afraid, God-loving one, you yourself are shining
just like I am; you too are now in the fulness of the grace

of the Holy Spirit, otherwise you wouldn't be able to see
me as you do.'

And leaning towards me Father Seraphim said quietly,

'Thank the Lord for his ineffable goodness: you may have
noticed that I did not even make the sign of the cross; only
in my heart I said this prayer to the Lord: "Lord, grant him
the grace of seeing clearly, with the eyes of the flesh, that
outpouring of your Spirit which you vouchsafe to your
servants when you condescend to reveal yourself to them in
the reflection of your glory." My friend, the Lord granted it
instantly – merely at poor Seraphim's prayer . . . So, my
friend, why not look at me?' . . .

Then I looked at the *starets* and was panic-stricken.
Picture, in the sun's orb, in the most dazzling brightness of
its noon-day shining, the face of the man who is talking to
you. You see his lips moving, the expression in his eyes, you
hear his voice, you feel his arms round your shoulders, and
yet you see neither his arms nor his body, nor his face, you
lose all sense of yourself; you can see only the blinding light
which spreads everywhere, lighting up the layer of snow
covering the glade, and igniting the flakes that are falling on
us both like white powder.

Motovilov then goes on for several pages describing to us how
he felt an amazing well-being, a peace which no words can
express, a strange, unknown delight in his heart, extraordinary
happiness, an amazing warmth in spite of the snow settling on
their clothes, and a fragrance out of this world. And then,
after a few more paragraphs of encouragement from Seraphim,
the *starets* said, 'Go in peace, and may the Lord and his most
Holy Mother be with you now and always, and from all ages
to all ages.' Motovilov continues, 'From the instant when
Father Seraphim's face became filled with light the vision did
not fade. The *starets* remained in the same position that he
was in at the beginning of the conversation, and this ineffable
light went on shining all the time he was talking.'

This conversation between Seraphim and Motovilov requires
extensive commentary, but for our present purposes no more
than two observations are, perhaps, necessary. The first is that
not only is Seraphim himself transfigured but so also is Motovilov, through an overflow of the Holy Spirit. This distinguishes

the present occasion from the ones mentioned earlier. On those occasions the separate witnesses saw Seraphim transfigured, but they themselves were not drawn into the transfiguration. In the second place it is noteworthy that when Motovilov asks Seraphim how he can know that the Holy Spirit is within him the *starets* does not give an answer in words. Instead he invokes the Holy Spirit, as a result of which Motovilov himself is full of the Holy Spirit – if he had not been he would not have been able to see Seraphim as he did. That action of Seraphim, the invocation of the Holy Spirit, needs highlighting if we are to reflect, however briefly, on his teaching, since it is an example of the ancient dictum that one showing is worth a thousand lectures, a dictum which is entirely in line with Seraphim's own deep conviction that a teaching divorced from life is worthless. He once remarked to a theologian (drily, one supposes) that expounding theology could be compared with dropping stones from a cathedral tower whereas fulfilling the precepts was like climbing up the steps of that same tower carrying a sack full of heavy stones on one's back. Hence it is not possible to construct a systematic abstract doctrine of spiritual teaching on the basis of the *starets'* sayings and the short observations which he wrote down at various times. His life is his teaching.

## Seraphim's charism for modern Russia

Nevertheless, the preceding account of Seraphim permits us to place some of his sayings in the context of his life, out of which they produce a note expressive of Seraphim's unique spirit.

To begin with, he says, you have to concentrate on the active life, which includes fasting, abstinence, and vigils. So, 'one of the things you have to do first thing in the morning is to sweep out your cell', adding, with his usual practicality, 'and make sure that the broom you use is a good one'. Prayer, of course, is itself a form of practice and can be carried out in combination with other practices; so 'whenever you are engaged in some work or other, or you are going on a journey, keep praying unceasingly, "Lord Jesus Christ, be merciful to me, a sinner!" And in the prayer keep your concentration: that is, gather your mind together and unite it to your heart. At first, for a day or two, or more, make the prayer with the mind alone, noting each word separately and specifically. Then, as the Lord warms your heart with the warmth of his grace and unites it in you into one Spirit, the prayer will flow in you unceasingly and will be always with you, cheering and nourishing you. This it is of which the prophet Isaiah spoke: "The dew that is of thee is to them a healing." '

But you must not carry out any of these practices so fiercely that you harm your body 'for we must look after the body so that it serves the soul well. If we exhaust our body to the point of also exhausting our spirit we are like madmen, even though we are behaving in that way so as to overcome our passions.' That is why it is a good idea to light the samovar (a Russian water boiler for making tea) first thing in the morning 'because warm water is good for the soul as it is for the body.'

There are many pernicious habits that you must refrain from if you are to arrive at a condition of unceasing prayer. For example, 'we should never judge a brother, even if we have seen him committing a fault, because we do not know how often we ourselves will be enabled to preserve purity of soul. As Saint Isaac says, "If you see your brother committing a fault, cast your cloak over it." By not judging and by silence the peace of soul is preserved.' Judging others is frequently the result of indulging in gossip, so we must remember that 'nothing so much as idle words has power to extinguish that fire brought by Christ and enkindled in men's hearts by the Holy Spirit.' This prohibition of idle words is especially necessary when it comes to the secrets of one's own heart: 'You should not open your heart if it is not necessary to do so. Only one person in a thousand is capable of preserving your secret. How can we hope that another person will guard our secret when we are incapable of guarding it ourselves? By every means possible we should strive to maintain inward guard over the spiritual gifts we have received; otherwise we may lose them and never again recover them. However, if necessity

requires it and the right moment comes, then we may reveal
them for the glory of God.'

Failure to observe such prohibitions results in a condition
that Seraphim time and time again castigated as the main block
to the Spirit, a condition 'born of faintness of soul, idleness
and vain speech': that is, despondency. 'For despondency is a
worm gnawing at the heart . . . and just as a pale complexion
betrays sickness so despondency reveals someone still mixed up
in his passions. It is cured by prayer, by abstaining from idle
speech, by working with our hands as far as our strength
allows, by reading the word of God, and by patience.'

What signs are there, then, to be seen and felt that indicate
that the practices we are undertaking and our abstentions are
bringing us closer to what Seraphim defined as the goal of
our lives; that is, the acquisition of the Holy Spirit? Beyond a
doubt all the signs point to the same experience – a real
change in one's heart, a change expressed by Seraphim himself
on one occasion when referring to a time spent before the
altar of the Lord: 'My heart melted in the heat of that ineffable
joy.' That melting of the heart took place because 'God is fire
which warms and inflames the heart and soul. So if we ever
feel coldness in our hearts then that coldness comes from the
devil, which means we have to call on the Lord who will
come and warm our hearts with perfect love not only for him
but also for our neighbour. And in the face of the warmth
the coldness brought by the hater of good will disappear.' For
'when mind and heart are united in prayer and the soul is
wholly concentrated in a single desire for God then the heart
grows warm and the light of Christ begins to shine and fills
the inner man with peace and joy.'

'The devil', says Seraphim, 'is cold'; and without the divine
fire 'the human heart grows cold and becomes like an icicle.'
No wonder he once said of his persecutor Ivan Tikhonovich,
'Ivan is cold. All his life his heart will be cold towards others.'
But those whose hearts are melted love not only God but also
their neighbours in peace and joy. 'My joy, I implore you',
Seraphim said to one devotee, 'acquire the spirit of peace. The
man in possession of that spirit is not troubled by anything.
He is as if deaf and dumb, and even dead when he is battered

by the sorrows, calumnies and persecutions such as any Christian who wishes to follow Christ has to endure and go through. Because it is by way of many trials that we have to enter the kingdom of heaven, where there is found eternal joy, victory and celebration.' But then, emphasizing that the victory is not one for the victor alone, Seraphim adds, 'Acquire the spirit of peace within you and thousands beside you will find salvation.'

Many of these counsels set out above can be matched with similar statements from the Fathers of the Church and the mystics, but Seraphim's teaching is distinguished by one characteristic for which it is not easy to find a parallel in the Christian tradition, other than Saint Francis of Assisi. That distinguishing feature is the note of tender, motherly love which is to be heard in all his doings and sayings.

Naturally this motherly tenderness so characteristic of Seraphim is most clearly manifested in the way he behaved towards the 'orphans' of Diveyevo, of whom he asked that they should address him not with the slightly distancing 'you' but with the 'thou' that allows familiarity. Ksenya Vasilievna Pulkova, for instance, writes,

> Speaking in general of the future, and of the universal weakness of mankind at the end, especially of our female weakness, *batiouchka* ordered us not to exhaust ourselves with fasting beyond our strength, as is the old custom. Rather, *batiouchka* told us to fear above all, and to run away from as from fire, and to protect ourselves from the very worst state – that is, despondency. 'There is no worse sin, Mother, and nothing more awful and perilous than the spirit of despondency', so Father Seraphim used to say, and that was why he told us – indeed ordered us – to be well fed and eat as much as we like, even to take bread with us to work. 'Put a piece of bread in your pocket', he said, 'and then when you get tired take a bite and set to work again.' Even at night, so he told us, put a piece under your pillows. 'When you fall into despondency and you can't stop worrying', he said, 'take the bread, Mother, and eat, and your despondency will pass; the bread will drive it away and give you good dreams after your hard toil.' That is why

*batiouchka* strictly forbade that anyone should be refused bread at any time.

But it was not only towards the Diveyevo 'orphans', or even towards women, that Seraphim reached a gentle hand. He recommended the same gentleness towards the monks of Vissokogorsk on the part of the superior, Anthony.

> Be a mother to your monks rather than a father. Every superior must act – and continue to act – towards his monks like an understanding mother. A loving mother does not live for herself but for her children. She supports the infirm in their infirmities with her love. She cleanses those who have become dirty, washing them calmly and gently; she dresses them in clothes that are clean and new; she warms them and then warms them again, feeding them, consoling them and trying to make sure that never the least complaint is heard from them. . . . That is how every superior should behave towards his flock, forever attentive to their needs, safeguarding their peace of mind so as never to hear from them any moan or complaint. Then they, on their part, will do their best to guarantee peace and tranquillity for their superior.

And with a wisdom rare in that epoch Seraphim warns us against being harsh towards ourselves, saying, 'A man has to be lenient with his own soul in her weaknesses and imperfections and suffer her failings, just as he suffers the failings of others – though he must not become idle, but must encourage himself to better things.' Similarly he used to tell penitents in middle life not to fall into despair at their constant failings:

> The middle of a man's life, when his worldly passions have full sway, matters least. At that time he only needs to learn indifference to success and failure, to his own happiness or unhappiness, so that he may step out from all these tribulations overshadowed by the still wings of muted joy. But in the beginning, as well as towards the end of life, every trifle is of the greatest importance.

He was the gentlest of confessors and it was typical that his very last words to his devoted friend and supporter Vasily, the confessor to the sisters of Diveyevo, should be on this matter.

'He urged me', writes Vasily, 'to be as tolerant as possible in the confessional, as I always have been, in spite of the critics.'

The preceding illustrations are an attempt to show how motherly tenderness might well be claimed as the note most characteristic of Seraphim's spirituality. And yet, as we circle around Seraphim, trying to penetrate to the secret of his holiness, one might very well claim other notes to be most characteristic. The note of joy, for instance, in view of his habit of greeting people with the words 'My joy! Christ is risen before embracing and kissing them. And did he not refer to his favourite icon as 'Joy of all joys': an icon not usual in the Russian tradition since it represents the Virgin Bride with no Christ-child present? It was the icon he kept in his cell at Sarov, and the one that he left to the sisters of Diveyevo at his death.

But, then, one might claim that determination is the clue to his secret, since when asked once how it is that we seem unable to live such holy lives as the Christians of old, Seraphim replied, 'It is because we lack the determination to do so. If we were resolutely determined as they were we would live like them, since the grace that God bestows upon those who seek him does not change.' And the same claim could be made for silence as the clue, or for freedom, or for his lightness which so accorded with his name in Hebrew – 'the flame'.

Yet all these characteristics are themselves only clues to the secret of Seraphim's uniqueness. The source of that uniqueness, surely, lies in the fact that Seraphim, more than anyone known to history, embraced the truth that Christ has abolished death; and so, even now, amidst this world and the flesh, Christians are already called to live the risen life, in communion with God and all his saints. The veil separating this present world from the reality of the kingdom of heaven has been torn in two for those who accept that Jesus is the first fruit of the resurrection and that it is up to all humanity to celebrate his victory and follow in his wake. Everything in Seraphim's life, his capacity for joy, for silence, for healing and gentleness, for freedom and peace, and the capacity to serve as a light for others, all come from the risen life which he had embraced. Even during the period of his greatest trial when he stood for a thousand days and nights, praying without ceasing in the dark forest, winter and summer alike, subjected to endless assaults on his mind and body, he never experienced gloom and despondency because he faced those assaults as a victorious, risen follower of Christ.

The theme of resurrection is dominant even in the midst of the dark future and terrible fate that he predicted for Russia. He predicted that the Tsar would come to Sarov with all his family and that the great bell of the Kremlin would go 'Boom! boom!' on that day, and that contrary to all the liturgical rubrics the Resurrection would be celebrated in the middle of summer. Again, on the very last day of his life, he transcended the limitations of the Church calendar, according to his helper Brother Paul. The day was close to Christmas, 1 January 1833, but throughout the whole evening Brother Paul heard Seraphim in the next cell singing hymns of the Easter victory: 'We have seen Christ's resurrection, let us worship the Lord Jesus!', 'Shine, shine new Jerusalem, for the glory of the Lord has risen upon you!' 'O Passover, great and most holy, O Christ, O Wisdom, Word and Power of God! Grant that we may more perfectly take of you in the day that knows no end, in your Kingdom!' Seraphim's final legacy to Brother Paul, to Russia and to the world was one of the risen life.

Indeed one of the most precious scraps of paper left by him underlines his faith in a risen life that is not to be hemmed in by the limitations of the visible world. Written by his own hand it is addressed in the first place to the sisters of Diveyevo but through them to all of us, of course, and it reads: 'When I am dead, come to my grave. Come whenever you have time, the oftener the better. Whatever is on your soul, no matter what may have happened to you, come to me and bring all your grief to my grave. Speak just as you do to the living. All your sorrow will pass away. For you I am living and shall be for ever.'

## The canonization and beyond

How very much Seraphim was living for Diveyevo, Sarov and all Russia was demonstrated after the passage of seventy years when in July 1903 300,000 of the Russian people flocked to Sarov by every means – by car, by cart, by boat, on horse and on foot – in order to celebrate the canonization of Seraphim. From the moment on 3 July when the metropolitan bishop of Moscow conducted the ablution of Seraphim's relics until sixteen days later, 19 July, the actual day of the canonization ceremony, the area around Diveyevo and Sarov was transformed into a vast camp. Sheds and tents were erected to receive the pilgrims; shops and stalls were set up so that everyone could be fed, and from morning until nightfall the sun shone as the faithful attended endless acts of devotion stretching even into the depths of the night. On 17 July the tsar arrived accompanied by the tsaritsa and many members of their family as well as companies of courtiers. It was the last time that Russia was at ease with itself before the storms of revolution broke over the land.

The years that stretched between Seraphim's death and his canonization had not provided for his flock a period of tranquil growth towards his moment of triumph. On the contrary they had witnessed a titanic struggle between the true devotees of the *starets* on one side, and on the other Ivan Tikhonov and all those sisters, nobles and hierarchs whom he had managed to seduce.

Even before Seraphim's death Tikhonov had succeeded in ingratiating himself into the Kazan community at Diveyevo through his skill as a choirmaster and his gifts as a painter: even sending some sisters to Moscow to learn the art of icon painting. Also from the beginning he realized that the sisters at the mill, along with Vasily, Motovilov and Manturova, had been forewarned by Seraphim about the evil plans of the painter of Tambov. And so, through the influence of certain gullible members of the nobility and their money, he managed to amalgamate the community of the mill with the sisters of the Kazan church in 1842 and, at least for a time, to install as superior of the amalgamated community a weak sister whom he could manipulate.

For the following twenty years the struggle continued between Ivan Tikhonov and his party on one side and, on the other, the devotees of Seraphim who were sometimes near to despair – though buoyed up always by a *iurodivi*, Pelagia, who was capable of disconcerting any bully no matter what his status. In May 1861 it seemed as though Seraphim's cause was lost because the Holy Synod of Russia had been persuaded to raise the community of Diveyevo to the rank of a monastery, thus allowing the local archbishop, Nectary of Nizhny-Novgorod, a friend of Tikhonov's, to install a superior wholly under the latter's thumb.

But at this very point of greatest danger to Seraphim's cause Tikhonov's schemes began to unravel. To begin with Archbishop Nectary was shaken in to second thoughts by the folly for Christ that he encountered in Diveyevo. On one occasion, for instance, as he was travelling in his carriage he noticed Pelagia sitting by the roadside and, knowing her reputation for sanctity, he stepped down to greet her. But she turned away from him. Then, since he would not go away she stood up and calmly slapped him on the cheek. He, mindful of the gospel injunction, turned the other cheek. But she simply said, 'One is enough for you', and took her leave.

And then, by a miraculous series of coincidences, Motovilov, on a visit to the Lavra of Saint Sergius, was able to convince Metropolitan Philaret of Moscow of the true state of affairs in Diveyevo. The very next day Metropolitan Philaret was dining with Tsar Alexander II when the affair of Diveyevo came up in conversation, which gave the Metropolitan the opportunity to disabuse the Tsar and the courtiers of their illusions concerning the painter of Tambov. As a result, in November 1861 Ivan Tikhonov was forbidden to set foot in the territory of Diveyevo. Nectary was moved to another diocese and the monastery was placed under the jurisdiction of Archbishop Theophan of Tambov, a man of the deepest spirituality. A gifted, highly-cultured sister of the noble Uchakov family was elected superior. She, under the name of Mother Mary, was to preside over the community for over forty years, including the year of Seraphim's canonization. By the time of her death the monastery, numbering over nine hundred sisters, was a magnificent complex of buildings and a vibrant centre of spiritual life, a magnet for thousands upon thousands of pilgrims.

Not everyone in Russia was delighted by the celebrations of 1903. In fact the most authorative ecclesiastical tribunal in Russia, the Holy Synod, was reluctant to sanction Seraphim's canonization; the head of it had no liking for what he described as 'the consecration of peasant ignorance'. Nor were the intelligentsia in general much impressed at the time, with even the religiously-inclined Dmitri Merezhkovsky writing scornful words about Seraphim. And yet it was not long before Seraphim began to win the hearts of many intellectuals. One of the most turbulent of them, Vasily Rozanov, visited Diveyevo soon after the canonization and reflected that in the period of Napoleon, Metternich and the great congresses, and at a time when Pushkin and Byron were being celebrated, 'there lived in these forests a man who revealed an amazing resurrection of that serene contemplative spirit which had been alive in the Lybian and Syrian deserts in the second, third and fourth centuries'. Rozanov was overcome, moreover, by that same contemplative spirit which he saw shining in the faces and in the gestures of the sisters, the 'orphans' of Diveyevo. The joy and goodness streaming from their faces seemed to Rozanov a reflection of the joy and goodness of paradise before the Fall. All of this had been engendered through Seraphim.

During the 1920s, in fact, some of the leading intellectuals still left in Russia formed a Brotherhood of Saint Seraphim, one of whom was Bakhtin, the famous philosopher of language, who kept a bust of Saint Seraphim in his study. Yet though the spirit of Seraphim was alive in Russia in the 1920s his mortal remains were treated by the Bolsheviks with utter irreverence. They examined them in 1920 and labelled them a means of deceiving the people. Then in 1927 the Bolsheviks scattered the monks of Sarov and the sisters of Diveyevo and placed Seraphim's relics in the Museum of Godlessness in Moscow as an exhibit of superstition. And for many observers, both in Russia and throughout the rest of the world, it seemed in those days as though everything that Seraphim stood for was no more than a relic of a world that was dead and gone for ever.

True, there were one or two living relics who still clung to that world, as illustrated by an incident that took place in the Museum of Godlessness about the year 1930, on 19 July, the birthday of Saint Seraphim. The attendant in the room where the relics were displayed, herself a believer, noticed an old peasant standing hesitantly in the doorway, holding branches of pine and fir. Thinking that the man must have lost his way the woman asked him what he wanted. He replied, 'It's this way, *matouchka*, they have taken away our *batiouchka* Seraphim, and I have heard that now he is here. I come from Sarov and I thought that it might please him if I brought him a bit of something out of the forest. He loved the forest so much!' The attendant pointed to the saint's casket and the peasant knelt and laid his branches there.

The following year he came again on 19 July, once more bringing branches. That was his last visit, but it was not the last time for Seraphim. During the 1930s the monastery of Sarov was used as a labour camp for various sorts of victims of the Bolsheviks, among them being a Russian woman of French lineage, Julia de Beausobre. After reaching the West in 1934 she was able to reveal that wherever she had travelled in and around the labour camp near Sarov, whomever she met, everyone spoke of Seraphim; she heard endless stories concerning him. Again, thirty years later, the famous Soviet dissident, Andrei Sinyavsky, was in the concentration camp of Dubrovlag in the same area and he, similarly, reports that he heard all sorts of legends and stories about Seraphim and his predictions for the future of Russia.

But no one could have predicted what was going to happen in December 1990 at the Museum of Atheism in Leningrad. The museum was undergoing a radical reorganization in the course of which a group of the museum staff came upon some old chests in a long-neglected store room. When they opened one of them they discovered a skeleton around the neck of which was a copper cross – the same cross that Agatha Mashnin had placed around the neck of her beloved son Prokhor as he was setting out in November 1778 to the monastery of Sarov. The relics of Saint Seraphim, long believed to have been irretrievably lost, had been found. Their discovery gave birth to an eruption of joy throughout the whole of Russia. Liturgies of thanksgiving were celebrated in hundreds of churches until the summer of the following year when the relics, now housed in a casket of appropriate dignity, were carried from Leningrad to Moscow by train and subsequently from 23 July until 1 August, were borne in procession from Moscow by road across the Russian heartland by way of Bogorodsk, Vladimir and Nizhny-Novgorod to the newly-restored women's monastery of Diveyevo. The procession was greeted by millions of people as it passed through towns and villages; and, indeed, as it moved out of Nizhny-Novgorod the throngs lined the route for nine miles in order to greet it.

The reason why Seraphim's reliquary had to be taken to the convent of Diveyevo rather than to Sarov was because Sarov lies within the military zone Arzamas 16, entrance to which has for many years been strictly controlled since it was here that Sakharov and his scientific colleagues invented the Soviet Union's nuclear bomb. Not surprisingly, the contraposition of Seraphim's relics and the nuclear bomb holds apocalyptic significance for many Russians.

## The *starets*: an infinitely daring man

But while the contraposition has obvious meaning for Russians it raises in our minds the question whether Seraphim might have a message not only for Russia, and not only for the Church, but for the whole human family. And since we have nowadays come to accept that the story of the human family needs to be understood in relationship to the whole of creation, we need to ask ourselves if we can discern some special significance in Seraphim's story as it relates to the story of the whole creation.

Moreover, though it may seem unlikely, against the background of billions of years of space-time, that any individual could be such a key factor in the larger story, nevertheless we

have lately come to recognize from the study of evolution that
the great changes in the evolving condition of the created
universe arise out of some minute and initially scarcely discernible change, a change that certainly could never have been
predicted on the basis of the previous state of the universe.
'The creation of the atoms is as stunning as the creation of
the universe', writes one cosmologist. 'Nothing in the previous
several hundred thousand years presaged their emergence.' And
the same can be said of the emergence of the galaxies and the
supernovas: in each case a small breakthrough leads to the
creation of a new heaven and a new earth. And when we
come to the story of the human family small changes take
place analagous to those in the realm of physics. But whereas
the latter events can be physically measured those in the human
realm cannot be measured, they can only be related – the
decision, for example, to stand upright or to bury one's dead
or to make fire. All such decisions give rise to what Teilhard
de Chardin calls the 'noosphere', a sphere of ideas and the
communication of ideas within which the human family lives,
just as much as it lives within the atmosphere enveloping the
earth.

Unfortunately, or so it seemed at first, the noosphere
impregnated human beings with anxieties of all kinds, which
rendered them incapable of trusting their instincts in the way
the other animals do. And over the centuries these anxieties
rapidly grew more intense until they reached a pitch that
threatened to make life itself unbearable. At this crucial
moment of decision one human being decided that if he could
live a life totally beyond the fear and anxiety that are at their
most intense in the face of death, and which breed hatred for
all who carry the threat of death, then the hold of death upon
the human family would be broken. And in consequence, so
would fear and hatred. As a result of his decision spiritual
energies were unlocked from within this man that enabled
him to see into the souls of other persons, to heal them both
from their sins and from their bodily ailments. In some
instances this release of energy enabled him to control the
wind and the waves and to change the substance of things.
Eventually, at the culmination of his life, he overcame his

instinctive fear of death by sacrificing his life. And he was raised from the dead. The last enemy, death, had been overcome and a new earth and a new heaven was opened up in which there are no enemies and where all are free to enter if they will.

Few have done so whole-heartedly. But outstanding among those who have done is Seraphim, an 'infinitely daring man', in the phrase once used by a Jew to characterize the true Christian. Indeed Seraphim was so daring in following his leader that many less whole-hearted Christians were scandalized by reports that he was doing the same things that Jesus himself had done, healing the sick in mind and body, being transfigured, and exercising powers of clairvoyance, for example. Moreover, towards the end of his life, when he was trying somewhat unsuccessfully to warn his devotees of his impending death, he had gone so far as to apply to himself some words of the gospels.

That happened when Mother Praskovya Ivanovna went to visit him in his nearer hermitage. She knelt beside Seraphim who was sitting on a tree trunk. Then he opened the New Testament and began to read from the fifth chapter of Saint Matthew: 'You are the light of the world...' (verses 14 to 19), after which he recited almost in its entirety Jesus' discourse to his disciples after the Last Supper (John 14: 1 to 16: 24), beginning 'Set your troubled hearts at rest. Trust in God always; trust also in me. There are many dwelling places in my Father's house; if it were not so I should have told you; for I am going to prepare a place for you. . . .' Seraphim ended his recitation with the words, 'In very truth, I tell you, if you ask the Father for anything in my name, he will give it to you. So far you have asked nothing in my name. Ask and you will receive, that your joy may be complete.' Then he stood up and said, not in Russian but in Church Slavonic, as if to emphasize the solemnity of the occasion: 'Follow me'. Mother Praskovya stood up and followed him, weeping.

# 2

# The supramoralist: Nikolai Fyodorov

'The greatest of Russian religious thinkers' was how Dmitri Mirsky, himself one of the most respected of Russian critics, described Nikolai Fyodorovich Fyodorov. In those words he was echoing the judgements of many others whose opinions deserve our respect. Tolstoy, for instance, said of Fyodorov, 'I am proud to have lived at the same time as such a man.' And the famous philosopher Berdyaev wrote, 'Nikolai Fyodorovich Fyodorov was a man of genius. Fyodorov was Russian to the core, one who epitomized the particularities of Russian thought and Russian soul-searching.' Indeed some impression of the impact that Fyodorov made upon his contemporaries can be conveyed by quoting the extravagant praise accorded to him by one well-known critic of the day, Volynski, who wrote, 'The thousand year existence of Russia has been justified by the life and death of Fyodorov.' And though such ardour of enthusiasm for Fyodorov has cooled somewhat by now, nevertheless Fyodorov in our own day has been immortalized by Boris Pasternak in his novel *Dr Zhivago* in the character Nikolai Nikolayevich, whose opinions inspire many of the novel's themes.

Clearly the thoughts that give rise to such startling evaluations could never have been begotten by a lukewarm, commonplace personality. They would have had to come from someone very unusual, as is certainly true in the case of Fyodorov, whose austere features and fiery eyes used to impel the painter Leonid Pasternak, father of Boris, to think of Saint Francis of Assisi. And there were many others who, on getting to know Fyodorov, thought of him as a saint. Leo Tolstoy's son, Ilya, for instance, wrote

No one seeing the expression of his face could ever forget it. His wise and penetrating eyes were in constant movement.

They radiated an inner goodness bordering on childlike innocence. If there are saints then they must be exactly like that. Nikolai Fyodorovich was not only physically incapable of doing anything bad, but, so I believe, he himself was impervious to evil of any kind – he simply could not take it in.

On the other hand Fyodorov was himself aware of having a fiery temper that led him to quarrel with some who most admired him. Eventually, for example, he broke off relations with Leo Tolstoy and refused to shake hands with him. But the most negative comment of all upon Fyodorov comes from the pen of the man entrusted by Scorpion publications to produce an edition of Fyodorov's writings, namely Cherno-gubov, who wrote, 'He was extremely intolerant and terribly distrustful. It was difficult, in fact almost impossible, to get on with him for more than a couple of days. He was by no means a calm philosopher but rather an angry prophet.'

The truth of the matter is that Fyodorov was an angular thinker in the sense that he had his own angle on virtually every question he addressed. This angularity of his has dis-comfited many of his commentators, who have been irritated with him because they have not known how to reduce his thought to some consistent, recognizable system. Notably, certain spokesmen for Russian Orthodoxy have denied that he can even be considered a Christian thinker. But the wiser and more open-minded Pavel Florensky surely puts his finger on the just and true way of understanding Fyodorov when he described Fyodorov's style of thought as 'contrapuntal'. Of counterpoint the definition runs, 'The ability, unique to music, to say two things at once comprehensively'; and further, 'with the blurring or virtual elimination of the boundaries between consonance and dissonance a much wider range of confluences is open to the composer'. In that sense the way Fyodorov's mind worked is more like that of a composer than of, say, a mathematician who proceeds from one theorem to another by way of inference.

Clearly, therefore, if we are to profit from the thought of this person it is essential for us to acquaint ourselves with some of those experiences which provided for Fyodorov the original angles from which he saw aspects of the world and from which he then drew conclusions as disturbing to many of his contemporaries as to their successors.

He was born in the village of Klyuchi, situated in the province of Tambov, on 26 May 1829. He was the illegitimate son of Elizabeth Ivanova, a manorial servant, and Prince Pavel Ivanovich Gagarin, a scion of one of the most ancient of Russia's noble families. Beyond a doubt his illegitimacy was one of the most crucial factors determining the angle from which Fyodorov looked out upon the world. As he was to write many years later,

> there appear to be two feelings which form the essential, distinguishing feature of a human being – the sense of mortality and the shame of one's birth. One may suppose that all of a man's blood must flood to his face when he becomes aware of his origin; and that he must blanch with terror when he is brought face to face with someone like himself, someone of the same blood. If these two feelings do not destroy a man immediately probably that is merely because he only comes gradually to a realization of the truth and cannot at once grasp all the terror and misery of his condition.

It is difficult not to suppose that the young Nikolai experienced some of that terror and shame whenever he faced his elder brother Alexander or whenever he thought of his patronymic, Fyodorovich. For it was the custom of the time that illegitimate children at their baptism should receive as their patronymic the name of the one who stood there as their godfather rather than of their natural father. All the same, while they were growing up together on the Gagarin estate of Sasov the brothers seem to have been well treated, in particular by their uncle Konstantin Ivanovich Gagarin, who constituted himself their protector. They needed him because the boys' father, Pavel Ivanovich, though a tender man in his own way, was so entranced by the theatre that he rarely stayed at home with his family.

Nikolai was seven years old and Alexander eight in 1836

when the two of them went to school in the neighbouring town of Shatska, and studied there until 1842, in which year they went on to the gymnasium in Tambov. There the brothers proved to be outstanding pupils, Alexander distinguishing himself in both the natural sciences and the humanities, and Nikolai in geography and history. Their history teacher was long remembered not only for his enthralling gift for presenting history but, even more, for his loving care towards his pupils. His influence on Nikolai's later life is clear for all to see.

In August 1849 the two young men left Tambov for Odessa and the Richelieu *lycée* designed to provide training in a wide range of practical and cultural disciplines appropriate for the sons of the minor artistocracy. However, after only a year there, towards the end of 1851, Alexander and Nikolai were withdrawn from the *lycée* 'on account of domestic circumstances'. Though we cannot be sure precisely what domestic circumstances led to the brothers' withdrawal it was probably on account of the death of their uncle Konstantin Ivanovich Gagarin who died that year. He had supported their education and afforded them a home in Sasov. But after his death the boys' father, Pavel Ivanovich, returned to Sasov with his new family and the brothers seem to have been left to their own devices.

Not surprisingly Fyodorov quickly realized, and was later to keep insisting that the experience of those events marked a turning point – indeed, *the* turning point in his life. Through the death of Konstantin Ivanovich he had experienced the terror of death and through that loss realized how precious is kinship, having learned by his natural father's behaviour the horror of disrelatedness. Many years later, in the last year of his life, 1903, he expressed these emotions in the following words: 'Since the days of my childhood I have preserved three memories. I saw the black bread, exceedingly black, on which (so I was told) the peasants sustained themselves in a year of famine. From my childhood I have kept hearing the explanation of warfare – in war people shoot one another. Lastly, I learned that there are people who are not kindred but strangers and that even some kindred are strangers to one another.'

For the following fifty years Fyodorov was to work out the implications of these experiences in a series of essays, not published until after his death under the title *The Philosophy of the Common Task.*

But the common task, the philosophy of which Fyodorov was to expound, did not immediately require of him that he should write about it or go to the centres of influence such as Moscow and St Petersburg in order to expound it to others. Instead, for some sixteen years, he taught in a series of village schools throughout the Russian heartland, there putting into practice the demands of the common task, the demands, above all, of brotherhood, kinship and relatedness. And the more one studies Fyodorov's later writings and the descriptions of him by contemporaries the more aware one becomes of how deeply he was impressed by living among the folk of Russia's heartland. He taught the children of the folk; he followed a way of life in regard to food and clothes and money every bit as arduous as that of the peasantry themselves; he worshipped among them in accordance with their traditions of worship, their local rituals and their devotion to local saints. The fusion of Orthodox tradition with time-honoured peasant practices which shaped their working and worshipping calendar became so precious to him that he would later make great play with the assertion that the word *khrestianin* (peasant) was synonymous with the word *khristianin* (Christian). And he retained throughout his life a peasant-like suspicion of the city as a place of luxury and frivolity, devoid of substance and symbolized by the Prodigal Son in Jesus' parable.

Although this period constituted Fyodorov's 'hidden years', a time when the seeds sown in 1851 were slowly being brought to fruition, we are fortunate in having a vivid portrayal of the man from the pen of a young revolutionary, Nikolai Pavlovich Peterson. Peterson was twenty years old in March 1864 when he met Fyodorov in the small town of Bogorodsk, Tambov province, where Fyodorov was teaching. The young revolutionary had already spent some time as a teacher in Leo Tolstoy's experimental school on the Tolstoy estate of Yasnaya Polyana, when he arrived with the intention of spreading revolutionary propaganda in Bogorodsk and was told about the striking personality who was teaching in the local school.

Peterson was not slow in going to meet Fyodorov, whom he describes as being some forty years old with attractive brown hair, of middling height and with the most beautiful hazel-coloured eyes. He wrote,

> He was a bachelor and lived as an ascetic: he not only did without a bed, but without even a pillow; he ate whatever his landlords, simple merchants, put out for him, the healthful but simple food that they themselves ate; during Lent N. F. ate Lenten dishes and on Wednesdays, Fridays, and other days of fasting, he fasted. N. F. never made any special demands and was always content with whatever he was given. In my first meeting with N. F. I immediately poured out everything about myself, and explained the purpose for which I had become a teacher at the district school. In answer to which I heard: 'I don't understand', N. F. said, 'what you are troubling yourself about. After all, you won't be able to give those for whom you are troubling yourself anything except material well-being, since you don't admit to any other kind of well-being. But, in the meantime, while working to secure well-being for others, you renounce it for yourself and, indeed, are prepared to sacrifice your life for the sake of that. But what if material well-being is no more important to those for whom you are troubling yourself than it is for you? What is the point, therefore, of all your bothering?'

Fyodorov's direct, logical response had Peterson in thrall almost instantly. As a result Peterson became Fyodorov's most faithful disciple for the rest of his days and was to spend many hours and days working to make *The Philosophy of the Common Task* and its begetter better known.

One anecdote told by Peterson concerning his friend's way of dealing with situations brings out the note of *iurodstvo* in Fyodorov. The story goes that the father of one of Nikolai Fyodorovich's pupils was critically ill but the family had no money for medicine; and so Fyodorov gave every kopek he possessed to purchase some remedy. In spite of which the sick man died, and it turned out that there was no money for his burial. So Fyodorov sold his one and only regulation teaching uniform, the proceeds of which sufficed for the dead man's funeral. The next day Fyodorov appeared at school in an ancient coat looking almost like a beggar. As if it were meant, that very same day the district superintendent came to the school and was extremely shocked by the teacher's appearance. He demanded an explanation; but, in vain, because Fyodorov refused to give one. So the superintendent demanded Fyodorov's immediate dismissal. Only the blazing intervention of the school director on this occasion protected the strange eccentric.

A similar incident, recounted by another faithful follower, Vladimir Alexandravich Kozhevknikov, was to precipitate the end of Fyodorov's stay in Bogorodsk. One day in June 1864 the regular inspection of the school was being carried out in the district by Malinovsky, director of the principal Moscow gymnasium, a strict disciplinarian notorious for hiring and firing teachers. Turning up at one of Fyodorov's lessons he was unfavourably struck by the teacher's dress (for although on this occasion it was strictly speaking correct it was also terribly worn), and he began to carp at the pupils' answers, unwilling to listen to the teacher's explanation of his own particular system of explanation and answer. So Nikolai Fyodorovich abandoned the class, leaving Malinovsky on his own with the pupils, and handed in his resignation. To his credit Malinovsky would not accept the resignation when it was made clear to him what an unusual human being and teacher Fyodorov was. All the same, after that incident Fyodorov no longer wished to stay in Bogorodsk but transferred to Uglich in Yaroslav province.

His friendship with Peterson was soon to land Fyodorov in prison. This was because Peterson had been arrested in May 1866 on the grounds that he had at one time belonged to the revolutionary student group centred around Karakozov, the former student who, in April 1866, had attempted to assasinate the Tsar. After being questioned for three weeks concerning his contacts with Peterson, Fyodorov was released, whereas Peterson served a six-month prison term for not having reported his knowledge of the group's earlier illegal activities. This unhappy incident did not affect their friendship, however, since in the summer of 1868 we find the two of them journeying together all the way to Moscow on foot, in the course of which, so Peterson tells us, there was no stream or river they came across that Fyodorov did not bathe in. Fyodorov loved bathing and continued to do so summer and winter alike.

Soon afterwards Peterson married. And, for a time, a certain coolness fell upon their relationship, the younger man being busy with his family affairs and Fyodorov absorbed from the spring of 1869 in his task as assistant in the Chertkov Library under P. I. Bartenev. From there he was to move in 1874 to Moscow's leading public library, the Rumyantsev Museum, where he worked for some twenty-five years, first as a call clerk in the reading room and later as a cataloguer. In taking up each appointment, both at the Chertkov Library and the Rumyantsev Museum, Fyodorov had stipulated that he should be paid only the minimum salary and never be promoted. As a result, when he resigned from his post at the Rumyantsev, in September 1898, the small pension he received was insufficient for even his minimal needs and he took up a position as a desk clerk in the hall of the Moscow archives of the Ministry of Foreign Affairs where he worked until the end of his life.

It was during the quarter of a century of his service at the Rumyantsev Museum that Fyodorov became a legendary figure in late-nineteenth-century Moscow. How that process came about is by no means difficult to explain. To begin with, Fyodorov was a quite outstanding librarian who regarded librarianship as a sacred calling because for him a library was not a 'book graveyard' as he said, but the presence of many human beings, for 'behind every book is a person'. And he was serving the persons behind the books just as much as he was serving the visitors to the library in search of the books. From this latter group we have spontaneous witnesses to the almost incredible ardour which Fyodorov invested not simply in finding the books they ordered but even bringing them books and articles on their subjects which they themselves had never heard of. He also had a vision of librarianship reaching far beyond the walls of the Rumyantsev, full of schemes for cooperation between libraries in Russia as well as between Russian libraries and those throughout the world so that every member of the human family might have access to all the knowledge stored in libraries throughout the world.

As a result of the help he provided for readers in an amazing range of disciplines Fyodorov's corner of the catalogue room of the Rumyantsev proved to be a magnet for many of the leading intellectuals of the day and came to be described as 'the spiritual centre of Moscow'. Indeed we are blessed with a living image of it from the hand of the artist Leonid Pasternak. He tried to persuade Fyodorov on a number of occasions to allow him to paint his portrait but Fyodorov resolutely refused, just as he always refused to allow anyone to take a photograph of him because he detested self-glorification. But in the end Pasternak piled a stack of books at the front of his reading desk in the library and sketched Fyodorov sitting at his desk. Fyodorov's arms are resting on the desk before him, his hands buried in the loose sleeves of his shirt. The artist also sketched into the scene the head and shoulders of the philosopher Solovyov and of Leo Tolstoy, so that the three are depicted rapt in deep discussion. Both Solovyov and Tolstoy were regular members of the gathering in Fyodorov's corner along with Nikolai Chernogubov, the custodian of the Tretyakov Gallery, the poet Agfanasii Fet, the poet and novelist Valery Bryusov, and many others.

One of the most endearing anecdotes about Fyodorov's work as a librarian comes from Konstantin Tsiolkovskii, the scientist whose name is now synonymous in Russia with the exploration of outer space of which he is regarded as the main inspirer. Tsiolkovskii once told an interviewer how he made Fyodorov's acquaintance at the library:

It happened on one of my first visits. I dropped in and here's what I saw: a dozen or so people, mostly students, crowding around the librarian. I was shy. I stood there waiting for the librarian to get free. I had time to look him over: a bald head, around it white curls sprinkled with grey, coal-black eyebrows and surprisingly young eyes. He looked about fifty, but he had youthful movements – quick and sharp.

When the last student had left, the librarian noticed me and motioned for me to come to him. Apparently I looked nervous, because he smiled encouragingly. If you could only have seen his smile! It changed him and brightened him up at once. It was so affable and open, the way a father smiles at a son, or one brother at another. But this was the first time he had seen me. I was immediately filled with affection for him, and, having forgotten my earlier shyness, walked up to him. He cheerfully asked,

'What do you want to read?'

'Give me, if you can, *The History of the Peasant War.*'

'That book is forbidden!'

'Please speak a little louder – I don't hear well.'

'The book is for-bid-den!'

The words sounded so harsh, as if to say, 'See here, now, with the kinds of readers we have – give out forbidden books indeed!' But his eyes were merry and smiling. Still, I hadn't been around people much and didn't know what to say. He went off somewhere, quickly returned, and handed me a book. I asked:

'What's this?'

'*The History of the Peasant War.*'

'But isn't this book forbidden?'

'Take it!'

Not only did so many distinguished thinkers gather around Fyodorov in his Rumyantsev corner but they also visited him in the house where he rented one room at a rent of no more than six roubles a month. And there his distinguished visitors were struck with wonder at his spartan way of life. Most of them were already aware that he gave away much of his already meagre salary to poor students since a handful of Fyodorov's 'stipendiaries' (as he termed them) were to be seen waiting outside the museum to receive their 'stipends' each month on the day he received his salary. But even so his visitors were often taken aback to discover that he had no bed in his room but slept on a trunk covered with newspapers. He lived for nine months without hot food, sometimes taking a piece of fish along with hard bread rolls, though he did like drinking hot tea and was given to smoking. The only coat he possessed was so threadbare that he was sometimes mistaken for a beggar and he would never spend money on a cab even in the harshest weather but insisted on walking everywhere. In fact when in

1903 he was persuaded by well-meaning friends to wear a more substantial coat and to take cabs he soon caught pneumonia and died.

It would be wrong to conclude from all of this that Fyodorov was a gloomy ascetic. Apart from the fact that he regularly carried sweets in his coat pockets to give to children whom he met, everyone agreed that he was full of fire and energy. Moreover his engagement in what others deemed an ascetic way of life was in no sense undertaken with the traditional ascetic aim of self-perfection – the very idea of self-perfection was anathema to him. Rather it was that whenever we eat anything or make use of anything whatsoever made by our fellow human beings we are appropriating their energies for ourselves and we should not take more than is necessary for our work in the common task.

We turn now from Fyodorov's life to his philosophy, even though to make such a distinction he might have found unacceptable since each is an expression of the other. The transition may be most firmly underpinned by a brief account of how his thought has been made available. The greatest obstacle to his thought becoming available was found in Fyodorov's own distaste for the practice whereby authors demand royalties. He was deeply aware of how much we receive from our ancestors and from our fellow human beings and so he was opposed to the use of copyright. For Fyodorov to have sold his writings under copyright would have meant committing the sin that he accused the intelligentsia of committing at all times: that is, turning one's every thought into coveted private property for sale. He could never accept that anyone prepared to sell his thoughts can maintain that he is not part of the capitalist system: by turning our thoughts into private property we restrict to ourselves something which should be freely available to the whole human family.

Consequently, in the years immediately preceding his death, when Petersen and Kozhevnikov proposed to gather his writings into a book, he insisted that the book should not be sold but should be distributed freely to libraries as well as to any individual who might ask for a copy. That is why no more than 480 copies of the first volume of *The Philosophy of the*

*Common Task* were published in 1906, and even then by a firm situated in a small town called Verny in central Asia. Not surprisingly the book became a great rarity, though the second volume, issued in Moscow in 1913, proved even more difficult to obtain.

And the philosophy of the common task itself seems to have proved as difficult to grasp as the book is to obtain for the reason we mentioned earlier, namely, that Fyodorov's manner of presenting philosophy is unusual, more like the counterpoint of a musical composition according to Pavel Florensky. Counterpoint, it will be remembered, was defined as 'the ability, unique to music, to say two things at once comprehensively'; and, further, 'with the blurring or virtual elimination of the boundaries between consonance and dissonance a much wider range of confluences is open to the composer.' Also relevant for an understanding of Fyodorov's thought is the comment about one particular form of counterpoint, the fugue: 'Two distinct sections of a fugue may not appear related unless the listener has received the entire work, at which time the music's internal logic makes clear the relationship.' In that sense the themes struck by Fyodorov's passionate feelings resonate with one another though they may seem only remotely related until one comes to the ultimate archetypal theme which arises out of the very deepest passion. It is appropriate, therefore, for us to list the dominant themes of his life and philosophy and to leave implicit until the end the archetypal passion which makes clear the relationships.

We begin therefore with an exposition of what Fyodorov has to say about *disrelatedness*, a condition that burned itself in upon his memory when, in his youth he 'learned that there are people who are not kindred but strangers, and that even some kindred are strangers to one another.' Next we turn to his thoughts on the idea of *progress*, for which the nineteenth century showed unbounded enthusiasm. This will be followed by an account of his attitude towards *nature* and man's place in nature, which again was a major preoccupation of European thinkers in the late nineteenth century. The fourth theme is that of *prophecy*, on which subject Berdyaev declared that Fyodorov's interpretation is profoundly original. We then come to Fyodorov's prescription for the ills of humanity – what he himself defined as *supramoralism*, one aspect of which is the *Liturgy*. The list ends with the archetypal, all-pervading passion that can only be understood at the end, and which, once understood, lights up all the previous themes.

## Disrelatedness (or non-kinship)

It was not only the fact of disrelatedness among the members of society that struck Fyodorov. Even more astonishing was the fact that most members of society seemed to regard the condition of disrelatedness as completely natural and therefore completely acceptable. For them, apparently, the struggle for existence makes it inevitable that human beings should treat one another as strangers, rivals and enemies. Hence divisions along economic, social, religious and national lines – as well as the divisions between rich and poor, learned and unlearned, city-dwellers and peasantry – can never, so they maintained, be overcome because they are natural. But even though such assumptions were widespread in the late nineteenth century, especially among the learned and governing classes, they were deeply offensive to Fyodorov, an insult to the very foundations of Russia; because for him the foundational story of the Russian people is that of the two saintly brothers, Boris and Gleb.

Boris and Gleb were two of the sons of Prince Vladimir, after whose death their brother Sviatopolk tried to claim the whole realm by force of arms. When Sviatopolk's forces came arrayed to fight against Boris and Gleb in 1015 the two of them independently refused to fight and both of them were slaughtered. They gave up their own lives so as not to create division within the people of Vladimir's lands. At least that is the interpretation given to their behaviour by the Russian people, no matter what doubts the learned class in the official Church might cast upon it. And the canonization of Boris and Gleb by the simple people was dear to the heart of Fyodorov, for whom it was an example of 'a brotherhood-creating act.'

Such 'brotherhood-creating', indeed, is embedded not only

in the foundational story of the Russian people but even in their everyday language and customs. The collective word in Russian for those who belong to a kin, for example, is *rod*, and their relationship with one another is *rodstvo*, kinship. They are all *rodnoi*, related, because they share a common ancestor from whom they derive their birth, *rozhdenie*, the same word almost as 'Christmas', *rozhdestvo*. By extension the common people (the *narod*), thought of all Russians as kin because they all belonged to the *rodina*, the same native land. This relationship with the ancestors is further underlined by the custom, peculiar among European peoples to the Russians and the Balkan Slavs, of every person having a patronymic, a name derived from the father's name, in addition to their own. Indeed, the simple folk would often use only the patronymic when addressing another, as, for instance, Ivanovich or Petrovich.

Another feature to which Fyodorov attached great significance as a manifestation of the Russians' desire always to establish a relationship was their custom, inbred among the peasantry, of using kinship names even when addressing strangers. They would habitually greet them with appellations such as father, uncle, brother or their corresponding feminine equivalents. And he pointed out that children spontaneously insert themselves into this web of relationship. 'In the child's feeling for universal brotherhood', he wrote, 'there is latent the conclusion that every human being is a son, a grandson, a great grandson . . . each coming from the forefather.' He continues, 'When we were small all adults were for us the brothers and sisters of our fathers and mothers, they were our uncles and aunts; indeed our parents spoke of them to us in this way . . .' Such 'childlike feeling of general relatedness is the criterion and starting point for the attainment of ultimate perfection', an 'ignoring of worldly distinctions; and instead, a deep awareness of inner relatedness, the wish to serve and not to rule'. So 'it becomes clear why the gospel makes childlike feeling a condition for entry into the kingdom of God'; 'unless you become as little children you cannot enter the kingdom of heaven'.

Surprisingly, and a sign of Fyodorov's original mind, he

found solid support for his thesis in a reflection on man's place in nature, a favourite theme of that epoch, stirred as it was by Darwin's current hypothesis on evolution. He pointed out that though human beings share with other animals both sexual love and love for their offspring yet only human adults remain related by affection for their parents when the time comes that they no longer need their parents' protection in order to survive. He goes on to say of 'the first man who, though he was capable of living separately and independently, yet did not leave his parents even after their death, that he can be said to have been the first son of man. And with him there began tribal life, tribal religion (ancestor worship) and our human society.'

When he defines man as the one 'who did not leave his parents even after their death' Fyodorov is referring to the fact that 'man is a burying creature', who buries his dead parents with ceremony and keeps up his relationship with them by further ceremonies throughout the rest of his own life: ancestor worship, therefore, is the basis of all true religion. Hence his severe criticism of Protestantism which forbids prayers for the dead. But man's attempt to sustain relatedness seems doomed to failure, a pathetic effort to resist disrelatedness (*nyerodstvo*), to quote a word specially coined by Fyodorov. Because man is faced with the inexorable power of nature which not only splits the living from the dead by bringing death upon man but also spreads division among the living through inflicting famine, disease, both sexual and natural selection, all of which set human beings one against the other in their struggle to survive.

Nature is ruthless. Left to itself it surges only *forward* and drives everything and everybody forward before it. Its law is that of the irreversibility of its process in time. ('Time, like an ever-rolling stream', in the words of an English hymn, 'bears all its sons away. They fly forgotten as a dream dies at the opening day.') But Fyodorov maintains that it is precisely such a forgetting of one's fathers and forefathers that constitutes the most terible crime possible for human beings since it consigns the ancestors to not-being. *Zabyt*, the Russian for forgetting, can be construed as 'not-be'. Yet there is something in human nature that refuses to go only forward and insists on moving backwards against nature's processes, against the grain of nature, searching ever backwards until every last leaf on the human family tree is to be seen with the eye of love. By its very nature such love is a spiritual, *supra*natural undertaking.

But since such an undertaking runs counter to the grain of nature and lays such enormous demands on human beings we find that in the course of human history there have been many miserable failures to do so. It is those failures that have brought about the condition of disrelatedness of which the most powerful symbol, in the eyes of Fyodorov, and to which he turns time and again, is that of the Prodigal Son whose story is found in Luke's Gospel. The younger brother in that parable commits exactly that crime which for Fyodorov is the most terrible possible for a human being: the son, in order to secure his inheritance, wishes his father not to be, *zabyt*, to be forgotten. That he does simply by demanding his inheritance, a demand that in first-century Palestinian society meant that he wished his father dead.

The younger son's actions are heavy with further sinister import when we examine his reason for demanding his inheritance. He does so in order to leave his rural community and the discipline of work on the land so as to live in the city where luxury is easily available to those who have plenty of money. To acquire anything through the use of such unearned money was, for Fyodorov, a form of stealing, because it means taking for one's own consumption the energy that some other person has invested in the goods obtained, into which he has invested part of his life. And the theft of someone else's life is even more blatant when the money is used to take another's body, as happens when prostitutes are being hired. In the parable the story is brought to a terrible, logical climax when the son, returning to the country after having used up his inheritance, says to his father, 'I am no longer worthy to be called your son', thereby signifying that he thinks he has broken the fundamental relationship, the one between father and son.

However, Fyodorov sees an even wider application for the parable, because the figure of the prodigal son and his actions offer a perfect symbol of the *nyerodstvo*, the non-kinship that strikes you immediately you enter a modern, commercial, industrial city. Such a city is an aggregate of non-brotherly states since the whole reason for its existence is to provide its inhabitants with opportunities to secure an advantage over others, whether by having more wealth than others, more status, more power, more sexual glamour or intellectual capital than they – in any case, possessing something that divides one from another, sets one in competition with them and provides one with an advantage over them.

Moreover, the modern city itself expresses a non-brotherly attitude towards the countryside. For just as the prodigal son is implicitly wishing his father to be dead so that he himself may go to the city and live a life of luxury so, likewise, does the modern city destroy rural life, including its fauna and flora, simply in order to enjoy its own endless, wasteful lust for more and more superfluous goods. And like the prodigal son the modern city is ready to declare itself no-son and no-brother, preferring instead to become a slave to the pseudo-religious cult of women, a cult whose holy of holies is the opera and the ballet, of which Fyodorov was scornful for being mere titillating spectacles where the spectators find pleasure for themselves as individuals but are not brought into any true relationship with one another. He drew the contrast between these spectacles and the Church's liturgy in the villages where everyone in the community used to participate. Lacking such communal, authentic life the city has perforce to tart every-thing up. This prompted Fyodorov to predict a day when the city would develop the practice of even tarting up the corpses of the dead so as to mask the reality of death. Such a city, he said, is not a democracy but a *pornocracy* in which the citizens will eventually finish by loathing one another.

Although Fyodorov was no poet – and, indeed, seems to have had no feel for poetry – nevertheless the form his thought takes is that of symbols. He was prepared to stretch the symbol of the prodigal son still further into the contrast he draws between the position of practical reason and the position of theoretical, abstract reason. 'The precedence that is given to theoretical reason', he writes, 'is a usurpation, a betrayal of its begetter, practical reason, from which the critical reason comes forth, just as the city arises out of the village and the city-dweller out of the peasantry. When the theoretical reason returns to the practical reason, that is, returns to the village, that will be the expression of its repentance for its betrayal or usurpation.' 'The transition from the city to the village will be a transition from present-day industrialism (based on sexual selection and set up by prodigal sons enticed away by female beauty) to rural industrialism, based on the combination of the science of nature and the working knowledge of the Fathers. Such industrialism would not be artificial but a natural weaving together . . . an organic creation.'

As we said previously, the majority of human beings seem to regard disrelatedness with equanimity and find the anguish caused in Fyodorov to be difficult to understand. One reason for that failure to understand may well be that few people have ever seen human relationships – with their potential for good and evil – so clearly in the light of the Holy Trinity as did Fyodorov, for whom the Trinity was the very heart of Christianity.

'The Trinity', he writes, 'is the ultimate expression of relationship' because the Father, the Son and the Holy Spirit are perfectly distinct persons but not separated; 'they are perfectly One without the persons being confused.' Hence the doctrine of the Holy Trinity not only offers us the image of the perfect society but within it is marked out for us the way to achieve such society. And 'the doctrine applies to the whole human kin (*rod*) since it embraces all the living (sons and daughters) and all the dead (fathers and mothers) and makes the latter (the dead) a task for the living (the sons and daughters).' And when the latter do their duty there will be achieved that communion in which the independence of persons is not founded on separateness but in unity, wherein there is no bondage and no oppression.

Since the doctrine of the Trinity, as applied by Fyodorov, offers us such a perfect definition of society we are bound to ask ourselves why the history of Christian Europe presents us with a picture so contradictory to Fyodorov's vision. One clue is to be found in an almost off-the-cuff remark he made. He

pointed out that traditionally in Europe peace treaties con-
cluding wars used to be made in the name of the Trinity but
never has there been a war *declared* in the name of the Trinity.
He does not expand his remark but by it he clearly indicates
that at some deep level people intent on war were obscurely
aware that the divisions between themselves and their
opponents were incompatible with the doctrine of the Trinity.
The explanation for their failure to understand the implications
of that obscure awareness was clear enough, however, to
Fyodorov.

He says that they

> have not given thought to the conditions for that firm and
> eternal peace contained in the doctrine of the Indivisible
> Trinity. For the more we enter into unity, the more Divinity
> is revealed, and vice versa. If our thinking and knowledge
> are formed by way of experience, but in the process experi-
> ence gives us an understanding of nothing but enmity and
> domination, then it is clear that only the triumph, the com-
> plete triumph, of moral law can make the Triune Being
> fully understandable to us. That is, we will understand him
> only when we ourselves (all mankind) become a multi-
> unified or, more precisely, a togethered being . . . only when
> unity no longer takes the form of domination and the inde-
> pendence of individuals is not expressed as enmity . . . only
> when there will be full mutuality and mutual knowledge.

That statement is very typically Fyodorovian in its declar-
ation that a certain truth (in this case the doctrine of the
Trinity) cannot be understood until certain actions are done,
hence the achievement of 'all togetherness'. On many
occasions he applies that same formula, in support of which
he would quote the sentence from his favoured gospel, John:
'He who does the truth comes to the light' – coming to the
light is conditional upon *doing* the truth. Or, as Jesus said of
his followers: 'May they all be one as you, Father, and I are
one', because otherwise they would not understand the
message that Jesus was trying to convey to them.

Nor do we have to search far in Fyodorov's writings to
discover a source of divisions in European society which have
made it a society most unlike that perfect society which is the

Trinity. 'Every society loses its likeness to the Trinity', he writes, 'and secretes within itself darkness (ignorance) and death if in that society things are given precedence over mutuality. The discord begotten by things alienates people one from another. The soul is turned into darkness, and outward appearance ceases to be an expression, a revelation of the soul, but instead becomes a shell to hide the soul, a deception.' You are left to guess what is really going on in the mind of the person facing you – a situation which Fyodorov saw as characteristic of western individualism. This last, alienated state of existence is based on the attempt to secure things at as low a price as possible and to sell them at as high a price as possible by taking advantage of the vagaries of supply and demand, a system that the learned class, in the shape of economists, have erected into a law of their science and to which rational human beings are supposed to subject themselves. Such behaviour is not only a form of stealing but is also, therefore, a way of separating oneself from the common task of society, since by stealing the fruits of someone else's work you save yourself from doing your share.

In the Europe of his day the most blatant example of the disrelatedness Fyodorov was referring to was, undoubtedly, Great Britain. Nor did he hold that opinion just because of Britain's humiliation of Russia in the Crimean War. When speaking of the death-bearing individualism of Europe he says, 'At the head of this civilization there stands England, which attempts to turn every other nation, and especially Russia, into unskilled labourers, into instruments for the exploitation of the earth, striving to make them provide the raw materials to which England then gives a glossy finish before going on to seduce the country bumpkins in the backwoods by means of the very same material the latter had provided in the first place. . . . The expressions of this civilization appear to be [1] an addiction to manufactured toys which itself gave birth to this whole civilization; [2] individual freedom, meaning the least possible restraint on playing with these toys': all of which leads to competition, opposition of one to another, polemic and, finally, warfare, which seems to be regarded as a condition of progress.

No doubt a number of other thinkers, contemporaries of Fyodorov, were drawing attention to the same processes as engaged his attention; but few ascribed the evils of these processes to disrelatedness arising from individualism (which was the accepted ideology), just as it is virtually impossible to name another thinker for whom those evils were to be seen by the light of the Trinity and for which the remedy was to live a trinitarian life. And it is one of the joys of encountering Fyodorov's thought that he so often sees such a situation from an entirely original angle while not striving in any way for originality.

Consider, for instance, another illustration given by him of the destructive process of individualism:

> Only towards the beginning of so-called modern times (new Protestant history) is the resurrection of Christ in painting separated from the resurrection of humanity saved by him which begins with the harrowing of hell. That is to say, only from the fourteenth and fifteenth centuries onwards is Christ depicted as ascending on high from the tomb with a victorious cohort: such an image represents an individual victory over death. But in ancient representations the resurrection is represented, in accordance with the canonical gospels, by the angel's announcement of the resurrection to the myrrh-bearing women – the first proclamation of Christianity, a call to unite for the purpose of resurrection. And in the apocryphal writings the resurrection is depicted as the united procession of the dead in hell being set free from hell: the start of resurrection for all. Such a resurrection is an expression of love, and to the common people it makes sense whereas an individual resurrection is a glorious resurrection only comprehensible to the learned.

Fyodorov could smell out individualism in even the most sacred places.

## The idea of progress

It is virtually impossible for those of us living in the late twentieth century to comprehend what an almost unbreakable grip the *idea* of progress held on the minds of most educated people during the lifetime of Fyodorov. For them the fact of progress was undeniable; the evidence for it stood before their eyes every day, whereas for those of us who have witnessed the horrors and catastrophes of the twentieth century the very idea of ineluctable human progress seems to be an insubstantial dream. In this matter Fyodorov has proved to be much closer to our own age than are any of his contemporaries. The threats to humanity from individualism allied to science and technology that are now taken as common place were already foreseen by Fyodorov by virtue of his extraordinary independence of mind, which would never permit him to fall into fashionable attitudes. By the same token the grounds upon which he based his critique of the idea of progress are not the same as the ones that are fashionable at the present day.

To some extent Fyodorov's critique of the idea of progress can be traced to what one western commentator has dubbed – without any sense of the double irony in the phrase – 'the privilege of backwardness in Russian thought'. The phrase is meant to point out that some Russian thinkers in the nineteenth century, the Slavophiles in particular, made a virtue out of what western European thinkers classed as the backwardness of Russia, a backwardness which those same Europeans thought to be self-evident in light of the fact that Russia had never known a Renaissance, a Reformation, or a Revolution such as that which spread throughout Europe from France as the fruit of the Enlightenment. From their vantage point on the eastern borders of Europe the Slavophiles maintained that they were able to notice grave errors and shortcomings in those very portentous events that western Europeans glorified as stages on the path of progress, along which they claimed they were destined to lead the human race.

Though he shared some of the Slavophiles' attitudes Fyodorov in no way shared their obscurantism. At the same time, not being a systematic thinker, he never provides us with a sustained critique of the westerners' presuppositions. So we have rather to piece together Fyodorov's own judgements upon them out of a series of his tangential observations.

In Fyodorov's eyes nothing was so disastrous as the pride in the nature of the human person that characterizes the Renaissance, and those humanist illusions by which the contradictions and evil of that nature, its entanglement in animal needs and passions, were ignored. Fyodorov saw clearly the danger in the Renaissance ideal: of an individual who could of his own nature develop all the virtues, creating for himself a balance of body and soul, light and darkness, good and evil, one capable of achieving endless progress. But the disasters of history have subsequently revealed the baselessness of that ideal. Few thinkers in Fyodorov's day realized that, however; and even fewer perhaps would have agreed with his further critique of the Renaissance legacy in the field of the arts. For he maintained that the Renaissance led to a split between the culture of the 'all-round' aristocrat and the aristocracy's subservient 'learned class' on the one hand and on the other the culture of the people, with the consequent loss of the very idea of a universal culture uniting all human beings in the search for higher values.

This split in European culture was rendered even wider by the event of the Reformation, since for Fyodorov Protestantism was inherently divisive. In Protestantism stress was laid upon *individual* interpretation of the Scriptures, undertaken outside the worshipping community (in the study, for instance, by one of the learned class). Equally divisive was the stress laid upon the personal salvation of the individual to the neglect of resurrection for all, an obsession aggravated by the Protestant formula 'faith alone' than which no phrase could have more alienated Fyodorov in view of his own passion for *deeds* of faith, and his insistence on the *common task*.

More divisive yet, perhaps, and certainly a cause of great bloodshed was the slogan of the French Revolution; Liberty, Equality, Fraternity. Some of Fyodorov's most passionate sentences on this subject were prompted by his disgust for the Paris Exhibition of 1889, which he saw as a shameless flaunting by the European bourgeoisie of its superiority not only over other classes of society but also over the rest of the world. The 'Alpine' bourgeoisie of the European peninsula looked down upon the rest of humanity, maintaining that its ideal was 'the greater happiness of the greatest number' – an ideal cloak under which to abandon the traditional longing for the happiness of *all*, thus providing an excuse for treating a conveniently undefined number of brothers and sisters as non-existent.

An honest exhibition to illustrate the story of the nineteenth century, according to Fyodorov, would have shown France, followed by other countries, turning away from traditional faith in order to worship mammon, the god of money, and doing so in the name of liberty. In the name of liberty the bourgeoisie established cities in their own image, cities which behaved like vultures in relationship to the country, exploiting the peasantry so that they themselves could live in luxury. Complicit in this exploitation was the learned class, which by means of economic science provided its justification as well as inventing weapons for industrial competition. This, in its turn, led to armed warfare, the means for which were provided by another branch of the learned class, the natural scientists. The shamelessness of the bourgeoisie was most evident at the Paris Exhibition in their idolization of woman, where women ceased to be revered as wives and mothers but were paraded in assemblies and ballrooms as objects for the lusts of the men who were present.

It is not that Fyodorov was in any way unsympathetic towards the ideals of liberty and equality and fraternity but rather that by placing them in the wrong order, giving priority to the demand for liberty and leaving the struggle for brotherhood to the last, the bourgeoisie had perverted those noble ideals and rendered them impossible to achieve. Here Fyodorov makes a very obvious point to which the bourgeoisie was wilfully blind. How can one speak of a right to liberty when the society claiming to guarantee such a right does not even guarantee that a man has a right to the means of living and thereby to find himself in a position to exercise that right? Before talking about the right to liberty a society has to provide work for anyone capable of it, and the means of survival for those who are incapable.

By giving priority to liberty the French Revolution had provided an excuse for the most influential groups in society to shed their obligations to other members of society, a fact which explains Fyodorov's unexpectedly severe judgement on the abolition of serfdom in Russia in the year 1861. In view of his identification with the peasantry one would have expected him to welcome their emancipation, but he could not do so whole-heartedly in the form that it took, because by basing the abolition on the abstract right to freedom the landowners' ties to the peasantry were greatly weakened. As a result the peasants were in many cases worse off after 1861 than they had been previously. What should have happened was that before freeing the peasantry from service all the other members of society should have been put under obligation to render service to common cause (the intelligentsia included) – above all, the nobility, who for the past century had secured liberation from one form of service after another. 'That was why', writes Fyodorov, 'there quickly took place a reaction against the liberation of the peasants, as is illustrated by Tolstoy's *War and Peace*, that poem which glorifies the life of those people who never acknowledge any obligation, never perform any service and live by means of what they take from their estates and from the labours of the peasants. They are people who are never obliged to work for their daily bread. Such is the reactionary Tolstoy even to this day, though he does not acknowledge it.'

To make matters worse, by according to equality a precedence over brotherhood the Revolution had rendered the ideal of equality death-bearing. As Fyodorov points out, the only absolute equality is equality in death; and so by according precedence to equality the revolutionaries were instigating a process whereby all the differences that are characteristic of living beings would be eliminated, bringing death nearer and nearer. The story of the nineteenth century in Europe is an exemplification of that process, for in it thousands of human beings were slaughtered through envy towards those who differed by being rich. The slaughter was certainly not done out of love for the poor, or out of a sense of brotherhood with them, since it is manifestly a self-contradiction to try to achieve equality and liberty by means of envy and violence, both of which are not simply unbrotherly, but a direct denial of brotherhood.

For Fyodorov it was crystal clear that the only way to

achieve freedom and equality was by first nurturing a sense of brotherhood among human beings.

> It is obvious that the brotherhood, in the name of which the revolutionaries made a tumultuous, bloody attempt to achieve it, was a failure because they identified brotherhood with freedom and equality (which are only the consequences of brotherhood) and which they thought they could achieve by violence: that is, by unbrotherhood. Love alone brings freedom; that is, turns obligations towards others into something desirable and makes the fulfilment of one's obligations pleasant: not something burdensome but something one strives for from the inclination of one's own heart. Similarly only love for all gives birth to equality, impelling those possessing great abilities and strength to apply them, through inner inclination, in the service of others, their fellow human beings.

But the revolutionaries were constitutionally incapable of understanding the very meaning of brotherhood because brotherhood is impossible without fatherhood and the Revolution was precisely a denial of fatherhood on the part of its adherents. It was a statement that they owed nothing to their Christian ancestors and were now about to construct a society as if their ancestors had never existed. It was necessary, they claimed, to wipe the slate clean if the human race was to progress. Therefore Fyodorov was perfectly justified in taking as the essence of the idea of progress derived from the Revolution a statement made by one of his contemporaries, Professor Kareev. Kareev wrote, 'Progress . . . is a fact of individual psychology which is also repeated in collective psychology, whereby the members of the whole society become aware of their superiority over their predecessors in that same society.'

Commenting on Kareev's definition of progress, Fyodorov writes with indignation,

> Yet the life of society consists in the old folk getting older and the young folk growing up. But if the younger generation when growing up are made to think of themselves as superior to their dead predecessors then they are bound also to think of themselves, in accordance with the law of progress, as superior to those who are dying and those who are

ageing. Now if an old person says to a younger person, 'you must increase and I must decrease' that is a good wish, for it bespeaks a father's love. On the other hand, if a young person says to an elder, 'it is right for me to grow up and for you to take yourself off to the grave', that is progress and is an expression not of love but of hatred, the hatred of prodigal sons for their fathers.

Fyodorov goes on to point out that this hatred of sons for their fathers was manifesting itself throughout the whole of Europe during the nineteenth century but nowhere more bitingly than in Russia, as was evident from the violent storm that raged throughout Russian society in the wake of the publication in 1860 of Turgenev's novel *Fathers and Sons*. The story of Russian society since that date, whatever else it may show, does at least underline the strength of Fyodorov's criticism of the *idea* of progress being taken as a reflection of a law of nature.

## Nature

Common to all mentally alert, educated persons in the latter half of the nineteenth century was a keen and deep interest in the findings of natural science. There was very good reason for that interest since the astronomers of the day had formulated the law of entropy, according to which the universe is steadily losing energy and, among other consequences, our sun will eventually cease to shine, thus bringing the human adventure to a cold end. Also the Darwinian theory of evolution by natural selection seemed to show that the position of high importance in the universe that *homo sapiens* had for ages attributed to himself was an illusion: man is no more than a lucky survivor in the struggle for existence.

These declarations about nature made by scientists never cease to be the background for all the thoughts of Nikolai Fyodorov also. But, in contrast to many of his contemporaries, he wrote, 'It is not possible to deny the facts, but it does not follow that we have to bow down before them.' By this he meant that he was not cowed by nature; he did not bow down before nature out of fear. Nor, however, did he consider nature to be perfect and therefore something to be worshipped or idolized. Quite the contrary, he repeatedly describes nature as 'blind', 'that force which, by virtue of its blindness gives birth to hunger, sickness and death, and does not distribute its gifts and products according to need, but brings rain where it is not needed and scorches where it is only necessary to warm.' Thus he did not 'deny the facts' embedded in Darwin's evolutionary theses: that in nature the governing factors are strength (or, rather, violence) and beauty – the motive of sexual selection. But what he did deplore was the unthinking conclusion that human beings were bound to accept those same factors as irresistible in the shaping of human society. That conclusion, combined with the individualism that had been producing disrelatedness ever since the Renaissance, seemed to convince many people that human society could never escape from militarism, the expression of natural selection, and from industrialism which produces luxury goods (beauty) in the service of sexual selection. The consequences of that attitude are plain for all to see: 'the destruction of the forests, the exhaustion of the earth, the spread of the deserts, the imbalance of the climate leading to floods and droughts'; and, as a consequence, 'the world is approaching its end; and man by his behaviour is even accelerating that end since his civilization is exploitative but not restorative, so there can be no other result but the hastening of the end.'

But Fyodorov did not believe that such a pessimistic conclusion was unavoidable and his ground for hope was that neither nature nor man is evil. Certainly nature is blind, and certainly man is a fallen creature, but man also has the capacity not only to ask 'what is?' but also to ask 'what ought to be?' and the very fact that he can ask that question demonstrates that he has some vision of how nature ought to be, in other words to remedy the blindness of nature. Fyodorov states very clearly, nature

has already begun *in us* to know itself, and even to practically regulate itself; and if it is expected that nature will produce catastrophes and the destruction of the world then the guilt for that is ours alone for not having united in the task of getting to know the power of nature and regulating it. However could such a bizarre – not to say absurd – teaching arise which urges rational creatures to adopt a passive attitude towards a blind, irrational power which is not really hostile towards us, but only seems so, and indeed *cannot be* hostile since it is in us that it knows itself? And if nature harms us it does so not consciously but out of blindness and through our guilt, through our doing nothing, through our disunity, because *we*, who are the very consciousness of this power, have so far *not united* to get to know nature: that is, to bring it to full consciousness, and so to regulate it that it is transformed from a seeming enemy, a temporary enemy, into an eternal friend.

With that statement Fyodorov displayed a vision of man's place in the universe being of such importance as to have astounded his contemporaries, who deemed man to have been dethroned by virtue of the advances in natural science. Yet many scientists of the present day are in agreement with Fyodorov insofar as they speak of the universe not as a static cosmos but as being in a condition of 'cosmogenesis'; that is to say, the universe is constantly creating new realities which themselves have the potential to create still further new realities.

One of these new realities, according to Fyodorov, is man, who is such a totally unexpected figure in the universe and, in a sense, is contrary to nature because man has none of the attributes by which other animals manage to survive. He does not have a thick coat of hair or scales; he does not have claws or a sting or a fighting beak. Moreover, years go by after his birth before he can forage for himself in order to survive. But Fyodorov argues that it was this very vulnerability and weakness which proved to be the making of man because he then had to struggle against nature, to stand on his own two feet, upright, and thereby to make himself. He then is a product of his own art – in combination with God, for 'the upright posture and prayer (that went with it) . . . were theo-anthropurgic art . . . which consisted of God creating man through man himself. For man is not only a product of nature but also a creation and concern of art. The last act of divine creation was the first act of human art, for man's purpose is to be a free being and consequently self-created, since only a self-created being can be free. In this act of self-creation . . . man discovers God and God reveals himself to man.'

Since he is a co-creator man is God's chosen instrument to cure the blindness of nature by exercising his responsibility for regulating nature. And the first sign that man was exercising that responsibility was given when man stood upright, a stand against the force of gravity which keeps the other animals restricted to horizontal vision. Left to itself 'the cosmos (how it is, and not how it ought to be) is power without reason, whereas man is reason without power. How then can reason become power and power become reason? Power will only become reason when knowledge, reason, regulates it. That is why everything depends on man.' To which the complementary statement runs: 'If a rational being is so related to irrational power that the first can never regulate the second . . . then there would be no choice except to see creation as an evil . . . intentional hellish mockery. Consequently only through faith in the love of God the Father (helping the sons of man with his power) is it possible to realize man's hopes.'

For our present purposes there is no need to enter at any length into the details of Fyodorov's plans for regulating nature, but in order to avoid misunderstanding one or two remarks upon his plans are desirable. First, he makes it clear that none of man's aims in this matter can be achieved until and unless the human race puts aside its divisions, its disrelatedness, so that every single member of the human race is engaged in the common task. Secondly, Fyodorov made a very clear distinction, rare in his day, between the regulation of nature and what he termed 'the exploitation of nature' (something he saw all around him) and 'the utilization of nature', by which he was referring to the industrialists' use of natural resources in order to make money out of their customers' lust for comfort and luxury and mindless toys. Indeed Fyodorov had a real compassion for all creatures, as is shown when he writes,

What practical meaning is to be found in recognizing the

kinship of man with the animals, if it does not even oblige man to protect the life of the animals? Not to do so only deepens the gulf between theory and practice, between the intellectual and the moral position of man, between word and deed. By taking up such an attitude the position of man becomes ever more false. The word of man is turned into empty chatter if, while recognizing his kinship with the animals he cannot even extend the command, 'Thou shalt not kill' to the animal kingdom.

Thirdly, it has to be acknowledged that Fyodorov's practical proposals for regulating nature, like the proposals of all visionaries, often seem wildly extravagant. One can, for instance, marvel at his prescience in predicting that man would travel throughout space by means of rockets and yet gasp with unbelief at his claim that humanity would learn so much about gravity as to be able to use the force of gravity to take command of the earth and to move it around as though the earth had become a kind of spaceship.

However, it would be wrong to conclude, as some commentators have done, that Fyodorov became inebriated by the promises of technology. Quite the contrary, the immediate technological future which he foresaw was one in which the human race would be governed by pornocracy. In that pornocracy men will have abandoned first the belief in God held by their grandfathers, and then the belief in man held by their fathers; and they will have come to regard themselves as 'zoomorphic', animals and nothing more. Then, 'having accepted that they are nothing but animals people will turn themselves into animals.' But technology will also make childless marriages possible as a result of which lust will be given free rein and will drive out love both for fathers and children. Since everyone will be concentrating on obtaining the maximum of comfort and luxury for themselves as individuals they will all come to compete against each other, and to loath one another, and finally to destroy one another. Thus the traditional prophecy of the 'Day of terrible Judgement' will be fulfilled.

But such a terrible outcome is not inevitable and will not happen if man repents of his disrelatedness, his individualism, and his failure to revere the ancestors and their traditions. Let him instead live up to his position as a co-creator with God, and recreate himself 'though not limiting his task simply to persons and society but extending it to the whole of nature. The task of man is to moralize everything that is natural, to transform the blind, involuntary force of nature into an instrument of freedom.'

At this point Fyodorov is inspired to one of the few poetic-lyrical passages to come from his pen when he

> postulates a paradise, the kingdom of God, not in the world beyond but here and now; it demands the transfiguration of this earthly reality, a transfiguration that extends to all heavenly bodies and brings us close to the unknown world beyond. Paradise, or the kingdom of God, is not only within us; it is not only a mental and spiritual kingdom, but a visible, tangible one, perceptible to our organs as developed by psychophysiological regulation (by the control of spiritual and bodily phenomena), organs capable of sensing not just the growing of the grass but the motion of atoms and molecules throughout the Universe, thus making possible the restoration of life and the transfiguration of the entire Universe.

## Supramoralism

Fyodorov's philosophical position, which gave him justification for such a bold vision of the universe and its potentialities, was named by him supramoralism. And his use of the prefix 'supra-' was justified on many counts. To begin with, he needed some term by which to mark the chasm that divided his position from that of the philosophers who had dominated European thought for over two thousand years. He charged those philosophers with having contented themselves with seeking to understand the world as it is and not working for a world as it ought to be. For 'one learns to understand only by doing', and it is only 'the one who *does* the truth who comes to the light'.

By dividing abstract theoretical reason from practical reason, and exempting themselves from God's command 'be ye perfect

even as your Father in heaven is perfect', the philosophers
had turned themselves into a learned class separated from
the unlearned, who were thereby left trying to carry out the
command of making the world perfect without the chance to
learn what was needed. 'At the present time', Fyodorov writes,

> there exist God and the world, and 'the world' [in Russian,
> *mir*] means the world in its present condition [not as it ought
> to be]: that is, the world in which we have not fulfilled our
> duty. When our duty is fulfilled, then the world will become
> the *perfect* world (*mir*).[4] When we say: 'God is not in nature,
> but God is with us', we are acknowledging the sovereignty
> of reason over blind force: that is, we are talking about the
> *perfect* world, and not about the world characterized by
> the opposite condition. The world is a fact, but the *perfect*
> world is our project.

But, he asks, is the learned class capable of becoming a ministry
of unification to carry out that project?

> Is that class which maintains itself with prejudices and whose
> religion is the acceptance of a dead, lifeless god and a lifeless
> immortality, whose ethic consists not even in egotism but
> in solipsism (which, when combined with the claim to an
> absurd 'altruism', makes this class the worst of all pharisees)
> – is such a class capable of such a transformation? Is that
> class capable of action which, even as it turns every thought
> and word into coveted private property (through copyright),
> also asserts that its renunciation of a future life is a laudable
> kind of disinterestedness; that class which, as it renounces
> belief in the future, pharisaically melts with emotion over
> its own cheap sacrifice?
>
> The learned class, freed as it is from compulsory military
> service, considers itself peace-loving; it even mourns the fact
> that people are unable to live in peace, and becomes indig-
> nant when they take up arms. This class preaches peace in
> the world, but does not notice that in whatever work it is
> doing, whether it be pure or applied science, it is itself
> promoting the business of war, either directly (if the appli-
> cation of its knowledge is related to the perfection of
> weapons) or indirectly (when the application of its knowl-
> edge is related to industry and commerce, which in
> themselves promote enmity and therefore serve to stimulate

war). But if the learned class occupies itself with pure science and is not concerned about application (which, incidentally, others will be concerned about, for no pure science will remain long without application to war or industry), it will be digressing from true knowledge, which is not just knowledge of general causes but is the knowledge of the causes of non-kinship, enmity and war. And these will be eliminated, not by preaching (no matter how persuasive), not by indignation (no matter how vigorous), not by banishing descriptions of war from the history books, but only by the elimination of the very causes of division, non-kinship, enmity and war. . . . The pinnacle of morality is the point where one does not separate oneself from others, does not separate 'one's own' from what is common; where there is no contradiction between thought and action. And the pinnacle of religion is Christianity, which does not separate the resurrection of Christ from the resurrection of all.

A further and even more profound justification for Fyodorov's term 'supramoralism' is rooted in another area of knowledge where the learned class again manifests the inadequacy of their philosophy by limiting themselves to what is rather than what ought to be. The area in question is that of history. For the learned, history is simply a telling of 'facts', from which nothing can be deduced as to whether history has any meaning or not. The unlearned, on the other hand, at least have the capacity to grieve over the 'facts', to protest that such facts are not what *ought* to be. And, in an instinctive though unenlightened fashion, they recognize that history is a project, something to be accomplished, and that they have a part to play in that accomplishment, in giving meaning to history. One may therefore elucidate the question about the meaning of history according to Fyodorov by invoking a formula characteristic of all his thinking: that is, 'if . . . then . . .'. So when someone asks whether history has any meaning the answer is neither yes nor no but, '*if* the human race fulfils the common task, *then* you will be able to answer in the affirmative'.

The issue on which Fyodorov most clearly displays this unique way of addressing a question is that which he entitles

*The conditionality of prophecies concerning the end of the world.* His treatment of the matter is described by Nicolas Berdyaev as Fyodorov's most original contribution to human thinking.

> The religious interpretation of the books of Holy Writ differs sharply from that of the learned. The priestly class does not find there dogmas but *law,* that is, it demands *action.* It does not divide history from the prophets, that is, action from word. But for the learned class a prophet is a contemplative, that is, one of the learned class whose object is knowledge of the future, a predetermined, fatal event. . . . The learned accept determinism, fatalism, the inevitable, and refuse to recognize history as a project for universal redemption, which would involve the negation of determinism and fatalism.

The most obvious example of the provisional nature of prophecy, of its being conditional upon certain undetermined actions, an example that Fyodorov frequently adduces, is that of the prophet Jonah. Jonah prophesied that the city of Nineveh was doomed to destruction. But, as we all know, the citizens of Nineveh repented of their sins and the destruction announced by the prophet of God, Jonah, did not take place. Whereupon Jonah, instead of being glad that the city had been saved, became indignant and flew into a rage. (We might comment that in this he behaved like one of the learned class, indignant that an event predicted on the basis of reliable evidence had not taken place.) There are many other scriptural passages cited by Fyodorov of such provisionality, one example being God's change of mind in Jeremiah 18: 7; and others are to be found in the parables of Jesus which are so often couched in the form of 'if . . . then . . .' warnings. But perhaps the most arresting instance of the application of the Fyodorovian formula is in regard to the question of God's very existence.

He claims that not even the most profound subjective mystical experience, nor any intellectual speculation, can afford convincing proof of God's existence. Only when humanity has fulfilled the common task demanded of human beings by God will man be worthy to stand in the presence of God. 'Only through great, exacting, prolonged labour will we acquit our-

selves of our obligation, especially to the resurrection, and
enter into communion with the Trinity, abiding in the likeness
of the Trinity, being distinct, deathless persons, both feeling
and touching our unity. And only then will we have ultimate
proof for the existence of God, seeing him face to face.'

It is clear from this passage why Fyodorov coined the term
'supramoralism'. He needed some term to point infinitely
beyond the narrow, individualist, pharisaical type of behaviour
conventional in his day. Instead he urges a moralism that
originates from and finds completion in the life of the Trinity
and that demands an intensity of work far beyond any conceived by contemporary society. In the achievement of that
work he attached supreme importance to the Liturgy, never
failing to point out that the very word, based upon the Greek
*leiturgia*, can be translated as 'the common task'.

## Liturgy

We have many witnesses to the ardour with which Fyodorov,
in contrast to most educated Russians of his day (even to most
of the believers) used to take part in the Church's Liturgy,
faithfully following the cycle of the Church year. He was often
to be seen in Moscow churches wrapt in prayerful concentration. And, since he used to define Christianity as 'the
religion of resurrection', for him the central moment of every
year was Holy Week culminating in Easter. That was why he
was so enraged with Tolstoy when the latter scornfully referred
to Easter as 'witchcraft'. It was his practice, whenever possible, to make his way to Moscow on foot for the Easter
Liturgy in the Kremlin, beginning with vespers and matins in
the Uspensky cathedral. In fact he spoke of himself as 'having
been formed by Holy Week and Easter morning' and went
on to maintain that 'the Liturgy can provide education of a
depth and breadth such as science never can do, so long as
science remains abstract. Because the Liturgy, by embracing in
prayer the enduring needs of man, does not remain indifferent
to the great questions of the day. Though in that case much
depends on the liveliness and sensitivity towards those questions

on the part of the churches' ministers themselves.' Typical of his own sensitivity towards the importance of right order in liturgical actions was his comment that you can sense the authenticity of people's faith by the way they make the sign of the cross – the hasty fashion of the present day was a sign of corruption, a falling away from the dignified manner traditional among the people.

But if we are to understand Fyodorov's thinking we have to abandon entirely any notion of liturgy as nothing more than a series of signals performed in a church. For him the 'liturgy' of man already began when man first stood upright and turned his body towards heaven. 'In the vertical position as in every act of rising upwards, man – or the son of man – reveals himself to be an artist and his artistic product is a temple . . .: that is, an aesthetic interpretation of existence and creation, and by the same token not only aesthetic but also sacred. Our life is an act of aesthetic creation.'

Those words, however, would be completely misleading if we were to assume that by 'aesthetic' Fyodorov meant the same as his contemporaries meant by the word 'cultural'. In fact he once wrote, 'the aim of life is salvation from culture', and he spoke so because, on this point at least, he agreed with Tolstoy that nineteenth-century society had made culture into a surrogate for religion and for life itself. The people, on the other hand, had always known that religion and life came first. That is precisely why the primary creators of culture are always the people; for the individual accredited with cultural achievements owes everything to the people; and the highest expression of art is not a novel or a painting or a piece of music produced by an individual – but a communal achievement, the temple, the church, the cathedral.

For Fyodorov the highest of the various forms of art was architecture, especially the architecture of the temple or cathedral because in it was provided the opportunity to celebrate life in stone, in wall paintings, in icons and in music, all of these in the service of life itself. 'The son of man represents boundlessness, power and life by perfecting sculpture, painting and the art of icons in the cathedral. Man resorts to sound, word and letter and, finally, to his own self to serve as living representations of the dead; and in that form common prayer is converted into the service of the Church.'

It tells us much about Fyodorov's vision of liturgy that the artistic representation of the truths of faith should take the form of paintings on the *outer* walls of the church and that such paintings should make clear what is the common task that is being initiated within the church. What is taking place inside the church is for the sake of the world outside the church, for the uniting of the whole human family in brotherhood, in a society which reflects the Holy Trinity. Indeed Fyodorov time and again, in one form or another, employs his 'if . . . then . . .' formula to the question of the real presence of Christ in the Eucharist. He always fiercely contested the Protestant theory that the action of the Eucharist is only *symbolic* but at the same time his own answer was to say that the question of Christ's presence will only be able to be answered in the affirmative when the Eucharist is not simply a ritual carried out in church on a Sunday but rather the guiding power animating the whole of life every day.

Bewailing the fall away from that vision, Fyodorov writes,

> The Liturgy creates the Church. When the teaching of the Trinity was made into a dogma, a philosophical thesis, the Church became no more than a temple (a building in other words), leaving everyday abodes outside its boundaries. And so the Liturgy became the business of the priests, of the clergy, and not of the whole people, at the same time deviating from the task of achieving deliverance from the reality of death, from the task of resurrection. So for the learned class, and for artists, the Liturgy became no more than a remembrance in the form of a drama while for the unlearned it was turned into a fetish: that is, an action that spreads neither knowledge nor action – and exercises no transforming influence.

However, authentic liturgy reaches out to all, 'not only to all believers but to non-believers also'. While the Liturgy is a divine service for believers, for non-believers it is education through art. But for the one as for the other it has the same sacred character because of the importance of the questions concerning health and nourishment inherent in the Eucharist.

And though the Eucharist is for believers the body and blood of Christ, whereas for non-believers it is simply bread and wine, nevertheless for the one as for the other it is a profound mystery whose working out is our task. The uniting of all peoples takes place through work together, through the Liturgy, both preparing a meal for all (the question of nourishment), and healing the soul and body of all (the question of health). And this liturgy, when completed by the whole of humanity, will be a prayer leading into action, thoughtful remembrance becoming reality. The altar of this liturgy will be the whole earth, itself the dust of the dead, and the 'heavenly powers (light and heat) will visibly (and not secretly) serve to transform the dust into the body and blood of the dead'.

For an explanation of these mysterious words we can now turn to that archetypal passion of Fyodorov which, like the final section of a fugue, reveals the internal logic in the relationship between all the previous themes.

## The common task: the resurrection of the dead

If Nicolas Berdyaev is right when he says that 'no one in the whole of human history has felt such pain at the thought of death as did Fyodorov, nor such a burning desire to restore life to all who have died', then it is only to be expected that passion for resurrection should be Fyodorov's ceaseless preoccupation. But, contrary to what might be expected of a Christian thinker, his exposition of resurrection neither begins nor ends with the story of the resurrection of Jesus of Nazareth – indeed he only rarely uses the personal name of Jesus, on almost all occasions preferring the title Christ.

For Fyodorov the task of resurrection begins with the very appearance of man upon the earth. 'Resurrection is not a new commandment but is as ancient as the cult of the ancestors, as old as the act of burial, which was an attempt at revivification' – hiding the dead in the earth like a seed, in the hope that it would revive and grow again. ' "Man is a creature who buries." That is the most profound definition of man that has ever been given.' The impulse to resurrect is simultaneous with man's consciousness of death and is sustained throughout the whole human story, sometimes only weakly but at other times with a passion like Fyodorov's own. That was why Fyodorov attached so much importance to the example given by the art of ancient Egypt, which to him was a clear vindication of his conviction that art, in its origin, is an attempt to imitate resurrection. There, 'the son would erect a monument to his father not lying in the horizontal position, like the dead, but in the vertical position like a living person, upright', the face full of life. Most of the statues in their tombs convey the individuality of the dead person, his special clothes, for instance: everything that could serve as a replacement should the mummy itself be destroyed. The portraits of servants and food and scenes from everyday life surrounded the dead person with everything necessary for life beyond the tomb. They express the profound need and effort which gave birth to art: the need to restore life to the one who has vanished, has died; and the effort to transmute fleeting life into incorruptible, eternal life.

But it was not until the coming of Christ that the representation of the dead as living, an imitation of the dead one, was turned into reality, and it began in Bethany. 'Bethany!', wrote Fyodorov, 'This small village must be placed above Bethlehem, which had no place within its walls for the new born Christ; above Nazareth, intent upon killing its prophet; above Jerusalem, which killed him and had no place for him in death, just as Bethlehem had no place for him at his birth. But Bethany recognized the rejected Messiah in the highest degree, as the Resurrection and the life.' For Bethany was the site of the resurrection of Lazarus,

> the miracle of love for a friend, the highest deed of heroic self-sacrifice and courage, since the only one capable of giving life back to Lazarus was the one who laid down his life 'for his friend'. In the whole life of Christ there was no more significant event than the resurrection of Lazarus. That was his triumphant declaration of himself as the Messiah, both in deed and in word. Hence, 'the Resurrection' is his true name.

So it was at Bethany, where he declared himself 'the Resurrection and the life' that Jesus *initiated* the specific task of resurrecting the dead. And one must stress that word initiated at this point because it affords a clue to Fyodorov's highly original understanding of resurrection as he expressed it, for instance, in his answer to his own question:

> Why did the universal raising of the dead not immediately follow upon the Resurrection of Christ? How is one to comprehend, how is one to imagine, why the Resurrection of all did not follow the resurrection of Christ? Christianity would not be Christianity (that is worldwide love); Christ would not be the Son of Man (the son of the departed fathers); he would not be heart and soul in the grave of the fathers (in hell); he would be completely incomprehensible, if the connection between his Resurrection and the universal reurrection were to be broken. But according to Christian teaching, as expressed not only in word but also in the whole celebration of Easter, the Resurrection of Christ is inseparably bound up with the universal resurrection. We must see the raising of the dead as a not yet completed action. But neither is it an action to be completed only in the future, as the Mohammedans believe. It is neither altogether in the past nor exclusively in the future, but a public action in process of completion. 'The hour is coming, and now is' (John 5: 25). Christ is its initiator and through us it is continuing even now. The raising of the dead is not a thought only, but also not an accomplished fact; it is a project. As a word, as a precept, as a divine command, it is an accomplished fact. But as a task or fulfilment of the command, it is an action not yet completed. As a work of God it is already finished; as a work of man it is not yet finished.

Fyodorov also provides us with reasons why the project of resurrection had to be ordered in the way it has been. If people in Europe have generally failed to see why it is so, that is probably due to the fact that Europeans have confused resurrection with the claim made by Socrates that there is a human soul which is immortal. That claim was regarded by Fyodorov with horror because it had given rise in Europe to the individualism that so enraged him: having infiltrated into Christian modes of thought the claim sanctioned the horrible belief that some individuals in heaven could be in a state of bliss while brothers of theirs might be in hell, suffering eternal torments: as in Dante's *Divine Comedy*, the apogee (to Fyodorov) of individualist fantasy and a denial of the common task, the complete renunciation of 'brotherhood-creation'.

Once we see the inadequacy of the Socratic position it becomes easier for us to recognize the positive character of Fyodorov's explanation as to why the resurrection of all did not immediately follow the Resurrection of Christ: that is, had it followed immediately then the process of creating brotherhood and, indeed, the redemption of all creation that is conditional on the brotherhood of all creatures, would have been aborted. Because 'it is only through our transforming ourselves into instruments of the Divine Work' that the transformation of all creation and the establishment of the kingdom of God will take place: 'Universal resurrection will only be achieved by means of the whole hearts, the whole thoughts, the whole actions, in fact all the powers and talents of all the sons of man.'

And if those demands posited by Fyodorov for the future of man in creation seem exaggerated and even impossible we need to remind ourselves of the enormity of what is at stake. And that can be grasped most clearly when we are brought face to face with Fyodorov's vision of what is possible for man and the universe around him. Whenever Fyodorov speaks about that vision he does so with an ecstatic joy that can only have arisen out of his experience of the Easter Liturgy in church, which convinced him that the whole of creation was destined for such an Easter. Here are two passages that express his conviction:

> Supramoralism postulates paradise, the kingdom of God, not in the world beyond but here and now. It demands the transfiguration of this earthly reality, a transfiguration which extends to all heavenly bodies and brings us close to the unknown world beyond. Paradise, or the kingdom of God, is not only within us. It is not only a mental or spiritual kingdom but a visible and tangible one, perceptible to our organs as they are developed by psychophysiological regu-

lation (by the control of spiritual and bodily phenomena), organs capable of sensing not just the growing of the grass but the motion of atoms and molecules throughout the universe, thus making possible the restoration of life and the transfiguration of the entire universe.

And in a still longer passage, entitled 'The end of orphanhood; boundless kinship', he writes:

That day longed for throughout the ages, one of jubilation throughout the boundless heavens, will only dawn when the earth – which has swallowed the generations into darkness, but is now moved and regulated by the heavenly love of the sons – will begin to give back those whom it has swallowed up and will people with them the heavenly starry worlds, which at present are devoid of spirit and coldly, seemingly sorrowfully, look down upon us. [It will dawn] when we gather together and revivify the dust of those who gave us life or – more truly – gave us their own life, instead of turning that dust into food for ourselves and our descendants, which [at present] we are bound to do because of the disassociation of worlds and the need to live on whatever resources have accumulated on our tiny planet. Through their knowledge of matter and its power the reconstituted previous generations will already be capable of regenerating their bodies out of basic elements and populating other worlds, overcoming their divisions. At that time the sun will truly dance, just as the simple folk even now think they see the sun doing as Easter dawns on the day of Bright Resurrection. Then innumerable choirs of stars will also join in the rejoicing. Figments of the poets, which have personified these worlds, making them into fathers, will become the truth. But personification – or, more precisely, patrification – will now be presented not in thought or imagination but in deed. Premature participation, alive in popular and non-popular poetry, clearly demonstrates that the day sought for is the hope of all peoples for ages and ages, expected from time immemorial. This day, which the Lord will create through us, will arise neither from some imaginary movements of the sun nor real movements of the earth but from combined acts of sons who loved their fathers and have been filled with deep compassion for the departed. Then the earth will become the first star in the heavens to be moved not by the blind force of the fall but by reason, which has withstood and prevented fall and death. There will be nothing further when in the totality of worlds we witness the totality of all previous generations. (The all-embracing reunion. That is the great future which the past awaits, when the present will take up its vocation, its task, its aim.) *All will be related, nothing will be alien*; yet nevertheless there will open up for everyone a world of immeasurable depth and height, though not an overpowering or terrifying one, rather one capable of satisfying limitless desire, a life without boundaries such as frightens the present-day exhausted, sick, would-be Buddhist generation. This life will be new, in spite of being ancient: that is, spring without autumn, dawn without evening, youth without old age, resurrection without death. Then, however, there will be not simply autumn and evening, there will be dark night, just as there remains a hell of suffering such as there has been in the present and past generations of humanity, but it remains only as representing the grief that has been lived through, which will actually heighten the value of the bright day of resurrection. That day will be glorious, marvellous – but not miraculous, since *resurrection will be an act not of miracle but of knowledge and common work*.

The sought after day, the day hoped for throughout the ages, will be *a command of God brought to fulfilment by man*.

At the same time as Fyodorov envisaged such a glorious fulfilment of all creation as a real possibility he was also acutely aware that human beings were in dire danger of destroying that possibility. With prophetic insight he warned of a time when scientific technology will have far outstripped the capacity of human morality. Indeed, before his very eyes, he could see developing a society that he often described as a pornocracy or, on other occasions, as 'anti-Easter' and 'counter-Easter'. Characteristic of this pornocracy, for instance, was humanity's ready collusion with the blindness of nature, which was leading to destruction of fauna and flora over the face of the whole globe, and, more sinister still, to the destruction of the human race. So Fyodorov writes,

The human race, remaining unperfected and in a condition of discord and having failed to unite in the task of confronting the blind force of nature but, instead, submitting to it, arrives in a *natural way* at a condition of degeneracy and eventually extinction. In a *supernatural way* it can expect only transcendental resurrection: one not achieved through us but from outside, taking place apart from us and even contrary to our will. That would be a resurrection of wrath, the Last Judgement by which some are condemned to eternal suffering (the sinners) while others (the righteous) are destined to the contemplation of that suffering . . .

Taking up the same theme in another place he writes, '*The celebration of Easter*, of filial and brotherly love, is a conscious, natural act. But the opposite, *the victory of pornocracy* (that is, of brutal and beastly passion concealing itself under the pretence of culture) is in fact an anti- or counter-Easter, a natural act devoid of consciousness which leads to a counter-natural condition.'

By various stages the members of 'pornocratic' society will turn away from theology towards anthropology; and then, in the next generation, from anthropology to zoology, at which point, 'having classified themselves as animals they will turn themselves into animals'. Religion will be regarded as 'belonging to the youth or infancy of the human race, so it will be seen as something incidental, an appendage, long since of no importance or use. . . . Sexual feeling, or lust, having created *childless marriages*, will then drive out love for both fathers and children.' With no concern either for past or future generations the aim of these human animals will be to prolong their own lives at whatever cost to others, and to eliminate anything which threatens their own comfort and pleasure. In this anti-Easter they will maintain that their vices are virtues, these 'permanent adolescents' who despise the dead but do not beget new life. Finally, they will 'turn upon themselves and others with loathing'; and 'having rendered their adolescence perpetual they will start to eliminate one another; and so the Day of Wrath will have been brought about.'

All that has thus far been related about Fyodorov's notions of the resurrection of the dead seems to have been greeted with keen interest, and even enthusiasm, by three of his greatest contemporaries, Tolstoy, Dostoevsky and Vladimir Solovyov.

But when it came to the next stage of the project of resurrection – the practical steps that have to be taken in order to accomplish the common task, then not one of his three admirers could follow him. It is not surprising, since it has been said that 'throughout the whole of world philosophy there has never been a project so audacious and mysterious'. And yet the project is perfectly simple. It is that all the present members of the human race must join together so that by combining all their talents, both intellectual, spiritual and physical, they can quite literally resurrect all their dead ancestors. And to anyone whose immediate, spontaneous response to this audacious prospect is a negative one, thinking first of all that it is impossible, impractical, or even undesirable, Fyodorov has a word to say: that is, 'A man who would not, if he could, return life to those from whom he received it is not worthy of life or freedom.'

Fyodorov bases his answer to the objection that the project of the common task is impracticable on the observation that the human body is a kind of mechanism, composed of particles of matter, and since these particles have not vanished out of the universe but are still in existence somewhere, it should be possible, with the aid of advanced science and technology, to collect those particles together again and reconstitute them in accordance with the blueprint of the particular ancestor one is trying to resurrect. For if you can put back together a machine from its constituent parts, why can you not do so with the human machine? Were Fyodorov still alive he might well justify his project by pointing to the work of the American mathematical cosmologist Frank Tipler, who envisages how intelligent life may harmonize the massive energies of end-time into an infinite capacity to process information which will create a total simulation of the universe in all its past stages for the personal enjoyment of every human being who ever was. Moreover, a similar vision is to be found in the work of the Belorussian biologist, Aleksei Maneev.

There are, of course, innumerable reasons for doubting the feasibility of the practical steps necessary for the realization of Fyodorov's common task, many of them so obvious that it would be superfluous to list them. For us, rather, it is the spin-off of insights into spiritual issues resulting from such an authentic and noble passion that we need to attend to. (One needs to point out that the amount of space devoted to the material aspects of resurrection in the *Philosophia obshevo dela* is far smaller than that which he devotes to the spiritual issues involved.) For instance, on the theme of unity he writes that 'One learns to understand only by doing. Our understanding of God increases with unity and, conversely, decreases with discord (in the human race)', and 'an understanding of the Holy Trinity can only be attained by achieving universal human multi-unity', and 'the blessedness of unity is essential for the blessedness of resurrection'.

And what is it that causes the fatal disunity and discord? Fyodorov answered,

Of all divisions, the disassociation of thought from action (which has become the monopoly of certain classes) constitutes the great calamity, incomparably greater than the division into rich and poor. Socialists, and our contemporaries in general, attribute the greatest importance to this division into rich and poor, assuming that with its elimination all of us would become educated. However, what we have in mind is not schooling, which will become more evenly available with the elimination of poverty. What we have in mind is universal participation in knowledge and research. The elimination of poverty is not sufficient to ensure such a universal participation, which alone can bridge the chasm between the learned and the unlearned.

So long as participation in knowledge does not embrace everyone, pure science will remain indifferent to struggle and depredation; while applied science will contribute to destruction either directly by the invention of weapons, or indirectly by endowing things like consumer goods with a seductive appearance, thus fostering friction among people.

There remains, therefore, a project within the great project, a step on the way to the realization of the latter. And that can only be achieved by overcoming the division between the learned and the unlearned, which will only happen when learned and unlearned, rich and poor, unite in the common task of resurrection. That, in its turn, requires the city and the village to unite, because the scien-

tists and scholars who are bent upon reconstituting the dead
will have to move their laboratories and studies into the
villages so as to be beside the graveyards or even the fields
where the dust of the ancestors is to be found.

So Fyodorov outlined in great detail the complex of community institutions where learned and unlearned, children and
elders, would all be engaged in the common task: the existence
of a church could be assumed, as also a school; and there
would be a museum and an observatory. The observatory
would be a crucial instrument in the task of regulating nature,
controlling the climate, earth and water of the district, and this
would require the combination of the theoretical knowledge of
the learned and the practical knowledge of the peasantry, as
well as of the children, who could help to gather information
about the fauna and flora of the locality.

But one institution in his ideal complex specially close to
Fyodorov's heart was the museum, a closeness partly generated,
no doubt, because when properly understood the museum
offered an alternative to the university – an institution so often
the object of Fyodorov's anger. 'Nothing more than backyards
of factories and army barracks, serving industrialism and militarism', temples of 'the new Pharisees', are among the
descriptions applied by him to contemporary universities:
symbols of the separation of thought from action, of theoretical
reason from practical reason, places where the question asked
was always 'What is?' and never 'What ought to be?'

The learned class in the universities had propagated the false
notion that a museum can never be more than a repository
for dead objects, which is the exact opposite of the truth. For
the progress advocated by the learned class

> is precisely the production of dead things, accompanied by
> the displacement of living people. . . . For the museum a
> person is infinitely higher than a thing, whereas for the
> districts of a city dedicated to factory civilization and culture
> a thing is higher than a person. The museum is the last
> remnant of the cult of the ancestors. . . . In a museum under
> the appearance of old odds and ends there is a gathering
> of the dead, of the departed. But these souls only reveal
> themselves to those who themselves have a soul. A museum

is *not* a *collection of things, but a community of persons*; its functions consist not in the accumulation of things but in restoring life to the remains of what is no longer living, in the restoration of the dead through their products and by way of living agents.

One of the objections raised to Fyodorov's requirement of a movement away from the cities was the fact that advances in technology were based upon city life and would became impossible should Fyodorov's project be attempted. Fyodorov, in a few brief lines, answers the objection in a way that reveals one of the fundamental spin-offs from the philosophy of the common task. He indicts sociologists for concentrating on securing higher wages and shorter working hours for workers and failing to realize that the whole of industrial civilization is based upon the energy derived from the mining of coal and iron, which sentences miners to a 'back-breaking labour' (*katorzhnii* in Russian also means penal, *katorzhninik* – convict). The situation requires not economic reform but a radical, technical reform; indeed, not so much a reform as 'a universal revolution based upon moral revolution'. Here he is once more challenging the domination of 'what is' by the question 'what ought to be?' – a question which produces the answer that the kind of work demanded of miners ought not to be demanded of human beings. Fascinatingly, the consequences he foresees are far from being disastrous. On the contrary, human beings will in consequence have to concentrate their researches upon the regulation of nature, using the energy of the wind and the waves and, above all, the energy of the sun to provide the energy needed by science and technology. After all, the sun was the source of the energy that is now condensed in coal; and its energy, as he pointed out, will last much longer than the deposits of coal. By asking what ought to be Fyodorov had proved to be many years ahead of his time.

One further instance of a profound insight arising out of Fyodorov's passion for the resurrection of the dead comes from the consequent need for a template of each of the ancestors to be established. Since each human being is a potential ancestor,

taking into consideration the enormous significance of the

law of heredity, it must be recognized that everyone has the most sacred duty of keeping a psychophysiological journal. And the first religious duty of a school is to teach children how to compose such journals. In order to establish the programme for the stated journal one needs nothing less than a full international conference of psychologists, physiologists etc. These journals will serve as the foundation for the psychocratic society.

The complementary aspect, obviously, of establishing a template for the use of one's successors is the need to establish templates of all the ancestors. Hence it is a sacred duty, which also must be taught in schools, to establish the genealogy of one's own family which could then be broadened into the genealogy of the whole human family, thereby bringing into unity all the sons of God (all the children) – a unity which would represent the Son of God, the Logos. 'If there were no divisions (if all sons were a single son) then the Logos would represent the corporateness of the individual images of all the fathers as one father: that is, would represent a genealogy, which was partly the case in the family life of old. The primitive life of man was a family life; the first word of man, the first knowledge of the race was genealogy ... the Book of Genesis is just such a genealogy.' But in order for a genuine likeness of God to be established 'the genealogical tree of mankind must not be just a tree of knowledge but also a tree of life, in which inner-kinship becomes clear, external, tangible, and not just a vague feeling as it is now.'

Despite the ambiguities in Fyodorov's proposals for the audacious project of resurrecting the dead, and despite the inconsistencies to be found in the 1,200 large-scale pages of his *Philosophia obshevo dela*, there are no solid grounds for accusing him of propagating a materialist project or for doubting the authenticity of his Christian profession, as some rather narrow-minded theologians have done. He states quite unambiguously, on many occasions, that 'for the blessedness of resurrection the blessedness of unity is essential', and 'resurrection is impossible where there exist sin, ignorance and other misfortunes resulting from man's dependence on the blind forces of nature'.

Doubts about Fyodorov's theological correctness arise out of a failure to appreciate his subtle, though admittedly undeveloped, attitude towards time and eternity: an attitude that leads to his unusual solution to the problem of God's transcendence and immanence. He writes, for instance, 'The problem of God's transcendence or immanence will only be solved when humans in their togetherness become an instrument of universal resuscitation; when the Divine Word becomes our divine action.' He is quite clear that one should not 'confuse God with a world where blindness and death reign', yet in the end resurrection is the work of God through man. Here he is saying once again that we cannot understand anything of these matters unless we act upon the divine commands, otherwise our words and concepts are empty of meaning.

Probably the most helpful formulation of his position is given in that passage (already quoted) where he makes play with the fact that the Russian word *mir* means both world and peace (or perfect world).

> Our view is as follows. At the present time there exist God and the world (*mir*), and 'the world' means the world in its present condition: that is the world in which we have not fulfilled our duty. When our duty is fulfilled, then the world will become the perfect world (*mir*). When we say: 'God is not in nature, but God is with us', we are acknowledging the sovereignty of reason over blind force: that is, we are talking about the *perfect* world, and not about the world characterized by the opposite condition. The world is a fact, but the *perfect* world is our project.

It has to be a matter for regret that Fyodorov, on account of his reluctance to allow his writings to be published during his lifetime, thereby deprived himself and his contemporaries of the opportunity to discuss and clarify them. In the meantime, we have to be content with his formula 'God is with us', a not unsatisfying one in view of the fact that it is the one used by Isaiah, *Emmanu'el* (with us, God) as the title of the child whose birth is announced in Isaiah (7: 10–17) as a sign of deliverance and which Christians have taken as a prediction of the birth of Christ.

Even more to be regretted in the context of the present book is that Fyodorov never expanded on the intriguing opening sentence of his very last article, written in 1903: 'How to describe the year when the Easter Liturgy was sung in the middle of summer in fulfilment of the prophecy of Seraphim?' Why Fyodorov sought some special way of characterizing that year was because it was, as he says in the article, 'the year of the pilgrimage of the Tsar and his family to the graves of the ancestors in the Kremlin; and, in addition, to the canonization of the great devotee of the Bright Resurrection [Seraphim], in which the Tsar took a vital part in the company of his people.' Not only that, however, for as he makes clear, the year 1903 marked the fiftieth anniversary of his realization that his own task in life was to fulfil the common task of resurrection.

The bulk of that last article written by Fyodorov was a troubled one revolving around various peace conferences, which seemed unable to help in overcoming that greatest obstacle to the universal brotherhood, that effect and cause of disrelatedness, the practice of warfare. And that year was to be the last year of Fyodorov's life. It was on 3 December that he died, in the Mariinsky hospital for the poor, the very same hospital where Fyodor Dostoevsky had been born on the 30 October 1831. He was buried in the Skorbyashchensky Zhensky monastery where a quarter of a century later his grave was to witness the fulfilment of one of Fyodorov's more melancholy predictions. For in the 1890s, during the course of his polemic against the American futurologist Bellamy, Fyodorov had singled out for special castigation, as an example of contempt for the ancestors, Bellamy's prediction that, as a sign of progress, men would dance on the graves of their ancestors. In 1929 the graveyard where Fyodorov was buried was razed to the ground by the Soviet regime and the area was turned into a playground.

# 3

# The writer: Fyodor Dostoevsky

In June 1880 the educated classes in Moscow were ablaze with excitement, among other reasons on account of the celebrations in honour of their great national poet, Aleksander Pushkin. And the climax of those celebrations was fixed for 8 June when Dostoevsky was to make a speech at the unveiling of the Pushkin monument. It was a period of triumph for the great novelist whose work, *The Brothers Karamazov*, was appearing in instalments, and now nearing its completion, reaching an ever wider public and causing readers to acclaim, 'You are a prophet. We have become better human beings since reading *The Brothers Karamazov*.'

But the novelist was himself by this time reaching the end of his own life. He was to be dead only six months later. The weight of all the suffering he had endured, the humiliation inflicted upon him in the late 1840s by Turgenev among others, the mock execution by firing squad to which he was subjected by Tsar Nicholas I, the years in the Siberian prison camp, the years of desperate grasping for a woman's love, his addiction to gambling (which he conquered), his life-long financial difficulties, to say nothing of his constant bouts of epilepsy and his worsening emphysema, all of these trials and tribulations had almost exhausted his body by the time he stepped on to the platform in front of a vast crowd at the Nobles Club on the evening of 8 June. He looked tired and grey, his body shrunken inside his dress coat.

Yet throughout the whole of his stormy life Dostoevsky had known himself to be 'a ball of fire'. When imprisoned in the Peter and Paul fortress, for instance, he had written, 'I have such a reserve of vitality that it cannot be exhausted.' And from the prison camp at Omsk he had told his brother that he retained 'healthy reserves of spiritual life'. While in the depths of his most trying years he was delighted to report that he had the 'vitality of a cat'. These words proved to be no idle boast when the grey, shrunken figure on the platform of the Nobles Club was transformed once more into a ball of fire as his words drew ever more thunderous applause from his audience. At the end of his speech they acclaimed him with cries such as 'You are our saint! You are our prophet!' and for a whole half-hour they recalled him back to the platform over and over again.

As one commentator has observed, 'After his speech about Pushkin, an enraptured ecstasy seized his audience. This amazing day does not have any parallel in the whole history of Russian spiritual culture.' And maybe it was the rapture of that day that imbued Dostoevsky with the energy to complete *The Brothers Karamazov* so brilliantly and convincingly. For by October he was able to hand in the last instalment of the novel, the ending of which had been awaited with bated breath by thousands upon thousands of the Russian people.

Even after the novel was completed there were many who hoped that Dostoevsky might write a second volume which would continue the story of Alyosha Karamazov subsequent to his departure from the monastery. Those hopes were based upon certain hints in the novel itself but they foundered on spiritual reality, in the order of which Dostoevsky had completed the life's work laid upon him by his vocation. In the timing of his death there is an appropriateness strikingly parallel to that of the great poet whose name during Dostoevsky's life was often invoked as a source for understanding the great novelist, none other than Dante Alighieri.

The whole of Dante's life had been a preparation for the writing of the *Divine Comedy*. At its culmination he died, even before the last cantos of the poem had been published. Indeed for a period those last cantos were thought to be lost until his sons discovered them. The timing of his death was right and proper because he had completed his earthly work. In the process, also, he had himself become as integrated a human being as he possibly could be. And so it was time for him to go. The same can be said of Dostoevsky's departure from the world in January 1881, which is why Herman Hesse wrote that it is as well no continuation of the Karamazov story was published 'because otherwise not only Russian literature but also Russia and all mankind would have exploded and evaporated'. In any case it could already be claimed, of *The Brothers Karamazov,* as Mochulsky does, that 'Never in all world literature has Christianity been advanced with such striking force as *the religion of spiritual freedom.'*

The parallels between the life and work of the great Italian poet and the great Russian novelist are worth some attention at this point because Dostoevsky himself was conscious of them. In 1863, for instance, Dostoevsky wrote an introduction to the Russian translation of Victor Hugo's *Notre Dame de Paris* in which he says that for years he himself has been contemplating the great novel of which the nineteenth century was in dire need, and of which he says, 'Such a great work of art will have to give voice to the aspirations and characteristics of our own age just as the *Divine Comedy,* for example, expressed fully and for ever the beliefs and ideals of medieval Catholicism.' So it is clear that Dostoevsky, in trying to give voice to the aspirations and characteristics of his own age in his determination to write the great novel that the nineteenth century needed, had in mind the achievement of Dante's *Divine Comedy.*

Both Dostoevsky's writing and the *Divine Comedy* share a further characteristic that is important to bear in mind if one is not to misread both his work and his life. That is to say, it is a misreading of the *Divine Comedy,* and particularly of *Hell,* to think of the characters described there as external to Dante himself or as enemies whom he is judging in a pharisaical spirit. The *Divine Comedy* is actually an act of confession. Not, of course, that Dante was guilty of all the vices which are punished there; but all the vices castigated there are incarnated in historical personages through the power of the poet's imagination, and in the light of those personages the poet is able to see the hidden energies for vice within his own person. And by bringing them into the light he transforms them and is able to integrate them as healing forces in his own self.

The same is true of Dostoevsky. In all the characters that occur in the many writings he produced we see reflected the vices, temptations, betrayals, despair and unbelief of his age –

by all of which he was touched as only an artist of great imaginative capacity can be. The fact that he was able to describe those forces for despair and nihilism so memorably is a sign of how profoundly he was touched by them. But the fact that he was at the same time able to incorporate them into what is possibly the greatest and most hopeful novel in all world literature is testimony to those 'healthy resonances of spiritual life' which enabled him to integrate them into his own life and transform them into a force for good. And, in his case, that transformation was heightened in intensity almost beyond his ability to bear it by the fact that, as Theodor Reik (then President of the International Psychoanalytical Association) once said, 'Dostoevsky knew more about human psychology than the whole of the International Psychoanalytical Association put together.'

Unfortunately the fact that Dostoevsky knew so much about human psychology and exhibited the profundity of that knowledge in his creative writings has provided psychologists, both professional and amateur, with a golden opportunity for them to ransack Dostoevsky's novels for material from which to pronounce upon the psychology of Dostoevsky himself, often with scant regard for the fact that it is not possible to draw a straight inference from the words of a character in a novel to the character of the novelist. The first scandalous and most influential example of that gross error is to be found in the writings of the literary critic, sociologist and editor, Nikolai Mikhailovsky, who gave Dostoevsky a reputation for sadomasochism on the basis of Dostoevsky's literary creations without any reference to the evidence of the novelist's own life. The second such example is provided by Sigmund Freud, who latched on to a story about the death of Dostoevsky's father and used it to paint a similarly lurid picture of Dostoevsky's psychology, though the story was without any serious foundation in reality.

Both Mikhailovsky and Freud deserve the rebuke that Dostoevsky puts into the mouth of Nikolai Stavrogin in the suppressed chapter of *The Devils*, a chapter describing Stavrogin's visit to Father Tikhon in his monastery in order to make a supposed confession. The chapter ends abruptly at the moment when Father Tikhon descends from the level of the Spirit towards which Stavrogin was seemingly striving and predicts, like an all-knowing psychologist, that Stavrogin is about to commit some dreadful crime.

> Stavrogin by this time was shaking with anger and almost in terror.
> 'Damned psychologist!' he broke in suddenly in a frenzy, and without another glance he walked out of the cell.

That incident pinpoints the blindness that has afflicted so many commentators on Dostoevsky. Instead of seeing, as the Russian saying goes, *konets venchaet dela* (the end crowns the deed); instead of seeing Dostoevsky's life and work in the light of his glorious triumph at the end, they fail to appreciate the triumph because their gaze is still riveted on the trail of dangers and temptations undergone on the road to the triumph. It is as though the radiant scene at the end of *The Brothers Karamazov* is itself a personal rebuke to them for their pessimism. It is as though a death such as that of Lev Tolstoy, in flight from his family, and surrounded by quarrelling on the obscure station of Astapovo, would have suited their brief better than the truth about Dostoevsky's death: at peace with his family and the church, with his wife reading to him from that very copy of the Gospels which had never left his side since he had received it during his time in the prison camp.

*Konets venchaet dela* was a truth that Dostoevsky never lost sight of, which is the reason why he was always so concerned to shape the endings of his novels so that they throw light on everything that has happened previously. 'Reality is not to be exhausted by what is immediately at hand', he wrote in one of his notebooks, 'for an overwhelming part of this reality is contained in the form of a still latent, unuttered future word.' And one of Dostoevsky's most rare gifts was precisely his intuitive ability to utter the still latent, unuttered future word. He demonstrated that intuition in real life when confronted in the prison camp with the figure of a nobleman named Ilinsky who had been convicted of the murder of his own father. The evidence against him seemed quite overwhelming to the judges and to those who knew the detailed evidence.

But there was something about Ilinsky that made Dostoevsky doubt the story nevertheless. And his intuition was vindicated some years later when a criminal arrested for another crime confessed to the murder of Ilinsky's father.

It was the end that threw light on everything that went before; and once Dostoevsky's own life is seen in the light of the Russian saying we realize that it presents us with an example of something for which in the vocabulary of Russian spirituality there is a special term. That term is *podvig*, which can be translated as meaning 'a great, heroic deed', though that bare translation does not, of course, convey anything like the full resonance that it bears in the Russian spiritual tradition. One example of it we have already given in our account of the thousand nights that Saint Seraphim spent in prayer. Another common exploit often described as a *podvig* was undertaking to go on pilgrimage, perhaps to Kiev, or Solovki, or even Jerusalem. Yet another, less common, was to take upon oneself the vocation of *iurodivi*.

The form which Dostoevsky's *podvig* took was less common still, and perhaps should not be described as such if what Cardinal Newman said is true. When someone spoke of Newman as 'saintly', the good cardinal, mindful of having himself written the novels *Loss and Gain* and *Callista*, responded by saying, 'Saints do not write novels.' However Newman's sense of what might constitute a *podvig* is revealed as typically English and constricted when set beside a pronouncement of the Russian poet, Joseph Brodsky: 'Whenever any author picks up his pen he does so with the aim of achieving sainthood.' And though it is not for us to judge who in this world has achieved sainthood there is at least some justification for Brodsky's dictum in the fact that the burning issues of theology during the past century have been articulated most convincingly not by professional theologians but by novelists, the most important and influential of whom is Dostoevsky.

However, if we are to grasp the essence of Dostoevsky's *podvig* in his vocation as a novelist we have not simply to describe what happened in the course of his life and work but to divine what was truly 'going on' throughout those happenings. We have to apply to Dostoevsky the words of William Blake when he wrote:

> I give you the end of a golden string;
> Only wind it into a ball,
> It will lead you in at Heaven's Gate,
> Built in Jerusalem's wall.

But finding our way into heaven's gate in the company of Dostoevsky is not so simple a task as it is with, say, Saint Francis of Assisi or Saint Seraphim, because the novelist was a much more complex character than either of them. Like all great artists Dostoevsky's mechanism for filtering out the beauty and terror, the sorrow and the joy, the pain and delight of a human life was far less powerful than that of most human beings, who are better endowed with a protective mechanism that tones down the intensity of experience to a bearable level. The greater imaginative capacity of great artists also makes them acutely vulnerable to the intensity of human experience, leaving them open to various forms of madness and the temptation to seek release in drugs or suicide. In consequence, if we are to discern the golden thread in Dostoevsky's life, we have to traverse backwards and forwards through the happenings in his life, finding a connection between various events in his life and then seeing what was 'going on' all the time beneath the surface of those events.

At least we are on solid ground when we claim that Dostoevsky was brought up in an atmosphere of profound, traditional Russian piety. The writer's father Mikhail, a doctor in the Mariinsky hospital for the poor on the outskirts of Moscow, came from a long line of priests and had himself received a seminary education. Dostoevsky's mother, Marya Feodorovna Nechaev, belonged to a well-to-do family of the Moscow merchant class who were equally faithful in their religious observance. Every Saturday evening the whole family used to attend the office of vespers in the hospital chapel as preparation for the Liturgy of Sunday. Often Marya Feodorovna used to take the children to visit the shrines in the Kremlin and other famous churches in Moscow. Every year, on 7 October, the feast day of Saint Sergius (who saved Russia from the Tatars), the whole family made the pilgrimage to Sergius' monastery dedicated to the Trinity, a journey of some fifty miles. There they spent two whole days attending the services, visiting all the chapels and sharing meals with the hundreds of other pilgrims in the hostels.

In later life Dostoevsky was to record that his very first memory was one of prayer, the prayer that he and the other children were taught to say every evening by their *nyanya*, Alyona Frolovna, while kneeling in front of the icons: O Lord, I place all my hope in thee. O Mother of God, keep me beneath thy protection! It was the prayer which he prayed throughout his life and which he taught to his own children. It may also have been Alyona who first impressed Dostoevsky with the capacity among the simple people of Russia for spontaneous goodness, on account of an incident which occurred in the spring of 1833. It was the day when the family were shaken by a message announcing that a fire had destroyed many of the huts, the barns and the cattle on their already impoverished estate in the province of Tula. Financially the fire was a real disaster and the news of it drove Dostoevsky's mother on to her knees, sobbing. But at this point Alyona touched her on the shoulder and whispered, 'If you need money, take mine. I have no use for it. I don't need it.' The money in question came to five hundred roubles – a nest egg which she had saved against her old age.

Yet already before that incident the heart of young Fyodor had been stirred by an impression calculated to disturb the seeming tranquillity of his religious formation. He was no more than eight years old when he read the book of Job, which left such a profound impression upon him by virtue of Job's daring to question God's claim to be a just God in face of innocent suffering. The image of Job and his suffering, which placed both Job and even God in an agonizing dilemma and struggle, is a theme running through the whole of Dostoevsky's life, to the very end when he puts into the mouth of Ivan Karamazov the most powerful arguments imaginable for rejecting God's claim to be loving and good.

Nevertheless his childhood home planted seeds of goodness so deep in the young Dostoevsky's heart that they were never to be completely uprooted at any period of his life, a fact for which he was always grateful. His gratitude is given expression in the many times in *The Brothers Karamazov* that a sacred memory saves certain characters at crucial moments while others go astray through forgetting what they should remember. His message about memory is contained in the speech which Alyosha made to the boys gathered around him – not unlike the disciples gathered around Christ – at the funeral of the ill-fated Ilyushechka of whom Alyosha says,

'He was a nice boy, a kind and brave boy, he felt honor and his father's bitter offence made him rise up. And so, first of all, let us remember him, gentlemen, all our lives. And even though we may be involved with the most important affairs, achieve distinction or fall into some great misfortune – all the same, let us never forget how good we once felt here, all together, united by such good and kind feelings as made us, too, for the time that we loved the poor boy, perhaps better than we actually are. My little doves – let me call you that – little doves, because you are very much like those pretty grey-blue birds, now, at this moment, as I look at your kind, dear faces – my dear children, perhaps you will not understand what I am going to say to you, because I often speak very incomprehensibly, but still you will remember and some day agree with my words. You must know that there is nothing higher, or stronger, or sounder, or more useful afterwards in life, than some good memory, especially a memory from childhood, from the parental home. You hear a lot said about your education, yet some such beautiful, sacred memory, preserved from childhood, is perhaps the best education. If a man stores up many such memories to take into life, then he is saved for his whole life. And even if only one good memory remains with us in our hearts, that alone may serve some day for our salvation. Perhaps we will even become wicked later on, will even be unable to resist a bad action, will laugh at people's tears and at those who say, as Kolya exclaimed today: "I want to suffer for all people" – perhaps we will scoff wickedly at such people. And yet, no matter how wicked we may be – and God preserve us from it – as soon as we remember how we buried Ilyusha, how we loved him in his last days, and

how we've been talking just now, so much as friends, so
together, by this stone, the most cruel and jeering man
among us, if we should become so, will still not dare laugh
within himself at how kind and good he was at this present
moment! Moreover, perhaps just this memory alone will
keep him from great evil, and he will think better of it and
say: "Yes, I was kind, brave, and honest then." Let him laugh
to himself, it's no matter, a man often laughs at what is kind
and good; it just comes from thoughtlessness; but I assure
you, gentlemen, that as soon as he laughs, he will say at
once in his heart: "No, it's a bad thing for me to laugh,
because one should not laugh at that!" '

'It will certainly be so, Karamazov, I understand you,
Karamazov!' Kolya exclaimed, his eyes flashing.

However, that resolution of the conflict was still many years
in the future in May 1837 when Dostoevsky and his elder
brother Mikhail were sent away by their father to the Academy
of Military Engineers in St Petersburg in order to pursue an
army career on which neither of the brothers was at all keen.
In the course of that journey an incident took place to which
Dostoevsky was later to attach great significance as a revelation
of the ills of his native Russia. 'My first personal insult', he
wrote in 1873, 'the horse, the courier.' In that note he was
referring to the moment when he and Mikhail, en route for
St Petersburg, were looking out of the window of an inn at a
government posting-station in the province of Tver. There
they saw an official courier drive in at breakneck speed, jump
down from the troika, dash into the inn for a glass of vodka,
dash out again and jump into a fresh troika. Then the courier
immediately began to beat the neck of the troika's young
peasant driver with his clenched fist, whereupon the young
driver in turn started in a frenzy to whip the unfortunate
horses. That crescendo of beating was maintained until the
troika vanished from the sight of the Dostoevsky brothers.
'That disgusting picture', Fyodor wrote, 'has always remained
in my memory. I can never forget that courier.' Nor did he,
because the man's brutality came to symbolize for him the
cruelty with which the official and upper classes in Russia
treated both man and beast.

Neither did Dostoevsky forget the horse, for the image of an unfortunate nag being mercilessly beaten recurs in his writings, underlining the evidence of his compassion for all God's suffering creatures. In his book about his years as a convict (1860–62) for instance, *Notes from the House of the Dead*, he devotes a whole chapter to them entitled 'The prison animals'. There he describes the sad fate of a goat and of the prison dogs which were generally treated cruelly by the other prisoners but were comforted by the friendship Dostoevsky bestowed upon them. In that same chapter he provides a moving account also of his vain attempts to comfort a wounded and fiercely independent eagle. The eagle survived for three months in the prison compound until one day when a group of the prisoners decided to see if it might indeed fly. They launched him from the ramparts and saw him flapping his way across the bare steppes to that freedom for which they themselves longed. 'Ay, he's free; he feels it', they cried. 'It's freedom. Yes, freedom.'

So when in his notebooks Dostoevsky wrote the sentence, 'The one thing in the world is spontaneous compassion. As for justice that is a secondary matter', he was revealing something about himself that goes far to account not only for the extraordinary depth of his insight into the feelings of all creatures but also for some of the excesses into which his intense feelings led him. The man who in his youth could say to his brother Mikhail, 'I intend to become a fool', already had a presentiment that he was never to be comfortable amidst the pretence and hard-heartedness of polite society, which in return was time and again to treat him as a ridiculous person (*iurodivi*), a truth of which he likewise became painfully aware.

That truth was soon brought home to him when in January 1838 he was plunged into the coarse ways of the Academy of Engineers in St Petersburg. The young men in whose company Dostoevsky was to spend the succeeding four years were drawn from the upper crust of Russian society and spent as much of their time as possible in the kinds of pursuits designed to fit them for advancement in that sort of society. They went in for dancing classes and outdoor sports, and plotted how they might one day marry into greater wealth and rank. And as they achieved seniority in rank they enjoyed bullying their juniors in the way that they themselves had once been bullied. Dostoevsky, on whom his uniform hung awkwardly, who never seemed at ease with his rifle and his gear, whose mind was full of poetry and drama, as well as being 'very religious' and 'zealous in the performance of all the obligations of the Catholic Christian faith', was soon dubbed 'eccentric'. He himself 'aroused anxiety and perplexity' both in his companions and in his commanding officers, not least because he protested against the bullying of the juniors and tried to protect them, earning the comment from one young officer that he stood out from the usual run of students on account of his 'spiritual qualities' and his 'compassion for the poor, weak and unprotected'. Those same qualities were revealed again when his company of engineers went to camp one summer in a small village not far from St Petersburg. Horrified by the poverty of the local peasants Dostoevsky and a friend managed to collect money from their comrades which they distributed to the most needy of the local people. It is clear that Dostoevsky's comrades, whether grudgingly or otherwise, eventually came to respect him.

As a clue to Dostoevsky's essential character, and to the thread running throughout his life, these years that he spent among the Engineers have been strangely neglected by most commentators. That can only be because they themselves have never spent years in army barracks and are, therefore, unaware of how much courage and independence of mind it takes for a young man, no more than seventeen years old at the beginning, to withstand the constant, everyday coarseness of army life, as well as to maintain the zealous practice of his religion, and yet eventually to gain the respect of his comrades. So even at this early stage one can rightly apply to Dostoevsky the words which the eighteenth-century philosopher, Skovoroda, asked to have inscribed on his own tombstone, 'The world hunted me, but it did not snare me.' And the words of Skovoroda continue to be applicable during the following years when various groups and personalities tried to draw Dostoevsky into their nets: radicals, monarchists, Slavophiles and powerful representatives of many different shades of opinion. Even though he was prepared to collaborate with many of them on appropriate occasions he always managed, however, to retain his independence. He was at all times his own man.

Nonetheless, when in 1844 Sub-lieutenant Fyodor Mikhailovich Dostoevsky took the courageous decision to abandon his secure position in the Army Engineers in order to chance his arm as a freelance writer without any financial backing or patronage in the perilous, bitchy world of letters, he was exposing himself to far more cunning and seductive a temptress than any to be encountered in an army – as he was eventually to realize, though only after undergoing painful public humiliation.

The intensity of Dostoevsky's humiliation was all the more profound as arising from the unbelievable success of his first publication, a short novel entitled *Poor Folk*, in 1846. It is the story of a poor unmarried clerk, in his middle years, Makar Devushkin, who has spent all his life working in a government office as a scribe. But he has never achieved promotion and so is forced to live in a squalid rented room, constantly pained by the coarseness of his landlady and his fellow lodgers. Yet he himself manages to remain goodhearted, and therefore vulnerable through his naive tenderness which, when the story takes place, leads him to enter into a love affair conducted by means of letters with a young girl, Varvara Dobroselovo, who lodges in another squalid house opposite. Varvara's own misery is that she had been seduced by her 'protector' and abandoned. Sadly for Makar she finally agrees for the sake of security to marry her seducer, the landowner Bykov, in order to escape her poverty. In the end Makar himself takes to drink and dies.

The story of *Poor Folk* is beautifully told and evidence of psychological insight remarkable in an author only twenty-three years old. More than that, however, it is the first work of Russian literature to give voice to the misery of the deprived masses who milled around the filthy streets and markets of St Petersburg, under-nourished, ill-clothed and often sickly, destined to sustain the luxurious and artificial lifestyle of the tsarist ruling classes. It was this last feature of the novel that led to Dostoevsky's fateful relationship with the man who at that time was Russia's most influential literary critic, Vissarion Belinsky – a man known to his friends as 'Vissarion the

Frenzied' on account of his extreme and rapidly changing enthusiasms. His journal *Notes of the Fatherland* could make or break a young author, and in 1845 he was fervently championing the latest western European fashion, the social novel.

No wonder, therefore, that Dostoevsky was thrown off balance when he heard of Belinsky's reaction upon reading the manuscript of *Poor Folk*. 'You see this manuscript?' Belinksy said to one of his editorial team, 'I haven't been able to tear myself away from it for almost two days now. It's a novel by a beginner, a new talent. What this gentleman looks like and what his mental capacity is I do not know as yet, but his novel reveals such secrets of life and characters in Russia as no one before him even dreamed of. Just think of it – it's the first attempt at a social novel we've had; and done, moreover, in the way artists usually do their work – I mean, without themselves suspecting what will come of it.'

During the six subsequent months the manuscript of *Poor Folk* was passed around the group of littérateurs centred on *Notes of the Fatherland* which, under Belinsky's orchestration, poured such torrents of praise upon Dostoevsky that the young man completely lost his head. He went around St Petersburg retailing to all and sundry the flattering judgements made upon him by Belinsky and his associates. He started behaving as though he were already a great writer.

But by the time of the actual publication of the book, in January 1846, the inevitable backlash had set in, and Dostoevsky was subjected to cruel mockery, by Turgenev and Nekrasov among others, both in print and in the social gatherings of the polite élite. One of them wrote later: 'Our little idol began to talk his head off, and, after we pulled him down, was completely forgotten . . . the poor fellow! We destroyed him, we made him ridiculous!' To do him credit, Dostoevsky, after a period of despair and near suicide, managed to recognize how the episode had revealed to him the depth of his own vanity. And in later years it enabled him to describe so convincingly how difficult it is for a human being to deal with rejection and humiliation without becoming eaten up by the desire to inflict cruelty upon the perpetrators in revenge.

But a different effect of the episode was to throw him so

far off balance that he had to spend the rest of his life struggling to recover it. In his own words, written twenty years later, acknowledging the influence Belinsky had exercised upon him, he wrote, 'I adopted zealously the doctrine of Belinsky [atheism] and transformed myself into a western liberal, and I almost lost Christ.' He then goes on to describe an occasion when he himself, Belinsky and a friend of Belinksy were alone. Pointing at Dostoevsky, Belinsky said to his friend, 'I'm really touched to look at him. Every time I mention Christ his face changes expression as if he were ready to start weeping.' Then, turning to Dostoevsky he continued, 'Yes, believe me, you naive person, believe me that your Christ, if he were born in our day, would be the most ordinary and insignificant person: he would vanish in the face of contemporary science and of the contemporary mores of mankind.'

The impact of those words upon the mind and heart of Dostoevsky was never to fade, even though in the end it was transformed into something that would have astonished Belinsky. But they were especially devastating for a young man such as Dostoevsky whose adherence to Christianity had never been tested at the intellectual level and so had never matured in the way, for instance, that the faith of his English contemporary, John Henry Newman, had matured through study of the great theologians and through familiarity with the scientific discoveries referred to by Belinsky. But the impact of Belinsky's personality and ideology did not entirely destroy the thread leading Dostoevsky towards heaven's gate, because that thread contained strands stronger than Belinsky's rationalism. As Dostoevsky himself was later to say, 'One may be mistaken in ideas, but it is impossible to be mistaken with one's heart, and, because of error, to be dishonest; that is, to act against one's convictions.' He may not have known that according to the Bible the centre of man is not the mind but the heart. He could not have known the words of a later thinker, Vysheslavtsev, that the heart 'is the centre not only of consciousness but of the conscience, not only of the soul but of the spirit, not only of the spirit but of the body, not only of the comprehensible but of the incomprehensible: in one word, it is the absolute centre of a human being'. Yet the practice of the

Christian faith in his parental home had inculcated these saving truths about the heart in his own heart.

The other strand of the heavenly thread that never frayed was that of his devotion to Christ. Often he doubted God's existence, but never did he waver in his devotion to Christ. As he was to say, in a much quoted statement:

> I have shaped for myself a *Credo* where everything is clear and sacred for me. This *Credo* is very simple, here it is: to believe that nothing is more beautiful, profound, sympathetic, reasonable, manly and more perfect than Christ; and I tell myself with a jealous love not only that there is nothing, but there cannot be anything. Even more, if someone proved to me that Christ is outside the truth, and that *in reality* the truth were outside Christ, then I should prefer to remain with Christ rather than with the truth.

The significance of that statement has often been misunderstood; and even Dostoevsky never elucidated it in the language of philosophy. But he did so through his artistic creations, thereby refusing to accept the either/or choice demanded of Job by his so-called comforters: 'either God is just or you, Job, are guilty', to which Job's answer was 'I know that my redeemer liveth' – an answer that transcends the choices offered by both the comforters and the rationalists, but which was only to be fully realized centuries after Job in the person of Christ. It is the same answer given by Dostoevsky towards the very end of his life when Ivan Karamazov, the rationalist, is trying to destroy the faith of his brother Alyosha. Alyosha accepts that he cannot answer Ivan's logical assault upon the claim that God is loving and just, but he points to a way out of the dilemma – the way of practical love as embodied, for example, in Father Zosima.

Intriguingly enough, at this very time the same dilemma in the realm of geometry was being transcended by a great Russian mathematician, Nikolai Lobachevsky. A pioneer in non-Euclidean geometry, Lobachevsky challenged Euclid's fifth postulate that one and only one line parallel to a given line can be drawn through a fixed point external to the line. He developed a self-consistent system of geometry in which

Euclid's postulate is denied by allowing more than one parallel through a fixed point. There is therefore a third way beyond Euclid's option. And it is a sign of Dostoevsky's flair for judging what was significant in the intellectual air around him that he appreciated Lobachevsky's discovery almost by osmosis and raged against being imprisoned in Euclidean categories. In the words of his reply to those who tried to drive him to bow down before the restrictive laws of mathematics, Dostoevsky's 'underground man' says, 'Good Lord! What have I to do with the laws of Nature, or with arithmetic, when all the time those laws and the formula that twice two makes four do not meet my acceptance? Of course, I am not going to beat my head against a wall if I have not the requisite thoughts to do so: yet I am not going to *accept* that wall merely because I have run up against it, and have no means to knock it down. Does a wall, indeed, constitute a full-stop, a signal for a cessation of the struggle, for the mere reason that it, like the formula that twice two makes four, exists.'

What has been said in the immediately preceding paragraphs is in anticipation of later developments in Dostoevsky's spiritual journey, but it serves to show how often later insights help to reveal what was really going on in previous years. What Dostoevsky himself, for instance, was able to say in 1877 about his novel *The Double* (which followed *Poor Folk*, and which was severely handled by the critics) was something he could hardly have recognized in February 1846 when the novel was first published. Nevertheless he wrote truly in 1877, 'Although my story was not successful, its idea was clear enough, and I have never contributed anything to literature more serious than this idea.'

This cherished idea of Dostoevsky's was embodied in Yakov Petrovich Golyadkin, once more a clerk though no longer the poverty-stricken, humble Makar Devushkin but a well-established assistant to the chief clerk of his office. Moreover, Yakov is full of ambition not only to rise in the corrupt world of the St Petersburg bureaucracy but even to marry Klara Olsufyevna, the eminently desirable daughter of Olsufy Ivanovich, himself a privy councillor. It is the disparity between his ambitions and his status which leads to a split in Golyadkin's personality and generates a Mr Golyadkin junior, a character whom Dostoevsky brings in and out of the story so brilliantly that by the end, when Golyadkin goes mad and is driven off to the lunatic asylum, neither Golyadkin nor his fellow characters nor the reader can be sure whether Mr Golyadkin junior is real or just a figure in an hallucination of Yakov's. But, whether real or imaginary, Golyadkin junior mirrors the suppressed wishes of his senior's subconscious and reveals that side of him of which he is ashamed. Not only that, but it demonstrates the split as one running through the heart of the reader and of every human being, as well as through the great institutions of society of which St Petersburg is only one instance.

However, the crucial sentence in the story comes from the chorus, so to speak – from the cab drivers who say, 'A good man tries to live honourably, not just anyhow, and never has a double.' The truth in that statement was one more strand in Dostoevsky's golden string on to which he was to cling all his life until he finally incarnated its truth in the story of Ivan Karamazov being visited by a devil who tells him far more than he wants to know about himself. And, of course, all of Dostoevsky's artistic creations, as we mentioned earlier, are stages on his own pilgrimage to live honestly, to achieve psychological integration in which no human experience is to be excluded as a spur to that process – not even the words of the devil. 'Stop lying', Father Zosima says to the villainous Fyodor Pavlovich Karamazov (to whom Dostoevsky deliberately joined himself by bestowing his own name upon the old villain). And Dostoevsky never rested in his strain to fulfil Father Zosima's command, to acquire such self-knowledge that even his subconscious was not allowed to lie. Time and again his notebooks tell us of his passionate desire to depict, to incarnate a positive hero, a 'radiant' person as he says, whose radiance is even energized by the dark, impure elements of his subconscious transformed by repentance.

However, *The Double*, an expression of what Dostoevsky himself later considered his most serious contribution to Russian literature, was not recognized as having any originality by the critics when it appeared but was dismissed as a sign that the genius detected in *Poor Folk* was illusory. And, indeed, it is doubtful whether Dostoevsky himself could have realized the full significance of his idea if his fate had confined him to the incestuous literary circles of St Petersburg. Instead, for the next twenty years, fate was to inflict upon him more trials and dangers than even John Bunyan's pilgrim had to overcome.

The first of these many trials arose because impetuous compassion for the downtrodden led him into the circle gathered around Mikhail Butasevich Petrashevsky which, on Friday evenings, used to discuss radical ideas for the reform of Russia, an activity regarded by the authorities in Nicholas I's tyrannical Russia as treacherous. Though not one of the more vociferous members of the circle, Dostoevsky was to be remembered among them for his blazing indignation at any form of violence inflicted on lowly and injured people, and especially against 'how the landlords behave with their serfs'. He advocated passionately abolishing serfdom.

But though he was not prominent in the Petrashevsky debates Dostoevsky played an active role in a more radical splinter-group from within the Petrashevsky circle, the Palm–Durov circle. Here a secret printing press was obtained with the intention of distributing pamphlets among the peasantry calling for changes in the structure of Russian society, a prospect which, from the point of view of the tsarist authorities, could forebode nothing other than revolutionary terror. That is why on 23 April 1849, Dostoevsky and thirty-two other members of the Petrashevsky circle were arrested and imprisoned in the grim Petropavlosky fortress on the north bank of the river Neva, where most of them were to spend the rest of the year in solitary confinement. The grimmest section of the fortress, the Alekseevsky Ravelin, was set aside for Dostoevsky and the other most deeply implicated prisoners.

It was during those following eight months that the true mettle of Dostoevsky began to show itself more distinctly. For whereas a good number of those arrested succumbed to depression, were tempted to suicide and even proclaimed their repentance in a plea for mercy, Dostoevsky's nerve never failed him. By contrast he seems to have decided to make the best of the situation and even to have enjoyed the thrill of trying to outwit his interrogators. It helped, of course, that Dosto-

evsky, with remarkable objectivity, did not think of himself as
a victim of injustice and so never showed any signs of resentment or self-pity. When, thirty years later, someone suggested
to him that he and his companions were victims of injustice
he replied, 'Not at all, it was justice. The Russian people
would have condemned us. And who knows? Perhaps the
Almighty on high wanted to send me to prison in order to
teach me what is the most important thing of all, without
which one cannot live?' Of course he knew moments of
dejection, and he continued to worry about his chronic pain
from haemorrhoids and other physical discomforts; but the
first letter he was allowed to write, after three months without
such permission, expresses his constant disposition throughout
his imprisonment. Addressed to his young brother, Andrey, it
reads, 'I hasten to inform you that I am, thank God, healthy,
and though bored am far from despondency. Every condition
has its consolation, so don't worry about me.' Again, three
months later still, he writes, this time to his elder brother, 'I
am still alive and healthy. . . . I expected it to be much worse!
and now I see that I have such a reserve of vitality that it
cannot be exhausted.'

And even his bouts of boredom seem to have come to an
end once the prisoners were allowed to read books. It was
some indication of the drift of his thoughts towards 'the most
important thing of all, without which one cannot live', that
he should have asked for two accounts of pilgrimages to the
Holy Land and the life and works of Saint Dimitry of Rostov,
a seventeenth-century teller of the lives of the saints, as well
as for the Bible in both French and Church Slavonic. Further
than that, once he received pen and paper, he was forever
working out plots for new works of his own. He reports that
he had worked out such plots for 'three tales and two novels'.
One of those tales, *A little Hero*, was actually written and was
to appear in print eight years later. It is a quite extraordinary
piece, unique among Dostoevsky's writings for its unrestrained
romanticism. The young hero in question, a boy no more than
eleven years old, constitutes himself the knight destined to
protect a fair lady, M, who is engaged in a hopeless affair. The
young knight saves her from exposure. There is an unmis-

takeable sense in the tale that 'every flower, every last blade of grass' exhales a sacrificial aroma, saying 'Father! I am blessed and happy!' One senses that the writing of it was a saving act on Dostoevsky's part for his confinement in the airless Ravelin.

But it was the manner in which this twenty-seven-year-old writer stood up to interrogation by the representatives of the brutal Tsar Nicholas I, first of all in the written 'Explanation' of his conduct demanded of all the prisoners, and then in his face to face encounter with his interrogators, which cannot fail to command our admiration even to this day. To begin with Dostoevsky took upon himself whatever taint of guilt the Commission of Enquiry may have attached to his elder brother Mikhail and his younger brother Andrey, who were soon therefore released. When he then addressed the charge that he had 'spoken in a free-thinking fashion' in the public discussions at Petrashevsky's he went boldly on to the attack by saying that 'if a desire for improvement is liberalism, free-thinking, then in that sense, perhaps I am a free thinker'. He was bolder still when he came to assert the need to reform the practice of censorship over the works of writers, a practice which the Tsar himself personally insisted upon. The note of defiance and even scorn in Dostoevsky's words is unmistakeable. But when it came to the main charge against him – of having read aloud at Petrashevsky's a notorious letter written by Belinsky to Gogol which contained insults against the Orthodox Church and the supreme authorities of the state – he had to be more cautious. And though he defended Belinsky's personal work, saying that 'he was the very best of men as a man', he skilfully distanced himself from Belinsky's world outlook and managed to distract the commissioners' attention from the most dangerous charge that might have been brought against him – his activity in the secret Palm–Durov group which had been planning to spread reforming propaganda among the peasantry.

During the following months the conspirators were on several occasions summoned for further questioning both on the basis of their written testimony and in the light of further evidence subsequently gathered against them. More ominous still, the commission now took the more forbidding

form of a military court. It is breathtaking to read through the
documents recording Dostoevsky's responses to these interrogators, so skilfully does he answer their probing questions, never
losing his nerve or his dignity. (One is reminded of Joan of
Arc in the court of Bishop Cauchon, not least by the similarly
coarse character of the interrogators.) The characters with
whom Dostoevsky was faced, and the atmosphere of the court
itself, are brilliantly evoked in a paragraph from the pen of
Leonid Grossman:

> A narrow table stood on a raised platform in the smoothly
> whitewashed hall. From the smoothness of the gold-fringed,
> blood-red cloth, the kind used on official occasions, rose a
> three-sided pillar inscribed with the decrees of Peter the
> Great, surmounted by a two-headed eagle. An enormous
> bronze cross with a carved ivory figure flattened against its
> bearers stood beside the table. At the foot of this carved
> image of an execution in ancient times lay heavy volumes
> of army decrees with their ruthless penalties of shooting and
> hanging. Above these paraphernalia of justice hung a dark,
> varnished full-dress portrait of an unnaturally tall cavalryman,
> negligently crumpling a glove in one hand, and holding a
> white-plumed cocked hat firmly in the other, gazing down
> from his full height with a deathly look that turned the
> spectator cold. Just below the rowels of His Majesty's spurs
> were five frowning elderly faces with sideburns and smoothly
> combed hair: Dubelt's wolfish maw; Nabokov's heavy skull;
> the moon-like face, with shaved upper lip and bird-like eyes
> of grey-haired old Senator Gagarin, who was wearing a
> frock-coat with a white star; fat Rostovstev's broad, sagging
> face; and dried-up Dolgorukov's steely, cruel gaze. The blue
> and green uniforms and the silver of braid and the gold of
> orders were everywhere.

In front of them stood the sickly, pale young writer in his
prisoner's garb of canvas shirt and trousers. Yet he proved a
match for them all, even when General Dolgorukov, notorious
for his brutal punishment of soldiers, barked at him:

'What was your rank when you left the service?'

'Field engineer-lieutenant.'

'Have you been at the front? Have you been on any campaigns? How did you perform your service in the army Engineering Corps?' To which Dostoevsky could only answer that he had been in summer camp with the Engineers. Other members of the Court tried to wheedle him into repentance by offers of mercy and special consideration. The oily Rostovstev, describing himself as 'a lover of literature', and flattering Dostoevsky as 'a well-known writer', said, 'The emperor will forgive you if you tell the whole story.' But Dostoevsky continued to maintain his silence. Eventually the exasperated Rostovstev jumped up from his seat and left the room, exclaiming, 'I cannot look at Dostoevsky any more.' No wonder that Rostovstev said in his report – not, perhaps, without a grudging note of admiration – that as a witness Dostoevsky had proved 'clever, independent, cunning and stubborn'.

Writing about his own trial two years later Dostoevsky was to write, 'I conducted myself honestly before the court and did not try to shift my own blame on to others; I even sacrificed my interests whenever I thought I could possibly protect others by my confession.' It was, in the circumstances, a modest claim, and shows how deep a transformation was taking place in this young man who only three years previously had allowed himself to be thrown completely off balance when his vanity as a writer had been exposed by other writers who had previously praised him.

After the last meeting of the commission in September the prisoners were left for several months in suspense, wondering whether they might be pardoned or whether they would be sent off to Siberia for a term. Dostoevsky took advantage of this lull in life to continue writing and working out plots for future tales and novels, but others seem to have experienced enervating boredom. So there was a sense of excitement and anticipation among the prisoners when, in the darkness of early morning on 22 December, they heard the pealing of church bells and unusual noise in the corridors, followed by the clatter of cell doors being flung open. Then each of them was presented with his civilian clothes and led out into the prison courtyard where a whole line of hired carriages was stationed, surrounded by squadrons of mounted police. The prisoners were quickly bundled into the carriages by soldiers in blue uniforms, and the line of carriages started trundling across the city. Although they could not see where they were going, on account of the hoar frost on the windows, they guessed from the noise of the horses' shoes that they had crossed the Neva on the floating wooden bridge.

When the procession had been moving for about half an hour it halted and the prisoners were ordered out. They found themselves on the vast drill field of the Semenovsky Regiment which was a foot deep under recently fallen snow and on whose edges was gathered a crowd of three or four thousand of the citizens of St Petersburg. Not having seen one another for months the prisoners began to greet one another joyfully, not suspecting that they were about to be victims of one of history's most cruel jokes on the part of Tsar Nicholas I. Although the auditoriat-general had sentenced the conspirators to death by the firing squad, accompanied however by a recommendation for mercy, and though the Tsar had secretly commuted the death sentences, nevertheless he had ordered that his pardon should not be announced to the condemned men until the original death sentences had been read out to each of them publicly and individually and all the terrifying preparations for their execution had been carried out right up until the actual command to fire.

The whole ghastly 'liturgy' was carried out to the end. A priest carrying a cross announced to the prisoners, 'Today you will hear the just decision of your case. Follow me!' and he led them all to the scaffold where for half an hour, in a biting wind, an official in full dress uniform stood in front of each of them and read out the sentence. Dostoevsky was the tenth of them to hear it: 'Retired Engineer-Lieutenant Fyodor Dostoevsky, twenty-seven, for participating in criminal plans, for circulating a private letter that contained infamous expressions about the Russian Orthodox Church and supreme authority, and for an attempt to disseminate writings against the government by means of a handwriting press: to be put to death by firing squad.'

And so the diabolical parody of a liturgy continued: the priest gave a sermon, 'The wages of sin is death', and offered a large crucifix for each of the men to kiss. After that each had to don his funeral shroud, a loose gown of coarse linen with a pointed hood and long sleeves reaching almost to the ground, which was calculated to make them look ridiculous, like clowns. Dostoevsky's emotions at this moment are described by him in words which he later put into the mouth of a condemned political prisoner:

It seemed to him that, in those five minutes, he was going to lead such a great number of lives that there was no place to think of the last moment. So he divided up the time that still remained for him to live: two minutes to say goodbye to his companions; two minutes for inward meditation one last time. He remembered perfectly having fulfilled these dispositions, just as he had calculated. He was going to die at twenty-seven, full of health and vigour. He recalled that at the moment of saying goodbye, he had asked one of his companions a rather indifferent question, but had taken a keen interest in the reply. After saying goodbye, he began the period reserved for inward meditation. He knew in advance what he would think about: he wished to focus his attention firmly, and as rapidly and clearly as possible, on what was going to happen: right now, he was existing and living; in three minutes, *something* would occur; someone or something, but who, where? He thought to resolve those uncertainties during the two final minutes. There was a church not far off, its golden cupola glittering in the bright sun. He recalled having looked with terrible intensity at that cupola and at the sun's rays flashing from it. He could not tear his eyes away: those rays seemed to him a new nature that was to be his own, for he imagined that in three minutes he would become part of them. His uncertainty and feeling of revulsion in face of this unknown was dreadful. But the thing that was most unbearable for him at the time was the constant thought: what if I did not die? what if my life were given back to me? what an eternity! . . . And all that would be mine! Oh, then I would turn every minute into a century, I would not lose a single one, I would keep track of all my instants and would not spend any of them lightly.

Curiously enough, Dostoevsky does not mention an incident involving himself that was recorded by one of the other prisoners, a man who stood next to him on the scaffold: 'Dostoevsky was quite excited. He recalled *Le dernier jour d'un condamné* of Victor Hugo [a book which for some years had been among his favourites], and going up to Speshnev, said,

"*Nous serons avec le Christ!*" To which the latter (who was an atheist) replied with a twisted smile,

"*Un peu de poussière.*" '

In the meantime the condemned men were formed up in threes, Dostoevsky being in the second row. The execution master called out, 'Petrashevsky, Mombelli, Grigoryev', at which the three shrouded figures were led down the steps from the platform to the ground where they were then tied to the three stakes with ropes. Their arms were pulled behind their backs and the long sleeves of their shrouds were tied together. Three platoons, each of sixteen men, took up positions along a chalk line about twelve yards in front of each of the condemned men. They were all to kill together so that no one of them should bear the responsibility for the bloodshed. 'Load!' came the command from the non-commissioned officer in charge of the riflemen, who quickly took their ramrods and loaded. Then came the next command, 'Aim!' 'That was a really fearful moment', one of the condemned men still standing on the platform recorded afterwards. 'My heart stood still in anticipation, but the terrible wait lasted for a full half minute.' The reason for that agonizing delay was soon apparent. One of the Tsar's aides-de-camp came galloping across the parade ground and handed General Sumarakov a sealed packet. A beat of the drums was sounded: the signal for the riflemen to abandon the firing position. The sealed packet contained the Tsar's pardons. But the tension had already proved too much for Grigoryev who went out of his mind for the rest of his life. Next the terms of the commutations for each of the prisoners were read out one after the other. 'Retired Engineer-Lieutenant Fyodor Dostoevsky . . . to penal servitude in fortresses for four years, and after that a common soldier.'

That same day Dostoevsky wrote to his brother Mikhail a letter remarkable for its composure:

Brother, I'm not depressed and haven't lost spirit. Life everywhere is life, life in ourselves and not in things external. There will be people near me, and to be a human among human beings, and remain one forever, no matter what misfortunes befall, not to become depressed, and not to falter: this is what life is, herein lies its tasks. ... Do not grieve for me. ... Never till now have such rich and healthy stores of spiritual life throbbed in me. But whether the body will endure, I don't know. ... There is no bitterness or malice in my soul; at this moment I gladly would love and embrace be it anyone from my past. It is a consolation; I experienced it today when in the face of death I said farewell to those dear to me. ... As I look back upon the past and think how much time has been spent to no avail, how much of it was lost in delusions, in mistakes, in idleness, in not knowing how to live; what little store I set upon it, how many times I sinned against my heart and spirit – for this my heart bleeds. Life is a gift, life is happiness, every moment could have been an age of happiness. ... Now, upon changing my life, I am being born again in a new form. Brother! I swear to you I will not lose hope and will preserve my spirit and my heart in purity. I'll be reborn to the better. This is my entire hope, all my consolation!

On Christmas Eve Dostoevsky's brother Mikhail and his friend, Alexander Milyukov, were allowed half an hour in which to bid goodbye to Dostoevsky and a fellow prisoner, Sergey Durov. Milyukov has left us an account of this farewell meeting. He tells us that Dostoevsky and Durov were already dressed in the convicts' customary travelling clothes, sheepskin jackets and felt boots, and that the prisoners were remarkably calm.

Witnessing the farewells exchanged between the Dostoevsky brothers anyone would have thought that the one who was to remain free in St Petersburg was suffering the most, not the one who was just about to set off to the Siberian *katorga*. There were tears in the eyes of the elder brother and his lips were trembling while Fyodor Mikhailovich remained calm and kept consoling him.

'Don't, brother', he said at one point, 'You know me. After all I'm not going to my grave and you are not accompanying me on my burial procession. And the people in the *katorga* are not beasts but people perhaps better than I am, perhaps worthier than I am. And when I get out I'll start writing. I have been through a great deal these last few months. Inwardly I have experienced a great deal and I expect I shall see and experience much more out there – I shall have plenty to write about.'

An hour or two later the two prisoners were taken to the fortress smithy and ten-pound shackles were fixed around their ankles at the exact moment when the chimes of the Peter and Paul fortress were playing 'Glory to the Tsar!' Then the prisoners were put into open sledges, each accompanied by a guard, and the train of horse-drawn sledges, headed by a government courier, set off on the eighteen days' journey to Tobolsk, the centre from where prisoners were despatched to their final destinations. For Dostoevsky and Durov that destination proved to be the military prison of Omsk, where they arrived on 23 January 1850.

When he had foreseen that he would 'experience much more out there' Dostoevsky spoke better than he knew. Even the journey alone involved such trials as most human beings would find enough to last them a lifetime. Indeed, on top of the trauma of the Semenovsky parade ground, they were proving more than enough for Jastrzembski, one of the other prisoners, who tells us that at one stage of the journey he had decided to commit suicide. But Dostoevsky's innate buoyancy helped Jastrzembski through the crisis, aided by a candle, matches, and some hot tea provided by a friendly officer! 'We spent a good part of the rest of the night in friendly conversation. The sympathetic, gentle voice of Dostoevsky, his tenderness and delicacy of feeling, even some of his capricious sallies, quite like a woman, had a soothing effect on me. I gave up any extreme decision.'

Looked at in the context of the whole of Dostoevsky's life the four years that he now spent in the prison camp can be seen as the most extreme form possible of a retreat such as spiritual guides urge upon their followers but which nowadays usually last only a few days and take place in comparatively

luxurious surroundings. At least Dostoevsky himself regarded
those years as a kind of retreat when looking back upon them:

> All that time, despite my hundreds of companions, I lived
> in terrible solitude and, in the end, I came to love that
> solitude. Alone, in my heart, I re-examined all my past life,
> sorted out everything to the last detail, carefully thought out
> my past, judged myself unyieldingly and sternly, and even at
> some times blessed fate for having sent me this solitude
> without which neither this judgement of myself nor this
> stern examination of my previous life would have taken
> place. And with what hopes did my heart then start to beat!
> I thought, I resolved, I swore to myself that in my future
> life there would be neither those errors nor those falls which
> had previously been made. I waited, I bade fate to hurry, I
> wanted to put myself to the test once again in a new
> battle. . . . Freedom, a new life, resurrection from the dead.
> What a glorious moment!

Dostoevsky always recognized that those four years of penal
servitude, of 'unspeakable, interminable suffering' were the
occasion of his personal 'regeneration' and the 'regeneration
of his convictions'. But he also said of that experience, 'It is
a long story.' And it was to take him the rest of his life to reap
the fruits of his experience as he teased it out by way of his
vocation as a writer in the endless stories and reflections that
he was to publish over the following quarter of a century.

To begin with he had to plunge us, his readers, into the
indescribably repulsive conditions in the barracks which surrounded him for four years. He writes,

> I spent the whole four years in the prison behind walls and
> never went out except to work. The work they found for
> us was heavy (not always, of course), and I was sometimes
> completely exhausted in foul weather, in damp and rain and
> sleet, and in the unendurable cold of winter. Once I spent
> four hours on urgent work, when the mercury froze and
> there was some forty degrees of frost. My foot became frost-
> bitten. We lived on top of one another, all together in one
> barrack. Imagine an old, dilapidated, wooden construction
> that was supposed to have been pulled down long ago, and
> which was no longer fit for use. In summer, intolerably

stifling; in winter unendurably cold. All the floors were rotten. Filth on the floors an inch thick; one was liable to slip and fall. The little windows were so covered with frost that it was almost impossible to read at any time of the day. An inch of ice on the panes. Drips from the ceiling, draughts everywhere. We were packed like herrings in a barrel. The stove took six logs at once, but there was no warmth (the ice in the room barely thawed), only unendurable fumes – and this all winter long. There in the barracks the convicts washed their clothes and the whole space was splashed with water. . . . We slept on bare boards and were allowed only a pillow. We spread our sheepskin coats over us, and our feet were always uncovered all night. We shivered all night. Fleas, lice, and black beetles by the bushel.

The food was abominable and, of course, the convicts were in shackles the whole time.

Not surprisingly, Dostoevsky developed arthritis in his legs and suffered epileptic fits.

What, however, at the beginning of the four years most pained Dostoevsky was the hatred of the convicts for the handful of 'noblemen' such as himself: 'They were coarse, ill-natured, cross-grained people. Their hatred for the gentry knew no bounds, and therefore they received us, the gentlemen, with hostility and malicious joy in our troubles. They would have eaten us alive, given the chance. "You are noblemen", they used to say, "iron beaks that used to peck us to death. Before the master used to torment the people, but now he is lower than the lowest, he has become one of us." '

But, of course, the fact that he could not become one of them further deepened Dostoevsky's loneliness since neither did he think of himself as a nobleman. After all he had long been aware of how tenuous was his family's claim to such status, and his awareness of that had twenty years previously been a source of his isolation from those noblemen he met at the Academy of Engineers. Here again, in the camp, he did not have anything in common with his few fellow prisoners who were noblemen, especially the arrogant Poles. And for that reason he tried many times to identify himself with the convicts. The clearest example of this was the time when

the peasant convicts had assembled as a group in the courtyard
of the prison to protest against the bad food. Dostoevsky's
attempt to identify himself with them was greeted with scorn.
They shouted at him, 'What are *you* doing here? . . . He, too,
has come out of his hole. . . . Look at that killer of flies! . . .
Don't you eat your own stuff in the kitchen?'

'But we should all of us be together in a comradely spirit',
Dostoevsky replied.

'Well, how could *you* be one of our comrades?'

Dostoevsky writes that he had never before been so insulted
in prison, 'And this time I felt it very bitterly.'

Gradually, however, chinks of light began to appear in the
darkness of his prison. One such chink came through in
the unlikely person of Sushilov, a peasant who found himself
in the Omsk prison by mistake. 'A pitiful fellow, spiritless and
downtrodden by nature', as Dostoevsky described him, Sushilov attached himself to Dostoevsky, serving him as though he
were his body-servant.

One day, in need of a small sum to pay off a debt, Sushilov
came to ask for money from Dostoevsky, who responded by
saying, 'You don't forget to ask for your money, but you don't
do what you are told.' Sushilov remained silent and did what
he was told. Two days later when Dostoevsky offered him
some money to pay off his debt, Sushilov:

> turned sharply on his heel and went out. Astonished at his
> behaviour, I followed and discovered him behind the
> barrack. He was standing with his head against the palisade,
> his arms resting on the stakes.
>
> 'What's the matter, Sushilov?' I asked. He made no reply,
> and to my great surprise I saw that he was on the verge of
> tears.
>
> 'You think', he said, in a trembling voice and trying not
> to look at me 'that I care only for your money, but I . . .'
> He turned away from me, laid his forehead against the
> palisade, and began to sob. It was the first time I had seen
> a man weep in prison.

At this point Dostoevsky experienced a moment of compunction, and recognized that he had been cruel. He did everything he could to console Sushilov.

Such rare sensitivity may well account for the attraction toward Dostoevsky felt by the most resolute and feared man in the prison, Petrov, a soldier whose colonel had struck him one day on the parade ground. Whereupon Petrov killed the colonel on the spot. Genuinely attached to Dostoevsky he suddenly remarked to him, 'You are a man with a good heart but you are so simple, so simple that one has to be sorry for you.'

But the brightest light for Dostoevsky in his early months in the camp was a young Muslim named Ali who should never have been imprisoned. 'How this young man preserved his tender heart, his native honesty, his frank cordiality without becoming perverted and corrupted during this period of hard labour', Dostoevsky writes, 'is quite inexplicable.' Dostoevsky himself taught Ali how to read and write Russian by way of the two of them reading the New Testament together. In the course of their reading Ali 'came to love Jesus so tenderly' that one can scarcely doubt that the light of Ali's love for Jesus must have quickened Dostoevsky's own ardour for the New Testament and its message. After all, what circumstances for accepting that message into his heart could have been more propitious than his isolation from the vanities of St Petersburg's literary circles? For four years he received no news of that world, not even one letter from his brother, and the only book allowed him was the New Testament.

It was as though such incidents as his cruelty towards Sushilov, his strange relationship with Petrov, his loving care for Ali, and his constant reading of the New Testament were all preparing him for a moment of 'regeneration', one to which Dostoevsky himself was twenty years later to attach the greatest significance. In his *Diary of a Writer* for February 1876 he tells us how on Easter Day 1852, when he was serving as a political prisoner in Siberia, he was so disgusted by the drunkenness and violence of his fellow-prisoners that he climbed on to his bunk and turned his back upon the hell of a barrack room. For a long time he nursed his loathing of the other prisoners until there suddenly arose within him the memory of an incident which he had completely forgotten from twenty years past.

As a child of nine he had one day been wandering alone across an open field on their estate when he thought he heard a wolf approaching. In his terror he ran towards the lonely figure of Marei, the serf who was ploughing the field. Marei quickly comforted the boy, stroking him on the cheek and murmuring, 'Don't be frightened, my dear. Christ be with thee. Cross thyself.'

'But I did not cross myself', writes Dostoevsky, 'the corners of my lips quivered; and, I believe, that was what impressed him most. Slowly he stretched out his thick thumb, with the black nail soiled with earth, and gently touched my trembling lips . . . and he looked at me with a long motherly smile.' And now, twenty years later, it was Marei's soil-blackened thumb that Dostoevsky particularly remembered:

> and if I had been his own son he could not have bestowed upon me a glance full of a more serene love. And yet, who had prompted him? He was a peasant serf, while I was a nobleman's son. No one would find out how he had caressed me and no one would reward him. The meeting was a solitary one, in an open field; and only God, maybe, perceived from above what a profound and enlightened human feeling, what delicate, almost womanly tenderness may fill the heart of some ignorant Russian peasant serf. And when I climbed down off my bunk and gazed around I felt I could behold these unfortunate men with a wholly different outlook, for suddenly, by some miracle, all the hatred and anger had completely vanished from my heart.

That is a classic illustration of the melting of the heart which is essential if one is to see one's fellow human beings in the light of the Holy Spirit. And the fact that Russians have a special word for such a moment – *umilenie* – is itself testimony to the frequency with which they have been alert to those moments throughout the long history of the Russian people's spiritual endeavour. That moment of *umilenie* in 1852 gave an impulse to the spirit of Dostoevsky that was to sustain him for the rest of his life throughout many trials and failures. For he was aware, first, that, however inchoately, he had found his way into the heart of the Russian people. Secondly, he had rediscovered Christ, and more specifically 'the Russian Christ'; and thereby he saw opening up before him, more clearly than ever, the trajectory of his vocation as a writer.

In the letter that he wrote to his brother Mikhail on 22 February 1854, Dostoevsky said,

> During four years in prison I at last came to discern human beings among the thieves. Will you believe me: there are deep, strong, beautiful characters among them, and what a joy it was to discover gold beneath the rough, hard shell . . . I have lived in the closest possible contact with them and, consequently, I think I know them pretty well. How many stories of vagrants and robbers and of poor, wretched folk in general! Enough to write whole volumes. What a wonderful people! I have not wasted my time in prison because I came to know, if not Russia, then the Russian people as perhaps few know them. That is what I pride myself on a little. It is, I hope, pardonable.

No wonder he henceforward always harboured a conviction that he was commissioned to speak to the people in a way not possible for 'the landowning writers', Turgenev and Tolstoy, or for the intelligentsia, as he showed some years later when he was a visitor at the home of the Suslovs. There a young doctor criticized Dostoevsky's 'mystical' ideas about the future role of the Russian people, asking, 'Who has given you the right to speak so assuredly in the name of the Russian people?' Whereupon Dostoevsky, with a brusque gesture, raised the bottom of his trousers and revealed his ankles on which the marks left by his shackles were still visible. He commented, 'These gave me the right.'

Those marks had given him the right not only to speak for the people, and by the power of his writings to bring their fate into the state's universe of discourse but, conversely, to bring the educated and upper classes to an understanding for, and warmth towards, the marginalized poor folk. In order to do so, he later wrote, 'we have to renounce our class prejudices and transform ourselves morally'. He warned against either 'a coarseness beyond belief towards the people or a pitying sugar-

sweet approach', for the people 'will not tolerate a politeness
à la française which they regard as an insult. One must love the
people but not with a sentimental love acquired in the study.'

However, one can well understand the reservations which
the young doctor at the Suslovs expressed concerning Dostoevsky's vision of the messianic role of the Russian people and
their 'Russian Christ', to quote what became a favourite phrase
of Dostoevsky's. Because out of gratitude towards the people
through whom he had found a deeper relationship to Christ
Dostoevsky easily gave the impression that the Russian folk
had a monopoly of the approach to Christ. But he did so out
of gratitude to them for having once more been able to take
hold of the golden thread of his childhood, especially by virtue
of the convicts' reverent observance of Christmas and Easter.
Speaking of Holy Week, for instance, he writes,

> that week was a great solace to me; we went two or three
> times a day to a church not far from the prison. I had not
> been in church for a long time. The Lenten services, familiar
> to me from early childhood in my father's house – the
> solemn prayers, the prostrations – all stirred in me the
> memory of things long, long past, and awoke my earliest
> impressions to fresh life. I remember so clearly how happy
> I was when in the morning we were marched off to God's
> house, treading the frozen earth, under an escort of soldiers
> with loaded muskets; the escort remained outside the church.
> Once within we were massed close to the door, so that we
> could scarcely hear anything except the deep voice of the
> deacon. Now and again we caught a glimpse of a black
> chasuble or the bare head of the priest. Then I recalled how,
> as a child, I used to look at the common people who stood
> huddled at the door; how they made way slavishly for some
> important fellow with epaulettes or some nobleman with a
> big paunch or an overdressed pious lady . . . It seemed to
> me then that it was only *there*, near the church door, just
> inside the porch, that prayer was offered with genuine
> fervour and humility; only there that folk prostrated them-
> selves with true self-abasement and a complete sense of their
> unworthiness.
>
> And now I myself stood in the ranks of the common
> people – no, not even that, for we were outcast and in

chains. Everyone shunned us. We were feared, and alms were slipped into our hands as though we were beggars. I remember that all this gave me the strange sensation of a refined and subtle pleasure. 'So be it!' I thought. The convicts prayed with deep fervour; every one of them had with him his poor farthing for a little candle or for the collection for church expenses. 'I, too, am a man', each of them said, perhaps, as he gave his offering! 'In God's eyes we are all equal.'

At the end of the six o'clock Mass we all went up to communion. When the priest, the chalice in his hands, recited the words 'Have mercy on me, even as thou hadst on the thief whom thou didst save', almost all of them prostrated themselves amidst the clanking of their chains. I think they took these words as applying literally to themselves and not as being just Scripture.

Once his heart was opened to its depths Dostoevsky continued to 'discover gold' amidst his fellow-prisoners. There was an old man from Starodub, for instance, one of the Old Believers, so-called because they clung to the old rituals of the Orthodox Church which were suppressed by Peter the Great when he subjected the Orthodox Church to the Tsar in the fashion of the German Protestants. 'This man', writes Dostoevsky, 'was about sixty years old, thin and growing very grey . . . his look was so tranquil and mild, and I always saw with pleasure his clear and limpid eyes, surrounded by a number of little wrinkles. I often talked with him, and rarely have I met so kind, so benevolent a being.' The other prisoners also trusted this old man so much that they all entrusted their money to him, convinced that he at least would not be robbed. Yet, though the old man was of a gay and expansive disposition and often laughed, Dostoevsky awoke at three o'clock one morning to discover him weeping. He was praying from a handwritten prayer book, 'Lord, do not forsake me. Master, strengthen me. My poor little children, my dear little children, we shall never see one another again.' 'I cannot say', writes Dostoevsky, 'how much this moved me.'

And the local town population also warmed him by their compassion. The ten-year-old girl, for instance, who had seen

Dostoevsky in the army hospital when she came to visit her dying father. On seeing Dostoevsky walking under escort she ran to give him a kopek. 'There, poor unfortunate', she said, 'take a kopek, for Christ's sake.' Dostoevsky treasured that kopek for many years and was very distressed when he realized he had lost it.

So when Dostoevsky was released from the Omsk prison camp on 15 February 1854, to begin five years of service as a soldier in Siberia, he really did feel that he had acquired a wealth of experience about which he could write. 'New life', he wrote, 'freedom, resurrection from the dead.' He expressed his eagerness 'to put myself to the test once again in a new battle'. However he could not possibly have realized that this 'new battle' for which he was so eager would last for the remaining twenty-seven years of his life. But if we ourselves are to grasp the magnitude of the man's *podvig* from that date onwards we have to see those years as a relentless struggle to integrate his experiences of the preceding years into writing that would promote the healing of the Russian people and their mission to the nations at the same time as bringing about the healing of his own battered soul, the reconciliation of the contradictions within himself.

Fortunately, whereas the biographer of Dostoevsky has to concern himself with every detail of those years and the personalities of all with whom the writer came into contact, for anyone trying to follow the course of his *podvig*, his spiritual growth, the task is made easier in view of the way the years fall into fairly clearly defined periods. Thus the period from 15 February 1854 until 15 February 1867, was a period of continuous chaos in Dostoevsky's life – 'holy chaos' maybe (to use a term sometimes invoked by biblical scholars in view of the seeming need for chaos to occur before new life can be generated) but chaos nevertheless. The second period begins with his second marriage on 15 February 1867 to Anna Grigoryevna Snitkin, and lasts until 8 July 1871. It was a period of self-inflicted exile in Europe which providentially served him as a retreat and renewal, much as his years in the prison camp had done previously. The final period of his life was one of increasing triumph which was crowned by his

Pushkin speech on 8 June 1880, and the completion of *The Brothers Karamazov* in the November of the same year.

But before filling in some details about those three periods it is helpful to indicate the method, the means by which he threaded his way through all those event-filled years so as to arrive at his crowning achievement. And that method was writing, which from his earliest days he had described as a 'holy art'. And at a later date he again declared the holy nature of the art of writing, at a time when he and his brother Mikhail were in urgent need of money and Mikhail was urging his younger brother to hurry and complete the novel he was engaged upon. In reply Fyodor wrote, 'I have decided, and have taken an oath on it, that nothing half-baked, nothing immature, nothing hurried (as before) will I publish because I need money: one should not trifle with an artistic work, one should work honestly.'

At whatever period of his life we follow Dostoevsky we see clearly that through the instrumentality of his writing he subjected himself also to a process of personal integration leading him towards both the 'sainthood' spoken of by Joseph Brodsky and the office of a prophet of reconciliation and unity, first for Russia and then for the whole human family. But that journey towards sainthood and prophethood could no more be achieved by means of a map of ideas than could Dante's similar journey towards the same goals in his *Divine Comedy*. In each case it had to be achieved by way of human characters serving as symbols, because symbols are a far greater source of life than are ideas. That is why Dostoevsky never tries to advance by way of abstract, disembodied ideas. As a friend once noted of him: 'He, so to speak, *felt thought* with unusual liveliness. Then he would state it in various forms, sometimes giving it a very sharp, graphic expression, though not explaining it logically or developing its content. Above all, he was an artist; he thought in images and was guided by feeling.' In order to achieve integration head and heart need to be in harmony. For, as Dostoevsky himself said, 'my seeds of artistic thought always occur and give notice of themselves . . . and are felt both in my head and in my heart. But, you see, this only occurs in a flash, and what is needed is a complete embodiment, which always arises suddenly and unexpectedly, but you can't calculate precisely when it will come about; and then finally, having received the complete image in your heart, you can undertake its artistic realization.'

Anyone who reads through Dostoevsky's writings in chronological order is bound to notice how the author slowly, searchingly, feels his way along a series of his own creations. There is the figure of a proud woman making her plight worse through the egoism of suffering (little Nellie in *The Insulted and the Injured*), who is later embodied in Polina (in *The Gambler*), then in Nastasya Philippovna (in *The Idiot*) and to the final incarnation in Katerina Ivanovna (in *The Brothers Karamazov*). A similar line is followed by one who sets himself aside from the common herd and takes pride in his isolation: it runs through Raskolnikov (in *Crime and Punishment*) to Stavrogin (in *The Devils*) and finally to Ivan Karamazov. Probing along such lines could not be done simply by taking thought but required years of personal maturing, as Dostoevsky himself recognized when in 1854 he wrote, 'The character that I created and which is the foundation of the whole story required several years of development, and I was convinced I would have spoilt it all if I had undertaken it feverishly and without preparation.'

One figure who haunted Dostoevsky in search of embodiment was that of 'a perfectly beautiful man'. Time and again he attempted to portray such an archetypal human being, much as Renoir, the great painter, longed to be able to paint a perfectly white canvas. Once it seemed to Dostoevsky that he was going to manage it in the person of Prince Myshkin, the hero of *The Idiot*. In the event Myshkin proves too smart for Dostoevsky. He turns himself into an angel who is incapable of fulfilling the longings of the full-blooded woman Nastasya Philippovna or, indeed, of the less-demanding Aglaya Ivanovna. It is as though the 'double' of Dostoevsky the proud psychologist is showing Dostoevsky himself that psychological ideas are not what it takes to achieve embodiment. That can only take place when Dostoevsky himself is no longer in thrall to a 'double', entangled in his own psychological ideas. And it does take place when the full-blooded Alyosha and the spirit-filled Father Zosima emerge in *The Brothers Karamazov.*

The method employed by Dostoevsky for discerning the true way through his forest of symbols was itself rooted in his own singular personality, a courageous personality that always led him to allow an experience to penetrate his heart and mind to its extreme, and never to abort it. 'As for myself', his *Underground* man says, 'in my life I have pushed to the extreme what you yourselves have never dared to take even halfway. Because you have constantly mistaken your cowardice for prudence and have constantly deceived yourselves with comforting reflections. The truth is that I have been more *alive* than you.'

Many years later Dostoevsky again jolts his readers out of any of those self-comforting reflections when we hear Father Zosima saying to the peasant woman who is weeping bitterly for her dead child, 'And do not be comforted; you should not be comforted. Do not be comforted but weep.' Dostoevsky was never one for 'all those easy speeches that comfort cruel men', to which his childhood reading of the Book of Job had alerted him. In answer to Job's challenge to God to justify his suffering, God had no answer. Humanity had to wait many centuries for an answer; and when it came it was not in the form of an argument but in the person of Jesus. This need to wait for spiritual enlightenment was asserted by Dostoevsky once again in 1878 in answer to a woman unable to rest because of her doubts concerning personal immortality: 'Remain in your unrest,' he writes to her, 'seek further . . . it may be that you will find.'

Moreover, just as Dostoevsky pushes emotion to its extremity so also he pushes ideas to their extreme, as in his celebrated arguments in the form of *pro et contra*, for and against. The outstanding illustration of this method is to be found in *The Brothers Karamazov,* where the whole of one of its twelve books is headed *Pro et contra* and contains the famous *Legend of the Grand Inquisitor* in which the arguments against the idea of a loving God are stated so powerfully that the over-procurator of the Orthodox Church, Pobedonostev, was alarmed. To him Ivan's atheistic arguments seemed unanswerable – as they were, indeed, to Dostoevsky at the level of logic and psychology. But by that year Dostoevsky had long realized a truth that was later stated so succinctly by one of his most gifted commentators, Vyacheslav Ivanov: 'Denial of God and faith in God are not two different interpretations of the same world, but two essentially different worlds of the spirit, existing side by side, like an Earth and a counter-Earth.' The great difference between those two worlds is that whereas one may easily drift into the denial of God you can only enter into the world of faith through a conscious, whole-hearted response to the Spirit. And by the time Dostoevsky emerged from the prison camp he had already, however inchoately, responded to the Spirit. So he was no longer floundering between two worlds like some psychologist who imagines he can belong to both.

That Dostoevsky was himself aware of having received the gift of prophecy is clear from the answer he gave in 1868 to a friend who had written to say that he found the characters in *The Idiot* altogether 'fantastical'. 'Oh, my friend', Dostoevsky wrote, 'I have a totally different conception of reality and realism than our novelists and critics. My idealism is more real than their realism. God! Just to relate sensibly what we Russians have lived through in the last ten years of our spiritual development – yes, would not the realists shout that this is phantasy! . . . Their realism cannot illuminate one hundredth part of the facts that are real and actually occurring. And with our idealism, we have predicted facts. It's happened.' The confident 'it's happened' was a reference to the case of the impoverished student Danilov who on 14 January 1866 had killed a moneylender, Popov, and his maid. This poor student of 'handsome appearance, with large black expressive eyes and long thick hair thrown back, was intelligent and well educated.' At the time of Danilov's trial a certain Glazkov suddenly testified that it was he and not Danilov who had killed the usurer. Soon after, however, Glazkov retracted his confession. That whole series of events uncannily reproduced the course of events previously described in Dostoevsky's *Crime and Punishment* where the blameless workman Nikolay had previously made a similar self-accusation. Reality had imitated fiction with uncanny precision.

And the facts of world history in the past century have also imitated Dostoevsky's creations in an uncanny fashion, leading Albert Camus to exclaim that anyone wishing to understand twentieth century history should begin by reading Dostoevsky; and one leading Russian critic of the present day asserts that it is Dostoevsky's novel *The Devils* that most illuminates the events of late-twentieth-century Russia.

Take, for example, his warning against the misapplication of Darwin's *On the Origin of Species* which Dostoevsky regarded as the most dangerous of all threats to true humanity and brotherhood. It runs as follows:

> If science is unable to provide for people's subsistence, and there is a shortage of space, people are going to throw their babies into latrines, or eat them. I won't be surprised if they do both, especially if science suggests it to them ... When food becomes scarce and science proves unable to provide for food and fuel, whereas the world population continues to rise, it will be necessary to stop the further growth of population. Science says it isn't your fault nature has arranged things that way, and the instinct of self-preservation being first and foremost, it follows that babies must be burnt. That is the morality of science. The burning of babies will become habitual, for all moral principles in man are only relative *if he has to rely on nothing but his own strength* ... Science by itself, as it reaches the point when it becomes insensitive to the death of babies, will deaden and brutalize mankind. But with Christianity even the shortage of food and fuel could be overcome – one can always choose to die oneself, for the sake of one's brother, rather than to kill off babies.

When one rehearses in one's mind the practices prevalent in the abortion clinics of the great powers – China, Russia, the USA and Europe – in our own day, one cannot but be astounded at the eerie accuracy of Dostoevsky's prophecy.

Having now anticipated some of the methods which eventually helped Dostoevsky on his twenty-seven-year journey from prison camp to his final triumph, let us return once more and survey the three periods of his journey that we characterized as chaos, exile and triumph respectively.

## 1854–67: chaos

For anyone who has served a number of years in warfare or in
a prison camp it is not in the least surprising that Dostoevsky's
exhilaration on his release from the stockade of Omsk should
quickly have turned into confusion as to which direction to
take in everyday life. To everyone in that situation either there
seem to be no signposts, or else there are too many of them,
all pointing different ways. *La diritta via era smarrita*, as the first
canto of Dante's *Hell* puts it. And there stood Dostoevsky,
an ex-prisoner approaching the canonical age of thirty-three,
without any profession, long out of contact with his family
and friends, having no firm prospects and never having experienced a stable relationship with a woman. These and other
factors constituted a recipe for disaster. Nor was it long in
coming; because within a few months Dostoevsky was wildly
in love with the neurotic wife of an out-of-work customs
official, Marya Dimitrievna Isaev. Unfortunately for Dostoevsky, Marya Dimitrievna's drunken husband died in August
1855, and hence, after a hysterical courtship, Dostoevsky found
himself in a position to tie himself to this consumptive woman
and her impossible son Pasha until the day of her death on 18
April 1864. Maria Dimitrievna's death filled Dostoevsky with
guilt because for the previous two years, even as she was dying,
he had allowed himself to be swept all over Europe in a wild
affair with Apollinaria Suslova, a young feminist writer, as
unbalanced as Dostoevsky himself was in this period. He also
fell victim to addiction to utterly reckless gambling at the same
time as his epileptic fits became more frequent and his incessant
smoking brought emphysema upon him. In financial matters
he proved to be no less undisciplined, as a result of which he
became a familiar of the pawnshops. At the same time,
however, he was always wonderfully generous with his money,
his time and his energy. When his eldest brother Mikhail died
some two months after Marya Dimitrievna's death, for instance,
he immediately assumed responsibility for Mikhail's widow and
children and for the debts of the journal *Epoch* which Mikhail
had piled up. Dostoevsky's younger brother Nikolay said of
him at this time, 'He has given himself entirely to the family

[of Mikhail], works all night, never goes to bed before five in the morning, works like an ox . . . You have to have lived a long time, and to have gone through a good deal, in order to know just how supremely honourable and noble is that man's soul . . . He never complains and says nothing about all that has probably piled up in his heart.'

Not unnaturally, in view of the way he was behaving, Dostoevsky does not make many references to his personal faith at this period (even though he continues to urge the superiority and importance of Orthodoxy) until, that is, 18 April 1864. That night he found himself sitting beside the corpse of Marya Dimitrievna, trying to make sense of their sad years gone by. In order to do so he resorted, as always, to his .pen, writing down his thoughts in a notebook as he sat there. He wrote, 'Masha is lying on the table. Shall I ever see Masha again?' What the tormented man then put down in his notebook is too confused for clear exposition, but the thrust of it is clearly expressed later in his *Diary of a Writer* (for November 1876): 'Without a higher idea neither man, nor any nation, can exist. But on earth there is *only one* higher idea; that is, the idea of the immortality of the human soul, for all the other "higher" ideas of life, by which man can live, flow from that alone. I declare that love for humanity is completely *unthinkable, unintelligible*, and altogether *impossible* without concomitant faith in the immortality of the human soul.' Here Dostoevsky had convinced himself that somehow, somewhere he would see Masha again.

But though Dostoevsky was undoubtedly shaken by his wife's death and felt that he had come to a watershed in his life, nevertheless his conduct of life in the following two years was as chaotic as ever. He was soon journeying to western Europe in a fruitless attempt to renew his relationship with Suslova, to whom he later proposed marriage but without success. At one time or another he proposed to two other young ladies and had an affair with a Sixties 'hippy'. In an attempt to pay off the debts and to support the family of his dead brother Mikhail he entered into a disastrous contract over his writings with a crooked publisher, Stellovsky, and then deceived himself into thinking that he might save the situation financially by means of another gambling spree in Wiesbaden.

As it happened, however, an unintended result of that fatal contract with Stellovsky was the salvation of the miserable novelist, because under it Dostoevsky was obliged to hand in the manuscript of his novella *The Gambler* by 1 November 1876, otherwise Stellovsky would have gained the right to publish a complete edition of all Dostoevsky's previous works and the scripts of all his writings for nine subsequent years. And yet, by a stroke of great good fortune, Dostoevsky was guided to a stenographer whose diligence enabled him to hand in the required script in the nick of time. Five months later Dostoevsky was married to the stenographer, Anna Grigory-evna Snitkin, and the next period of his life was inaugurated in the form of an exile which was to serve as a great retreat for renewal comparable to his earlier exile in Siberia.


## 1867–71: exile

Marrying Anna was the most sensible act of his whole life; for Anna herself, of Swedish Lutheran stock, was the epitome of common sense. Within two months of their marriage she had sorted out Dostoevsky's publishing rights as far as was humanly possible and made sensible arrangements concerning Mikhail's family and Dostoevsky's step-son Pasha. And, with great firm-ness for a mere twenty year old, she had prized Dostoevsky out of their grip by departing with him for a break in western Europe on 14 April 1867. Their intention was to spend a few months there. In the event their exile from Russia lasted four years.

Those years of moving around Germany, Switzerland and Italy were by no means comfortable ones. Often their lodgings were cramped, their lack of money often forced them into the pawnshops from which Anna could not always then redeem her precious possessions. They suffered loneliness and lack of contact with Russia. In Switzerland they buried their first-born, the three months old Sonya. But in spite of all their hardships Anna weaned Dostoevsky from his addiction to gambling; and together they enjoyed the cultural richness of Europe, especially of Italy. He was able to write *The Idiot* and work out the scheme for *The Devils*. But, above all, Anna's reliability, her common sense and unpretentious piety steadied Dostoevsky and helped to ground his emotions upon the soil of family happiness. When the two of them, along with their little daughter, Lyubov, returned to Russia in July 1871 Anna had every reason to be gratified by the change in Dostoevsky. That change was recorded by one who knew Dostoevsky well, Nikolai Strakhov:

> I am completely convinced that the more than four years which Fyodor Mikhailovich spent abroad were the best time of his life, that is, the time that yielded the most profound and purest thoughts and feelings. He worked with great intensity and was often in need; but he had the peace and joy of a happy family life and lived almost exclusively in total solitude, that is, remote from all occasion to deviate from the straight path of development of his thinking and his profound spiritual work. The birth of the children, concern for them, the sharing of man and wife in one another's suffering, even the death of his first born – all these were pure, sometimes exalted experiences. There is no doubt that it was precisely abroad, in that setting, amid those long, serene reflections, that the peculiar revelation of the Christian spirit which had always dwelt in him was consummated.
>
> This fundamental change was revealed very clearly to all those who knew him then when Fyodor Mikhailovich returned from abroad. He would constantly bring the conversation around to religious themes. Not only that: his manner changed, acquired greater mildness, sometimes verging on utter gentleness. Even his features bore traces of that frame of mind, and a tender smile would appear on his lips ... It was evident that the highest Christian feelings dwelt in him, those feelings were expressed in his works more often and more distinctly. This was the man who returned from abroad.

In that passage Strakhov pre-dated 'the consummation' of Dostoevsky's 'particular revelation of the Christian spirit' because it actually took all the remaining ten years of the novelist's life to achieve it. But at least Strakhov's statement points to the fact that the last ten years of Dostoevsky's life are best understood as one continuous 'public civic *podvig*', as Dostoevsky himself expressed it.

## 1871–81: Sobornost

If we search for one sign under which we might understand those years as a whole none better can be found than the word which has played such a profound role both in expressing and in shaping Russian spirituality: *sobornost*. The word is derived from *sobor*, meaning 'cathedral', and refers to the feeling one experiences in the cathedral, or the church, when the Liturgy brings all the worshippers into a common unity so that each of them feels to belong to everyone else there and to the organic whole that they form. It is derived from the Russian verb *sobirat*, meaning 'to gather together', and expresses exactly what Dostoevsky was attempting to do. He grieved over the separation between the various sections of Russian society and longed to gather them together: parents and children; peasants and merchants; rich and poor; Orthodox and Old Believers; revolutionaries and monarchists; westerners and Slavophiles; women and men; educated and ignorant; the living and the dead, gathered together in a spirit of forgiveness and reconciliation that he dared to describe as 'universal communion in the name of Christ' – not a *mechanical* communion but a spiritual communion, a new form of Church where all peoples will be gathered 'in a great, universal, brotherly fellowship in the name of Christ'.

Being the writer that he was Dostoevsky set about his task soon after returning to Russia by 'preparing to write a very big novel' that would both express and promote *sobornost*. And by the time he came to write *The Brothers Karamazov* he knew precisely what he wanted to say, a fact reflected in the absence of any substantial difference between his notebooks for the novel and the actual text; whereas in the case of other novels there is usually a considerable difference between the notebooks and the published version. In fact all Dostoevsky's previous writings ever since the publication of *Poor Folk* in 1846 can be seen as preparation for *The Brothers Karamazov*. And although some of those works, especially *Crime and Punishment*, *The Idiot* and *The Devils*, are recognized as great novels, all of them were markedly imperfect in his eyes. But with *The Brothers Karamazov* we move somehow into a new dimension, into a new atmosphere of spiritual freedom and of joy, for as the translators of the most successful English version of the novel say, '*The Brothers Karamazov* is a joyful book . . . joyful in its energy and curiosity, in its formal inventiveness, in the mastery of its writing. And, therefore, in its vision.'[5]

But if it was *The Brothers Karamazov* that most perfectly expressed *sobornost* for his Russian readers at that time and which still continues to do so both for them and, indeed, for all of us to this day, nevertheless it was the *Diary of a Writer* that taught him how to achieve that 'public civic *podvig*'. Because when he started to issue his *Diary* in 1873 he did something unprecedented in Russian life: by breaking the barrier that stood between the writer and his readers he established an intimacy with them that not only enabled him to speak directly to *them* but also encouraged them to write to *him*. The very openness with which he expressed his convictions and fears called forth similar openness on the part of his readers who, in their hundreds, confided their fears and hopes to him, almost as though they were making their confessions to a priest. And the remark made by those who had heard Dostoevsky's Pushkin speech applied equally to his words in the *Diary*: 'He did not use the high-flown manner customary on such occasions but spoke about ultimate questions, almost as if talking to himself in the presence of friends.'

As soon as the *Diary* began to appear the readers sensed an urgency in Dostoevsky's writing that was missing 'in the aristocratic landowners' literature' of Turgenev and Tolstoy which 'had already said everything it had to say'. There was need therefore, Dostoevsky maintained, for 'a new word' that could help redeem the tragic situation of Russia; and he was called to pronounce that new word. For Russia, in his view, was on the edge of an abyss, as he had tried to demonstrate in *The Devils*: Russia had become possessed by devils like the

man in the gospel story of the Gadarene swine. As the possessed man was healed when the devils had been driven out
by Jesus, so would Russia be healed if Russia would only listen
to the 'new word' that Dostoevsky hoped to speak. Because
there is no doubt that Dostoevsky saw himself as a prophet of
healing and reconciliation. So it was no accident that in these
years, whenever he was asked to do a public reading, he
invariably included his favourite piece, *The Prophet*, by Pushkin,
a poem invoking the prophet Isaiah in words taken from
Church Slavonic.

Dostoevsky also recognized clearly that being a prophet
involves taking enormous risks, such as that mentioned previously, when in the *Diary* for 1873 he inserted an item
that Mochulsky has described as 'an act of public penance
unprecedented in the history of Russian spirituality', adding
'there is a grandeur in this boldness and order of the spirit'.
Dostoevsky was commenting upon the Nechaev affair: that is,
the murder in 1869 of a student named Ivanov (a member of
a revolutionary cell) at the instigation of the organizer of the
cell, Nechaev, himself the most cold-blooded, ruthless nihilist
imaginable, whose whole life was devoted to destroying the
ruling system in Russia, no matter what the cost in human
lives. Nechaev was the original for the sinister Peter Verkhov-
ensky in *The Devils* which appeared in 1872. Yet here was
Dostoevsky in January 1873 acknowledging in the journal *The
Citizen* (which belonged to the reactionary Prince
Meshchevsky) that he himself, in his younger days, might well
have become – not a Nechaev, certainly – but possibly a
Nechaevist, a follower endeavouring to cover the whole of
Russia with a network of secret cells in order to create bloody
insurrection, or overthrow the government and abolish
religion, the family and property.

Even in issues closest to Dostoevsky's heart, issues of faith,
he was prepared to expose his own vulnerability. This was
illustrated in his reply to a letter from Pobedonestov who
was obviously fearful that in the instalments of *The Brothers
Karamazov*, Dostoevsky was not providing any rebuttal of Ivan
Karamazov's arguments for atheism. Dostoevsky answered that
the section entitled 'The Russian monk' was intended as such

a rebuttal. But 'I tremble for it in this sense – will it be a *sufficient* answer? The more so that this answer is not direct, not point by point, to the theses expressed in "The Grand Inquisitor" and before, but is only implied. This is what disturbs me – will I be understood?' Again, as he says of Ivan's arguments, in answer to a troubled student, 'In Europe there has never been such a powerful expression of atheism, nor will there be. The truth is that my faith in Christ and my proclamation of my faith is not that of an infant: my hosanna has passed through a furnace of doubts.'

In the process of thereby weaving a web of *sobornost* for the Russians the warp that Dostoevsky used was his own intense experience of life and the experience of the people, while the weft he employed was drawn from the whole range of threads that are particularly treasured in the spiritual tradition of the Russians: *umilenie, iurodstvo, prozorlivost*, repentance, pity, forgiveness, divine motherhood, and the beauty of Christ. One of the most moving instances of how Dostoevsky drew his readers into his own experience and helped them to ease their own sufferings is contained in the chapter of *The Brothers Karamazov* entitled 'Women of faith'. There Father Zosima asks a woman weeping over the death of her three-year-old boy where she comes from. 'From far away, far away', she said in a sing-song voice. In response Father Zosima gently speaks to her in such a way as to draw the bitterness out of her heart. And then he asks the woman what was the child's name. 'Alexei, dear father.' 'A lovely name! After Aleksei, the man of God?' says Zosima. 'Of God, dear father; of God.'

Aleksei was actually the name of Dostoevsky's three-year-old child who had himself died only a few months previously. And doubtless Father Zosima's words were akin to those spoken by the *starets* Ambrose of the Optino hermitage to Dostoevsky himself when he went there in June 1878 accompanied by his young friend, the philosopher Vladimir Solovyov. And we are privileged to catch a glimpse of a singular thread linking the peasant woman to the writer, to the *starets* and the court of the Tsar when we learn of Dostoevsky, in April 1880, reading the chapter 'Women of faith' to a gathering of a court circle. Among them was Princess Marya

Feodorovna, the wife of the future Tsar Alexander III. She had herself not long before lost a little son. She was moved to tears by Dostoevsky's reading and grateful for the balm he brought.

Yet Dostoevsky would not have been capable of touching hearts in such a way had he not himself been a devoted husband and father, a quality not specially cultivated among educated Russians where the 'haphazard family', to use a favourite term of Dostoevsky's, was so often the rule. The fathers of these haphazard families are often mercilessly satirized in his novels, none more fiercely than in the person of Fyodor Pavlovich Karamazov, who virtually forgets that he has any sons, as a result of which the sons themselves grew up strangers to one another, not brothers. The revulsion Dostoevsky felt toward the phenomenon of the haphazard family in Russia goes far to account for his increasing concern during his later years to speak to, and on behalf of, women and children. He who was most respectful towards women – refusing, for example, to follow the practice of kissing their hands, which he regarded as a sign of condescension – was emboldened to speak on their behalf by virtue of the many, many women who opened their hearts to him in letters. Sometimes they even visited him in person. 'Our women', he writes, 'are beginning to arise, and maybe they will be able to save much . . . Women are our great hope. Perhaps, at the decisive moment, they will render a service to all Russia . . . In Russian woman resides our only great hope, one of the pledges of our revival. The regeneration of Russian woman during the last twenty years has proved unmistakeable. The rise in her quests has been lofty, candid and fearless.' However, the principal fault in her striving, he goes on, 'is her extraordinary dependence upon several essentially masculine ideas'. So the remedy he proposes for that fault is by no means a retreat out of the modern world back into the patriarchal one. Quite the contrary he argues, because higher education should be made available for all women accompanied by all the rights granted by higher education – since it is only such knowledge which is 'capable of answering women's questions'.

Not that Dostoevsky acquiesced in the one-dimensional

view of women characteristic of many of the liberal advocates of women's rights. Being so thoroughly Russian he could hardly fail to see woman as a symbol of Mother Russia, and as herself illuminated by the country's wealth of folklore according to which the divine feminine principle, Wisdom (*sophia*), is embodied in woman, in the Mother of God, and in mother Earth. The best known evocation of these connections in Dostoevsky's works, delicate and indirect, is when Alyosha emerges from his dream of Cana in Galilee and under the night sky 'waters the earth with tears of joy'. But its more explicit expression is to be found in his earlier novel, *The Devils*. There an old woman coming out of church speaks of the Mother of God as 'the hope of the human race', for 'the Mother of God is the great mother moist Earth and great joy is contained in that for man . . . And when you water the earth beneath you a foot deep with your tears, then you will rejoice over everything.'

Several similar passages in his writings have led a number of theologians to accuse Dostoevsky of pantheism. But surely it is more correct to see those passages as evidence of a deeper and broader sense of what is sacramental than is to be found in catechisms. 'There is something sacramental in the earth, in the soil', he wrote in an article entitled 'The Land and Children'. That article shows Dostoevsky to have been an ecologist before his time, since he called upon the Russian people to recognize that 'land is everything', and that the bourgeois takeover in the nineteenth century with its 'horrible cities . . . banks, budgets, polluted rivers and mills' constitutes an aberration in the development of the human family by cutting people off from the land. And so 'something must change, because everyone must have land . . . if you wish to regenerate mankind into something better, if you wish to make men virtually out of beasts, give them land, and you will achieve your purpose'. And not only do the people need land but they also need forests, hence Dostoevsky was one of the first to sound the alarm for the forests of Russia and to protest against deforestation. That is why he insisted to Anna Grigoryevna that if ever they managed to buy a small estate it must have woods, not manicured woods, either, but natural ones.

As a further extension of his ecological concerns he keenly supported the Russian Society for the Protection of Animals. Significantly one of the main reasons he gave for doing so was that whereas children were nowadays being brutalized by the present practice of cruelty towards animals they would become humanized if they saw animals being treated humanely. That reason, namely its effect upon children, echoes what he had already written about the need children have for land: 'Children must be born on the soil and not on the pavement . . . every decent, healthy urchin is born together with a little horse; every decent father must know this if he wishes to be happy . . . a nation in its vast majority should be born and *sprout* on the earth, on the soil upon which corn and trees grow . . . There is something sacramental in the earth, the soil.'

In these words of Dostoevsky we hear a note of passionate concern that children should be treasured and accorded dignity and compassion at all times. That note did not arise out of remote, sentimental theorizing but out of his own experience, not only in the forbidding back streets of St Petersburg but also from the many visits he made to homes for orphan children and illegitimate children, as well as to settlements for juvenile delinquents. His never-failing compassion for these unfortunates must often have startled the educated classes who read his *Diary* – as, for instance, when he proposed that since foundling children had been given such a raw deal from birth it was incumbent upon society to make up for their misfortune by ensuring that they were given privileged access to university education and afterwards helped to find a stable position in society. Nor within the whole 'theology of faces' permeating *The Brothers Karamazov* is any more powerful than the one expressed by Father Zosima when he says, 'Every day and every hour, every minute examine yourself and watch over yourself to make sure that your appearance is seemly. You pass by a little child, you pass spitefully with foul language and a wrathful heart; you may not have noticed the child, but he has seen you, and your face, ugly and profane, will perhaps remain in his defenceless heart. You may not know it, but you have perhaps sown an evil seed in him and it may grow.'

Even more startling to his readers must have been his long articles on the many criminal cases in which he took such a deep interest – not merely attending the courts but also going to visit the accused, both in prison and, in the case of Katerina Kornilova, in her home. Herself pregnant she had thrown her small stepdaughter out of the window in a fit of rage against her quarrelsome husband. The stepdaughter had survived. But when the case came to court and it seemed that Katerina would be sent to prison in Siberia for seventeen years, Dostoevsky intervened, especially through raising the case in his *Diary*. By virtue of a powerful description of the morbid psychology frequently encountered in a pregnant woman, he managed to convince the jury to acquit Katerina.

Another case on which he commented at length was that of Vera Zasulich, who was indicted in 1878 for her attempt to assassinate the brutal military governor of St Petersburg, Trepov. Under the jury system newly introduced into Russia Zasulich was acquitted, much to the delight of many liberals but to the horror of Dostoevsky's conservative friends such as Pobedonostev, and Katkov his publisher. For both of these groups, though for very different reasons, Dostoevsky's own comments constituted a scandal, an occasion for ridicule. Dostoevsky concluded that Zasulich should not have been acquitted, because she was certainly guilty. Instead the court should have said to her, 'You have a sin on your conscience because you wanted to kill a person, but go; you are free; but do not do such a thing again.' He did not want her to be made a heroine, but at the same time he wished to raise the matter from the juridical to the moral level.

It was precisely because he was in the thick of such events throughout the 1870s that Dostoevsky could address the Russian people not as one of the scribes but as one who spoke with authority. Above all, he was able to speak words of hope to a confused people, for as he said as a result of his experience in writing the *Diary*: 'Contrary to what I used to think two years ago it has proved that we in Russia have incomparably more truly Russian people . . . So many more, that even in my most ardent dreams and fantasies I could not have imagined this result. . . . Much in Russia is not at all as gloomy as formerly it seemed, and most important, there is much that testifies to a yearning for a new, just life.'

That he could speak so hopefully despite having been in the thick of so many threatening events was only possible because, throughout them all, his life and writings were shot through with all those threads of traditional spirituality that he had woven into the warp of Russian society to produce the promise of *sobornost*: those moments of *umilenie*, the insights of *iurodstvo*, the people's seemingly inexhaustible capacity for suffering and forgiveness, but, above all, the figure of 'the Russian Christ'.

The use of the term 'the Russian Christ' in no way implies that the Russians enjoyed an exclusive understanding of Christ. In fact Dostoevsky specifically rejected any such exclusive claim (such as was made by Danilevsky and the Slavophiles), because it limited the universal mission of Russia to share its unique historical experience of Christ with all humanity. It was rather that Dostoevsky had been born again into Christ through the Russian folk whose sufferings he shared in the prison camp. 'Our people know their Christ-God', he writes, 'perhaps even better than we do, though they did not attend school. They know because through many a century they have endured much suffering, and in their sorrow, from the earliest days unto our own time, they have been accustomed to hear about this Christ-God of theirs from their saints who laboured for their people.'

It has rightly been said that the feeling of a new period of forgiveness and reconciliation dawning in Russia marked by Dostoevsky's Pushkin speech and the completion of *The Brothers Karamazov*, a sense of *sobornost*, was the crowning of Dostoevsky's life. As we all know, that feeling did not last. Yet for another moment it was sustained and even deepened by Dostoevsky in his death. For by one of those strange turns of fortune that characterize his destiny, Dostoevsky's very death and burial seemed to confirm the feeling of Russians as a people gathered together. The strange turn of fortune began when Dostoevsky's wife Anna began to search for a place where her beloved husband might fittingly be buried. Husband and wife had once spoken about the question when he had said he would like to be buried in the cemetery of the Novod-evichy monastery (among the most historic in his native Moscow). Whereupon Anna, who disliked discussing the matter, had jokingly said, 'No! You will be buried in the Alek-sander Nevsky Lavra' (in St Petersburg, founded by Peter the Great, and of course reserved for only the most select in Russian society) 'and the monks will come out to greet your funeral procession!' Dostoevsky laughed and said, 'They only do that for Tsars.' In the event the nun at the head of the Novodevichy monastery not only demanded an exorbitant fee but she also made it clear that Dostoevsky's fame was of no importance in the eyes of nuns.

But at that distressing message Dostoevsky's destiny took a hand. Pobedonostev, for reasons of his own, put pressure to bear upon the ecclesiastics to allow Dostoevsky's body to be received into the Aleksander Nevsky monastery, for the monks to greet the coffin and to sing the Liturgy just as Anna had predicted in jest. At first, it is true, Metropolitan Isidore coldly demurred at Pobedonostev's suggestion, saying that Dostoevsky was 'a novelist, and no more, and had never written anything serious'. Eventually, however, from 28 January until 1 February, from the day of his death until the moment of his interment, in St Petersburg and throughout Russia an outpouring of spontaneous grief took place such as had never been seen, not even at the death of a Tsar. All lectures at the university were cancelled; memorial services were held there and in Moscow, and altogether some four hundred tributes to him were penned throughout Russia. Estimates of the number of people who accompanied the coffin vary from thirty thousand to a hundred thousand, but all agree that it was the largest that had ever been held in Russia. Even more important, as one who was present wrote, 'In Saint Vladimir's at the first sound of prayers being intoned everyone bowed their heads and many of us were moved to tears . . . at that moment everyone somehow truly felt the breath of God, unbelievers no less than believers.' 'This was no burial', wrote another, 'it was a celebration of life, the resurrection of life.'

That sense of resurrection and of hope was maintained unabated in meetings, in newspapers and in journals for a month, and might have continued longer still had it not been for an event that Dostoevsky had long feared. For on 1 March the liberator Tsar, Alexander II, was assassinated, and a period of terror from the authorities was set in place that eventually led to the revolution of 1917.

For many people the instigation of terror from above signalled the end of the *sobornost*, and therefore the end of Russia as a 'Church of universal brotherhood', towards which all Dostoevsky's energies had been consecrated. But at least for one person it was not the end, because he understood why Dostoevsky had chosen as the epigraph for *The Brothers Karamazov* a sentence from his favourite gospel: 'Unless the grain of wheat falling to the ground dies, itself remains alone, but if it dies it bears much fruit.' That person was the twenty-seven year old philosopher Vladimir Solovyev, the man closest to Dostoevsky in the writer's last years. There can be no doubt that the daring action Solovyev took on 28 March 1881, only a few weeks after Tsar Alexander's death, was the fruit of his friendship with Dostoevsky. On that day Solovyev was delivering a lecture in the crowded hall of the Credit Union in St Petersburg when he suddenly broke off from his abstract theme and said,

> Today the Tsar's murderers are being judged, and, probably, they will be condemned to die. It is within the power of the Tsar to pardon them and if he really feels to be linked with the people he should pardon them. The Russian people does not accept two moralities . . . The decision in this affair does not lie with us . . . We are not called to judge . . . but if the reigning power disassociates itself from the Christian principle and proceeds to the shedding of blood we shall be abandoning it, disassociating ourselves from it and denying it.

Solovyev's words brought deathly silence in the hall, followed by cries of 'traitor', as officers led him out – never to lecture again in a Russian university.

Yet were not Solovyev's words an echo of those pronounced

by Dostoevsky in the case of Vera Zasulich: 'You have a sin on your conscience ... but go ...; you are free; but do not do such a thing again'? And who is to say that the history of Russia might not have been totally different had the new Tsar heeded the words of Solovyev and inaugurated that 'Church of universal brotherhood' for which Dostoevsky longed? Indeed, the whole course of world history might have been profoundly changed had the new Tsar, Alexander III, allowed a moment of *umilenie* to melt his heart and to follow the urging of Solovyev and Dostoevsky. Instead Tsar Alexander unleashed a wave of white terror that was to result later in the hanging of Lenin's older brother and the fatal stoking of Lenin's hatred for the traditional social order of humanity.

# 4

# The scientist martyr: Pavel Florensky[6]

It has been said that 'Russia in this century has provided more martyrs than all the preceding centuries of Christianity put together.' And since the Greek word *marturos* means 'witness', that striking statement leads us to ask what it is, precisely, to which the martyr bears witness? The answer to that question was memorably provided even before the opening of the present century by none other than Lev Nikolayevich Tolstoy, in his marvellous retelling of a traditional folk take to which he gave the title *That by which human beings live*. In that story Tolstoy shows that a human being does not live by bread alone but by a presence which human beings throughout the ages have named Spirit, or the Holy Spirit. Tolstoy's answer is of crucial importance at the present junction in the history of the human family because the past two centuries have seen the destruction of human beings on a scale so vast as to have induced a feeling that a human being is a disposable quantity, devoid of Spirit.

And to compound that feeling recent centuries have also brought about the spread, among the educated and half-educated classes, of vulgarized versions of scientific theories. At one time we were being reduced to economic units and at another time to items of psychology. And then the sociobiologists busied themselves in trying to prove that even the seemingly unselfish acts of human beings were nothing more than expressions of the species' desire for survival. Now, in the wake of progress in genetics, it has become widely assumed that a human being is simply a bag of genes.

But every one of these theories regarding human beings breaks down when brought face to face with the martyrs. For if we adhere to such reductionist theories we are bound to say to the martyrs, 'You are fools, under the illusion that there is a Spirit of truth in whose name you are giving up your lives.

What is more, your behaviour is actually immoral because by giving up your lives you are throwing in your hand for ever, and so can no longer have any influence whatsoever on the destiny of the human family.' Yet surely no one in their right mind would say such a thing to a Thomas More or a Janani Luwum?

Of course, the example of the martyrs does not prove the presence of the Spirit. Only abstract theories are susceptible of proof. For truths concerning life and death you need witness, manifestation, a showing. In matters of life and death one showing is worth a thousand theories. And such a showing is precisely what martyrs provide, one of whom is Pavel Florensky. He was almost unknown outside the ranks of Russian specialists until the last few years. But nowadays he is being hailed, on account of his multi-faceted skills, as 'the Russian Pascal'.

Pavel Alexandrovich was born in 1882 of a Russian father and Armenian mother who provided him with a quite extra-ordinarily wide and deep education in the sciences of nature: geology, botany, biology, physics, chemistry, mathematics. But they tried to steer him away from any interest in religion. In his late teens, however, Florensky boldly faced the question: What is it by which human beings live? and was thereby led, despite considerable success in his thesis on discontinuous functions in mathematics and the offer of a professorship at Moscow university, to become in 1911 a priest in the Russian Orthodox Church. He likewise became one of the outstanding figures in the circle of Orthodox intellectuals in Moscow who counted such luminaries as Berdyaev, Bulgakov and Trubetskoy among their number.

In 1922, when most of these luminaries left Russia, Florensky deliberately chose to stay in his homeland to share the destiny of his people, even though he had a prophetic sense of what it might cost him in the end. His decision of commit-ment led him to give himself to scientific and technological investigations in the service of the Soviet State. He became a major figure in the electrification of the Soviet Union; he was an editor of the ambitious *Soviet Technological Encyclopaedia*; and even when in 1933 he was arrested, he maintained his scientific researches – in Siberia investigating the problems of permafrost and in the Solovki labour camp working on the extraction of iodine from seaweed. Nevertheless, this 'priest-professor and unenlightened mystic' (as the NKVD called him) continued to stick in the craw of the Bolsheviks, and on 8 December 1937 he was executed by a firing squad near Leningrad.

It is obvious that only a person as variously gifted as Florensky himself could do justice to his insights into the whole astonishing range of fields in which he became a specialist, but I believe that even ordinary mortals can glean some grains of wisdom from those insights. What follows is my attempt to glean after him in the fields of natural science, theology, art and semiotics.

## Natural science

Florensky always preferred to speak of 'natural science' rather than 'science', because for him the experience of nature was immeasurably more significant than experiments in laboratories – though he valued those also. But, as he was later to express it in a letter from Solovki to his son Kyrill, 'The terms atoms, electrons, and so forth are very useful but nevertheless they do not belong to direct experience but represent an abstraction, a regulating idea. And the more that experience is thereby unravelled, the further away the idea deviates . . . For myself, I have no love for such diagrams, though recognizing that they are useful for us. If I may say so, they dematerialize the world . . . and induce the fatal habit of replacing perceived reality by limiting schemata and fictions of an abstract order.'

In those words we catch an echo of his childhood on the shores of the Black Sea at Batum, where he became aware of the world as a whole, as a living whole in which every particle was mysteriously alive and related to every other particle. The phrase 'dead matter', which was common currency in the period of his youth, was to him completely meaningless, if not worse. He never lost that childhood sense of wonder, and it led him to question the conventional assumption that the pursuit of science is primarily motivated by truth. He maintained that the original impulse for investigating nature is the experience of delight in seeing, hearing, smelling, touching and tasting, which arouses wonder at the *beauty* of the world revealed through the senses. And since it is characteristic of beauty to be attractive, consequently the beholder is drawn towards the embodiment of beauty, feeling an intimacy with it which is already a kind of love. Without such love one cannot enter into the inner mystery of anything, into the *truth* of anything. Without that intimacy one's relationship with the whole creation is inevitably external. So the process of scientific investigation, according to Florensky, flows from beauty to love and is consummated in truth, in intimate relation with reality.

Having such a vision of science it is scarcely surprising that he was very suspicious of the direction that science had taken since the Renaissance. For, as he saw it, scientific thinking since the Renaissance had been dominated by the enormous success of mechanical inventions. And what is characteristic of machines is that they work by means of pressure of one part or another, the parts having to remain separate if the machine is to work properly. Consequently, overwhelmed by the success of machines, thinkers absorbed the notion that the universe is a great machine in which the parts, including human beings, can only have external relationships with one another.

Moreover, within such a *Weltanschauung* scientific terms are essentially tools by which to manipulate nature for the purposes of human beings. As a result human beings are constantly destroying nature in the attempt to know it, using scientific terms as their tools. And this is the point at which Florensky is most diametrically opposed to the post-Renaissance view of the world. Because for him scientific terms are not primarily tools but *symbols*; not primarily for application but revealers of reality. And just as a window is a window – and not just glass – in so far as the light is seen beyond it, so a scientific term is a symbol in so far as it reveals the spirit energizing reality.

Predictably enough, Florensky's suspicion of anything which threatens life and spirit in the name of mechanics was rooted in childhood experience which he describes most vividly. He tells us that he used to be entranced by the stalls at which traders sold their goods in the market at Batum. But from the very first he sensed a deep gap between those articles that were machine-made and those that were handcrafted. He acknowledged that the machine-made articles were often beautiful; but it was a sterile beauty, whereas there was something attractive about most of the handcrafted articles that drew one further. Reflecting on that experience in later years he commented that the handcrafted articles manifested a spontaneity which was of the spirit and drew from you a response that led you through beauty to truth.

Florensky's reflections on handcrafted articles remind us of a remark made by a Japanese Zen Buddhist named Saichi who was renowned as a maker of *geta*, a type of wooden shoe. He used to say that since modern articles of production are not accompanied by joy in their making, they bring no joy to those who wear them. But Saichi's *geta* were made with joy and so carry joy wherever they go. In that respect, for Florensky, nature is handcrafted.

## Theology

The area of specialization for which Florensky is best known is that of theology because the crippling circumstances of Soviet life prevented him from completing a major, systematic work in any other field. The work in question, *The Pillar and Ground of Truth* (Moscow 1914), is certainly a major one, consisting of some six hundred pages of text and two hundred pages of notes in the tiniest of print.

One feature of the volume that shocked many theologians and philosophers of that day was the very form in which Florensky presented his thought. For it is in the form of twelve letters written from a friend to one or several friends. The letter on the Holy Spirit, for example, begins, 'Do you remember, my quiet one, our long walks through the forest, through the forest of that dying August? . . . Do you remember our deep-searching conversations, my distant but always present friend? . . . Now it is winter outside. I am working beside a lamp and the evening light is blue and grand, like Death . . .'

It is hardly surprising that such introductory words to a chapter on the Holy Spirit should have proved most disconcerting to a philosophical and theological community conditioned to assume that the only proper form in which to present serious thought was, more or less, in the form of propositions – preferably after the model of Spinoza's *Tractatus theologico-politicus* (virtually a form of linguistic geometry) or after the style of Hegel's dialectic of thesis, antithesis and synthesis.

But Florensky, with his bold independence of conventional thought, did not believe that there should be any gap between the form and the content of communication. So if he was to treat of friendship, both human and divine, then presentation in the form of letters to friends was an appropriate one – communication on such matters can only be achieved along the path of friendship. Moreover, for Florensky friendship was a theological category, since friends are upheld in their friendship by the Trinity, the truth of which is at the very heart of his life and thought. Indeed he maintained that the doctrine of the Trinity is not only the guarantee of true theology, but likewise of all true thinking whatsoever. Indeed, he went so far as to say that the human family is going to have to choose between the Trinity and madness.

The basis for that startling prediction by Florensky is his claim that western philosophical thought is itself based on a law of identity that has disastrous consequences for human life in general, which can only be remedied if we begin to operate upon the basis of a principle of identity which reflects the doctrine of the Trinity.

Obviously the traditional formulation of the law of identity, which asserts that A is only A and not non-A, makes nonsense of the doctrine of the Trinity, which asserts that three distinct persons, Father, Son and Holy Spirit, are at the same time one God. But for Florensky it is not the doctrine of the Trinity which does not make sense, but the traditional law of identity which he describes as 'miserable', 'static', 'inorganic', an expression of 'death, emptiness and nothingness'. He justifies these statements by claiming that the traditional law of identity reflects a way of perceiving the world in which each thing is an isolated monad. The world, therefore, is a world of individuals that are only externally related to one another. (The term 'monad', it should perhaps be explained, is a term coined by Leibnitz for the ultimate constituents of the universe.) Monads, since they are simple, are incapable of action and have neither doors nor windows, and therefore any apparent interaction is only to be explained through a principle of pre-established harmony.

Such a way of perceiving the world runs completely counter to Florensky's whole experience of the world right from the time when, as a child in Batum, he had been aware of some bond of organic unity that allows the free flow of being from one object into another. In particular, the Leibnitzian thesis empties of meaning the device that Florensky placed as the epigraph to his great work, *The Pillar and Ground of Truth: Finis amoris, ut duo unum sint* – the consummation of love, that two become one. Yet that consummation is only possible if it is true that nothing can exist by itself alone, totally independent from the rest of being.

The true, organic, dynamic law of identity is stated by Florensky in terminology that is unfamiliar to the general reader, but the sense of it may be gathered from a practical illustration. You often find two lovers to whom it seems that they alone exist. Yet it is only a third reality, the outside world beyond their mutual relationship, that guarantees that they do not absorb one another and thereby eliminate the mutual, dynamic relationship that constitutes their identity.

That practical example affords us a clue as to why Florensky felt so passionately that the traditional law of identity, if pursued to its logical conclusion, could only lead to madness, since it promotes a philosophy of external relationships according to which there can be no mutual indwelling of persons. And perhaps he would have felt his forebodings justi-fied if he had noticed the definition of marriage given by one philosopher who did take the traditional law of identity to its logical conclusion. That philosopher wrote: 'Marriage is a contract for the exchange of the mutual use of the sexual organs.' The word 'contract' does, of course, permeate the language of modern thinkers who regularly invoke it in the hope that it might be used to draw individuals out of their separateness from one another so as to form a society. But the history of the past two centuries has shown how impossible it is, on such a basis, to establish an organic society characterized by mutual aid. The resultant organization, on the contrary, seems to be one in which *every* relationship tends to become an external, contractual relationship, a matter of bargaining and haggling.

There are many other aspects of our society which Florensky, if he were still living, could point to in justification for his prediction that we have to choose between the Trinity and madness.

## Art

In view of the *éclat* that greeted Florensky's work on theology it might well have been expected that he would spend the rest of his life in that field. Instead of which the needs of the Church during the early years of the Revolution impelled him into the philosophy of art, and especially of icon painting. This was because the Bolsheviks were beginning to take over the churches' treasures, and Florensky was the churches' main defendant in disputing with the state commissioners, showing that their plan for incorporating the churches' treasures into state museums was intellectually a nonsense.

In performing this new task Florensky showed himself capable of withering scorn. He said that he could at least understand a fanatical socialist who wanted to destroy the churches, stone after stone, but he could not respect those who wanted to preserve spiritual artefacts in order for them to be admired in a museum. Such museums are characteristic of a bourgeois culture that defines icons as 'self-standing objects which are generally to be found in churches'. Again, what would one think, he asked, of an ornithologist who, rather than study birds in their habitat, chose to devote himself to collecting their beautiful feathers? Or of someone who, in order to fit a large painting into a limited museum space, proceeded to cut it up into several sections? Or would try to catch some of the sun's rays, label them and put them under a glass cover? An icon, when taken out of church, ceases to be an icon and becomes a caricature of one, because an icon is a symbol with which one has to come face to face in a place where its presence is interwoven with all the other symbols – of architecture, music, incense and the light of candles – that comprise a church.

Since the misunderstanding of icons prevalent in polite society was rooted, according to Florensky, in the widespread assumption that icons are simply a crude attempt to imitate the religious paintings of post-Renaissance Europe, part of his task was to show that icon painting is a radically different undertaking. Hence his sustained critique of the rules that were claimed by the theorists of post-Renaissance European painting to be the only acceptable ones; that is, the rules of naturalistic perspective. But naturalistic perspective cannot claim to be the only valid perspective any more than the Euclidean geometry on which it is based can claim to be the only valid geometry. Indeed, says Florensky, the naturalistic rules are far from natural since accordingly all psychophysiological processes in the observer are to be excluded from the act of seeing. According to the rules 'the eye is meant to look at the object to be represented unmovingly and dispassionately as if the eye were an optical lens. There are to be no accompanying feelings or memories. The process is a purely external, mechanical one, having nothing in common with the human act of *seeing*.' The result, if the rules were followed, would be a photograph. But fortunately the great painters knew better; and instead of representing things in frozen immobility, they represented the life of things through their own impressions of them.

Having thus cleared the grounds of misunderstanding in this fashion Florensky goes on to provide a description of the icon and icon painting that enables us to understand them as never before. The clue to that understanding is given in his statement that 'all my life I have thought about only one problem – the problem of the symbol'. And for him the symbol is a window on reality, so that when, for example, people describe the iconostasis in an Orthodox church as a barrier between the congregation and the altar they are failing to understand the function of a symbol, which is to open up the realm of light. They do not understand that in a church *without* an iconostasis the congregation is actually separated from the altar, from the realm of light, by a brick wall of dumbness. To eliminate the icons is to brick up the windows. Similarly he writes that 'the mystery of the world is not hidden but is precisely revealed in its true essence through symbols – that is, as a mystery. Just as a beautiful body is not concealed but is revealed by clothing, and revealed as glowingly beautiful, for it is revealed in its chaste modesty.'

But it is when we ask what it is that is revealed by the icon that we are brought up against the most intractable obstacle to understanding icons, at least as Florensky explains them. That obstacle is illustrated in what he says about many – perhaps the majority – of post-Renaissance painters who purport to paint religious subjects. He says that the mere fact that they have to look to contemporary models for the figures in their religious paintings shows that the artists do not truly see what they claim to be painting.

In what sense, then, do icon painters, by contrast, truly *see* the holy ones who are represented in icons? In order to answer that question we must recognize that strictly speaking those who wield the brushes are not the primary painters. The primary painters are the Church's ascetics, who 'see every creature in its first-created, victorious beauty. The Holy Spirit reveals himself in endowing them with the ability to see the beauty of creation.' That first-created image seen by the ascetics is then embodied in the Church's tradition, including the rules for iconography, which are the means for the fixing of heavenly images, 'the solidification on a board of that living cloud of witnesses surrounding the altar.' The one who wields the brush, therefore, is really a technician whose hand is to be guided by the Holy Spirit. This is why he has to prepare himself by fasting and praying, gazing on what has been revealed in the past until he also learns to see the original image in the present. One cannot paint what one does not see.

In his description of the technical aspects of icon painting

Florensky is at his most brilliant, showing, for instance, how gold – which, of course, is not a colour – is used to evoke the play of spiritual energies in the icon in the way that, for instance, a pattern of iron filings on a sheet of paper reveals magnetic forces. But the technical aspect for which he is most renowned is his exposition of reversed perspective, the device by which a reversal of conventional lines of perspective results in every line and colour in the icon serving to highlight the presence in reality of the holy ones.

And for a student of Florensky's thought it must be emphasized that for him the word present means *really* present. For, as he says regarding the icon of a saint, 'No matter where the remains of a saint may be, and no matter what condition they are in, his risen and transfigured body is in eternity; and the icon, revealing him, is not just a picture of the holy witness but is that very holy witness.' Or, as he says on another occasion, 'When I gaze upon the icon of the Mother of God it is her whom I see – not her picture but she herself – contemplated by means of, with the aid of, iconographic art. As through a window, I see the Mother of God.'

## Semiotics

The last field of knowledge I have chosen to convey the temper of Florensky's mind is one in which his genius has been generously acknowledged, a field only marked out in recent years – that of semiotics, the science of signs. In fact one of the leaders in the field, Vyacheslav Ivanov, has described Florensky as a predecessor of modern semiotics. Ivanov also tells us that Florensky, just prior to his arrest, was working on electrical devices for computation and sign processing, and even seems to have been on the verge of inventing a primitive electrical prototype of a computer.

However, if Florensky was indeed a predecessor in the development of semiotics, that only underlines what a pity it is that he did not live to guide the science of signs along the philosophical path that he himself had long followed. Here I am thinking of how typical semioticians define culture as 'a mechanism of information received, decoded and translated from one system to another', and define man as 'a mechanism that intersects with his surroundings, processing information within himself and with other members of the collective'.

This whole manner of thought and speech is worlds apart from Florensky's world, in which the model of all communication is the communion of the persons of the Trinity. The consequence for human communication of the trinitarian model is that a message in communication is not an item that can be transferred from a transmitter to a receiver in a mechanical fashion, but is a meaning, which is a relationship that arises from the being of at least three persons for whom to be means to be in communion. In such a relationship the very message that one of the persons intends to send is itself conditioned by sensitivity towards the person to whom it is being sent, and demands a reference towards a third reality.

Yet according to the most famous modern semiotician, Umberto Eco, semiotics cannot point to any reality outside its own system: a statement that recalls the mordant observation of a Zen master, 'I pointed to the moon, and the fool kept looking at my finger.'

But it is a sentence from Vyacheslav Ivanov which inadvertently betrays the fundamental divergence between himself, as a semiotician, and Florensky, when he says, 'Florensky was among the first to understand the role of signs ("symbols", as he calls them) in all the spheres of spiritual life.' Here Ivanov seems unaware that sign and symbol are far from synonymous for Florensky. Florensky writes, 'The symbol not only signifies something other but is itself the bearer of this other . . . two worlds are united in the symbol – the one to which the symbol belongs materially and the one to which it points, whose signifier it is . . . the symbol is endowed, if only partially, with the spiritual power of the signified. Therefore it does not simply signify, but also really manifests the reality of what is signified.'

For Florensky, unlike Umberto Eco, had learnt how to distinguish illusion from reality. Indeed such a distinction had been his life's work ever since, in his youth, he had set out to answer Tolstoy's challenge to discover that by which human beings live. In his own case the answer is given, indirectly, in a letter from Solovki about Pushkin, when he speaks of how society deals with its great ones: 'The great one's gift is not paid for by memorials and posthumous speeches, nor by honours or money. On the contrary the great one has to pay for his gift with his own blood. . . .'

When he wrote those words Florensky was in the process of paying for his own many gifts in the *Gulag*. For in reading his letters you can see that the *Gulag* provided him with a most unerring touchstone for distinguishing reality from illusion. And some of what he wrote about the illusions indulged in by human beings, especially by bourgeois society, gives the reader a jolt. Take, for instance, what he says in answer to the request made by his daughter for his opinion of Tchaikovsky and Scriabin. Florensky acknowledges their great power but is repelled by them, since:

I have to ask myself about the ultimate worth of their productions! What difference would it make if these productions did not exist? Would the world lose anything in that case? Would even one ray of light be lost from human life? For example, if Mozart, Bach, Beethoven and even Schumann and Glinka had not composed, the world would be a darker place. But if Tchaikovsky and Scriabin had been silent I fear the world would be more illuminated. So, although I consider *The Queen of Spades* an outstanding opera, that makes it all the worse since its despair is that much deeper: it expresses despair so powerfully; and despair is the most poisonous of emotions. The refined dress and the brilliant form do not alter the essential point, which is *death*, crawling into one's soul and which, by skilfully concealing itself and never naming itself with its own name, prevents any resistance to itself. Both Tchaikovsky and Scriabin are un-realists, surrendering to despair and illusions, such illusions as you cannot afford to indulge in if you are engaged in the struggle for the word against chaos and for life against death.

But in view of Florensky's severe words about the compositions of Tchaikovsky and Scriabin we ourselves may legitimately ask him what was the reality of which he was so convinced that it saved him from any hint of despair even though he was denied the realization of his untold gifts?

In his letters from the *Gulag* there is not the mention we might have expected of the Church, for the obvious reason that it would have endangered his correspondents; but there is one theme that recurs time and again throughout his life, summed up in the phrase *proshloe ne proshlo* – the past has not passed away. He first expounded the phrase in 1919 and later invoked it in separate letters to his wife, his daughter and his mother.

For instance: 'The past has not passed away, but is eternally preserved somewhere or other and continues to be real and really influential. It is only in books that the boundaries of personality are fixed, since in reality everybody and everything is so closely interwoven that separation is only approximate, with continuous transition taking place from one part of the whole to another part.'

How such a transition might take place was brilliantly conceived by Florensky in one of his works which caused a great stir, *Imagination in Geometry*. In that treatise, after referring to the theory of special relativity, according to which any normal object must move at a speed slower than the speed of light, Florensky goes on to posit the case in which a body exceeds that speed. Then, 'just as the air breaks at the movement of bodies with speeds greater than those of sound', so 'space *breaks* at speeds greater than those of light', which gives rise to 'qualitatively new conditions' and is consequently accessible to creatures located on the other side of the first surface. There occurs 'a *breaking* of the space, in which the body turns *inside out* through itself'.

Does that passage from Florensky's pen – with its image of a body breaking, disappearing and passing to the other side of the surface, thus becoming accessible to creatures located on that other side – not enable us to envisage how Florensky himself may now have become a real presence for the human family through his martyrdom?

Some fifteen years previous to his execution at the hands of the NKVD Florensky had spoken of Christ as 'the first martyr' and had quoted Saint Paul as urging the Roman Christians to

sacrifice their bodies as a *logiken latreian,* which most commentators translate as 'reasonable service' but which Florensky
translates as *slovesnoe sluzhenie,* which in Church Slavonic
means 'symbolic service', which Florensky interprets to mean
'possessing the word freely and witnessing to the truth'.

He then adds a further sentence of explanation which was
to resonate throughout his own life and beyond: *khristianin
govorit telom,* 'a Christian speaks with his body' – not merely
by black marks on paper or by breath through his lips, but
with his body. That is what Florensky did, thereby embodying
the symbol of which he said, 'The symbol not only signifies
something other, but is itself the bearer of this other . . . two
worlds are united in the symbol: the one to which the symbol
belongs materially and the one to which it points, whose
signifier it is. The symbol is endowed, if only partially, with
the spiritual power of the signified. Therefore it does not
simply signify, but also *really manifests the signified.'*

Florensky, in his death as in his life, manifests the Spirit,
which is why he is really present in the cloud of witnesses by
whom we are encompassed.

Some time after this text was prepared and delivered as a
lecture more information concerning Florensky has appeared
in Vitaly Shentalinsky's *The KGB's Literary Archive* (Harvill,
1994). The archive reveals that in 1933 a certain professor
named Gidulyanov had, in order to save his own life, falsely
accused Florensky of organizing a nationalist-fascist conspiracy
against the Soviet regime. In a subsequent document Gidulyanov makes it clear that Florensky, when faced by his accuser
in the presence of investigators, deliberately incriminated
himself in order to save others accused of the conspiracy.
Shentalinsky comments:

> All of Florensky's life had prepared him for this decision.
> When the release of several people from the hell of the
> Lubyanka and his own self-humiliation were weighed on
> the scales of his conscience he could only choose the latter.
> He preferred to sacrifice himself for the sake of others.
> Florensky once wrote: 'In the past there have been right-
> eous men with a particularly acute awareness of the evil and
> sin that floods the world who did not consider themselves

to be free of this corruption. Deeply grieving, they bore within them a feeling of responsibility for the sins of the world as well as their own shortcomings.' Now he too became just such a righteous man.

In one of his last letters from Solovki, Florensky wrote: 'The universe is so organized that only at the price of suffering and persecution can the world be given anything. The more selfless the gift, the harsher the persecution and the more severe the suffering. That is the law of life, its fundamental axiom . . . Greatness must pay for its gift in blood.'

# 5

# The holy folk

It will be clear from the preceding chapters that each of the towering figures who are portrayed here derived much of their spiritual strength from the traditional culture of the Russian peasantry, those who described themselves as 'the dark people' on account of their illiteracy, and of whom Metropolitan Filaret said, 'They have much warmth but little light.' Both those judgements underline what a delicate task it is to trace the spiritual strand that runs through the warm, 'dark' traditions of the Russian people during the century preceding the Bolshevik revolution. That delicate task is rendered impossible and vain if what we try to measure is the extent to which all, or even the majority, of the peasant population adhered to the strand of spirituality. For the life of the Spirit is beyond measure, like the wind which blows where it wills: you hear the sound of it, but you do not know where it comes from or where it is going. All we can do, and need to do, is to concentrate our attention so as to perceive the traces of the passage of the Spirit, whether in one person or in a multitude of persons, since one breath from the Spirit is enough for multitudes to be born of the Spirit.

It is true, of course, that the very effort of trying to trace the passage of the Spirit is itself an arduous spiritual undertaking, because in this sphere 'one only sees truly with one's heart'. Moreover the 'dark people', being illiterate, do not themselves record in writing their struggles to live by the Spirit, and so we have to listen carefully to them as they talk to one another in their folk stories and songs and prayers. But the rewards for having to listen so intently are all the more precious, because in all writing there is an element of self-display whereas, by contrast, in folk tales and songs and prayers the speakers are often facing a familiar audience, so that listening to them is like the experience of accidentally hearing someone saying their prayers. Moreover, people who live in a vibrant oral culture do not see any need to record their highest aspirations since everyone within that culture imbibes those aspirations from childhood onwards through the community's songs, rituals, tales and everyday observances. Often it is only when an alien culture has made an incursion, or when members of the home culture venture abroad, that it becomes obvious to them how precious are the elements of their own inherited culture. Meeting another culture always carries with it a danger to one's own; and under the threat of its loss one feels the need to record the richness of it before it vanishes.

Some such awareness seems to have arisen in the Russian writer Vladimir Rozanov, as a result of his experience in western European churches, after which he pronounced the judgement already quoted in the introduction: 'In the West they don't actually worship. Instead they have a lecture followed by a concert.' Without attempting to gauge what justification there might be for Rozanov's remark, at least it alerts us to the fact that in contrast to the West the Russia in which he lived was the home of a *worshipping* people. One needs to emphasize the word *worship* in this context because if Rozanov was right about the West then there is always a danger that western observers who have not experienced real worship, and therefore attach minimal importance to it, will fail even to notice it, much less recognize worship as being the foundation of life for the people of Russia. Such failure is not merely hypothetical, as was shown lately in the case of a book devoted to those peasants of the Moscow region who in the years preceding the Revolution were urbanized, becoming Muscovites. Out of the book's more than four hundred pages only two mention religion, and even then only tangentially.

The omission is breathtaking because for the great majority of Russians at that time the spiritual landscape was shaped by the familiar outline of a church, usually situated on a rise or beside a river or in a forest clearing. The beauty of the building and the sound of its bells were ever-present reminders of the invisible world, as were the icons to be found not only in the 'red corner' of every household but also outside public buildings, inside inns and on the platforms of railway stations.

Moreover there were special places within the sacred space afforded by the Church such as the monastery of the Caves in Kiev, or the Solovki islands on Lake Ladoga, or the shrine of Saint Sergius near Moscow to which every year hundreds of thousands of pilgrims went on foot, instinctively tracing the shape of Holy Russia.

In a sense every journey made by a Russian at this time took on the air of a pilgrimage, if only on account of a ritual, universally observed throughout the whole people, of the 'three minute farewell'. In accordance with this custom, whenever a member of the family was setting out on a lengthy journey the whole family would gather and say their farewells to one another, kissing and blessing one another. Then they would all settle down in silence for a period before taking their leave of one another. The English writer Maurice Baring wrote a beautiful short essay about such a leave taking, *The Three Minutes*, in which he weaves together the thoughts and feelings, fears and hopes of those who are sitting at the common table in the silence.

Such a ritualization of the journey meant that it is a mistake to describe as 'nomads' those innumerable Russian peasant families who crossed and recrossed the Russian plains in search of land. For the rituals meant that every journey, in a sense, became a pilgrimage with a clear goal. So it became virtually impossible to draw a distinction between a wanderer, a vagabond and a pilgrim since the ideas of wandering and pilgrimage had become fused. When we also remember the common folk's word for a prisoner, *neschastyi*, unfortunate, and their communal feeling revealed in the folk proverb, 'Doing anything in common is good, even dying', then it is less difficult to understand how peasants might set off on arduous journeys confident that in spite of their lack of resources they would somehow find food and shelter.

Not often do we come across an account by someone who actually experienced such a journey, but there has lately been discovered the diary of a peasant woman who, as a young girl of fourteen, made a journey of thousands of miles from Smolensk province to central Asia along with her mother and the rest of the family, her father having gone ahead the previous year in order to provide a place for them. In her later years Domna, as the girl was named, wrote of the kindness and communal solidarity with which their poor, defenceless family was embraced during the months of travel on trains, carts and boats, over rivers and steppes, and through sandstorms. To quote just once instance: having weathered a sandstorm through the selflessness of a Kirgiz carrier they found themselves near a Cossak village. Their mother, Thekla, sent Domna and her brother Demian to try to buy some food. Nervously they approached a long building near the village. Outside the building stood a tsarist soldier on guard. When he asked them what they were doing they explained who they were and that they wanted some bread.

'Go and stand by that stone', the soldier said. 'Soon I am going to be relieved and then we'll work something out.'

He went off as soon as the new sentry took over. Domna and Demian waited and waited for him until they began to think he had just been making fun of them.

'After all,' Domna thought 'what am I to him? Just a foreigner.'

Still they waited, until suddenly they saw the soldier approaching accompanied by two of his comrades. The first soldier was carrying a pail, the second a bag and the third a basket.

'Well', said the first one, 'lead us to the new immigrants', which the children did. The soldiers were amazed when they saw how many of them there were, saying,

'You could recruit a lot of soldiers out of this lot. But don't let them sign up with the Cossaks – they'll gobble you up!' Then the first soldier added,

'I'm a countryman of yours, from Kusek. I told your tale to my mates and the whole company agreed to give up their day's ration of kasha for you to have. So eat up. Bread is not easy to get around here.'

The soldiers sat with them as they ate and drank their fill and then said their farewells, all the time expressing their admiration for mother Thekla's courage in undertaking such a journey. She then blessed them and led her family back to collect their horse. To their astonishment they found their horse already tethered, and munching a pile of oats. It startled them until an old man came out of some nearby bushes, saying,

'Don't be alarmed. I put out the oats. We have plenty for ourselves.'[7]

And not only did the people live in sacred space, they also lived in sacred time. Though few of them were aware even of what year it was by the reckoning of governors and their officials, they were all aware of the cycle of the Church's calendar. Their year was shaped not only by the great feasts and fasts of Christmas, Lent, Easter, the Transfiguration and the Ascension of Jesus but at the same time also they calculated the tasks of their everyday lives in the farmyard, the fields and the forest by saints' days – fixing them according to 'three days after Saint Peter' or 'two weeks before Great Lent' etc.

Because they dwelt in sacred time and sacred space the peasants of Russia, whatever their doubts, sins and failings, lived a life that had imprinted upon it the 'liturgy' of the church of mother nature, of work on the land and in the family home. Liturgy is a far more powerful factor in shaping human beings than is formal education, since through its visual beauty, its music and its poetry it touches a person at a far deeper level than does formal education. And so the person who over the days, weeks, months and years has been formed by liturgy enjoys a much firmer identity than is to be found in someone who has received nothing more than the instruction of school and university.

Fortunately for our present purposes the contrast between an aristocrat who has received much formal education yet lacks firm identity and a peasant of no education who yet enjoys a firm identity by virtue of his peasant culture has been portrayed for us in a classical episode of world literature. That episode is the first encounter between Pierre Bezukhov, the illegitimate son of Count Bezukhov, and the peasant soldier Platon Karataev so unforgettably described by Leo Tolstoy in *War and Peace*.

It will be remembered that in September 1812 the French army under Napoleon was occupying Moscow when great fires broke out in the city, destroying some two thirds of it.

The French believed the fires to be the work of Russians who wanted to leave the French deprived of a winter base in Moscow, and among those arrested as an incendiary in Tolstoy's story was Pierre Bezukhov. Through a stroke of good luck Pierre escaped execution by a hair's breadth and was led by the French into a filthy shed which was being used as a prisoner-of-war barracks. Here, still completely stunned by the senseless executions he had witnessed, 'he now felt that the universe had crumbled before his eyes and only meaningless ruins remained . . .'.

At this point he found himself in a dark corner of the shed, sharing a heap of straw with a little man who turned out to be called Platon Karataev. For the following few hours Pierre attends fascinated to the small actions of the little man: his way of tying up his leg bandages, the unfussy way he shared his baked potatoes, his cheery concern for the grey-blue bandy-legged dog he had rescued and, above all, his wonderful sayings and stories, 'told in the tender sing-song caressing voice old Russian peasant women employ'. Eventually Platon says,

'Well, I think you must be sleepy', and begins crossing himself rapidly and constantly repeating: 'Lord Jesus Christ, holy Saint Nicholas, Frola and Lavra! Lord Jesus Christ, holy Saint Nicholas, Frola and Lavra. Lord Jesus Christ, have mercy on us and save us', he concluded; then bowed to the ground, got up, sighed, and sat down again on his heap of straw. 'That's the way. Lay me down like a stone, O God, and raise me up like a loaf', he muttered as he lay down, pulling his coat over him.

'What prayer was that you were saying?' asked Pierre.

'Eh?' murmured Platon, who had almost fallen asleep, 'what was I saying? I was praying. Don't you pray?'

'Yes, I do', said Pierre. 'But what was that you said: Frola and Lavra?'

'Well, of course', replied Platon quickly, 'the horses' saints. One must pity the animals too. Eh, the rascal! Now you've curled up and got warm, you daughter of a bitch!' said Karataev, touching the dog that lay at his feet. And again turning over he fell asleep immediately.

For a long time Pierre did not sleep, but lay with eyes open in the darkness listening to the regular snoring of

Platon, who lay beside him, and he felt that the world that had been shattered was once more stirring in his soul with a new beauty and on new and unshakeable foundations.

Of course it may be objected that Platon Karataev is a figment of Tolstoy's imagination and that his character affords no clue as to the true spirituality of the Russian peasantry. But the objection is not valid. Apart from anything else Tolstoy is not, in the conventional sense, an imaginative writer. On the contrary his temperament, like his prose style, is very matter of fact. But because he had a genius for observation he noticed clearly those things that ordinary mortals can only dimly imagine. It was that capacity which led Turgenev, after reading Tolstoy's story about the horse Strider, to exclaim, 'I knew it. Lev Nikolayvich must have *been* a horse.' It also explains why anyone wishing to understand what was going on beneath the surface of events in Russia during the struggle against Napoleon is better advised to read *War and Peace* than the work of any professional historian. In any case we have plenty of evidence outside of Tolstoy's novels and stories of how closely he paid attention from his earliest days to the lowly folk who wandered into, out of and around his ancestral home of Yasnaya Polyana, as, for example, in his autobiographical work *Childhood*.

In that book, recording the death of his mother when he himself was still an infant, he tells us how ashamed he was to notice that his grief over his mother was not pure. It was mingled with something false and self-regarding, a desire to show that he was more sorrowful than anyone else. Moreover, he detected the same element of display and egotism in everyone else there, including his father, except for one person. For as the family and friends gathered in the room where his mother's body lay in her coffin, 'there in a far corner of the room, almost hiding behind the open door of the dining room, there knelt a bent, grey-haired old woman. Her hands clasped together and her eyes raised to heaven, she was not crying but she was praying. Her whole soul was straining towards God. She was begging him to unite her with the one she loved far more than anything in this world, and she ardently hoped that would come soon. ' "There is someone who truly loved her", I thought and I began to feel ashamed of myself.'

That indelible impression of utter simplicity made upon him by an anonymous old lady is matched by the portrait which Tolstoy paints for us of Grisha: a wandering *iurodivi* who went barefoot throughout summer and winter alike, who wore chains next to his skin as a mark of penitence, and who made more of a mark on the young Tolstoy than did the boy's own free-thinking, highly-educated, libertine father, who despised Grisha.

Tolstoy tells us how he and his brother Volodya once concealed themselves in the lumber-room from where, unobserved, they could watch Grisha in the room below saying his prayers. As Grisha was finishing his night prayers, so Tolstoy writes,

> I noiselessly thrust my head in at the door, without daring to breathe, Grisha was motionless; heavy sighs rent his breast; a tear stood in his dim, squinting eye.
>
> 'Thy will be done', he suddenly exclaimed with an expression that cannot be described. And falling with his forehead against the floor, he burst into sobs like a child.
>
> Years have gone by since that time. Many a remembrance of the past has lost its importance and has become but a fancy for me. Even the wanderer, Grisha, has long ended his last pilgrimage. But the impression produced upon me by him, and the feeling aroused in me, will never die out of my memory.
>
> Oh, Grisha! thou great Christian! Thy belief was so deep; that thou couldst feel the nearness of God; thy love was so great that the words flowed from thy mouth freely; thou didst not control them by thy reason . . . And how greatly didst thou glorify his greatness when, unable to find any words, thou didst fall on to the ground with tears.

At almost the same time as Tolstoy was drawing his portrait of Grisha, the fool for Christ, his somewhat older contemporary Ivan Turgenev was sitting in an inn not very far from Tolstoy's home of Yasnaya Polyana. While there he was greatly moved by something told to him by one of the locals and which he embodied in his beautiful story, *Living Relics*.

Turgenev places at the head of his story some lines from a poem by his older contemporary, Fyodor Tyutchev:

These poor villages,
This humble landscape,
Native land of long-suffering,
Land of the Russian people.

The foreigner's haughty glance
Will not understand or notice
That which shines mysteriously and dimly
Through your humble nakedness.

Weighed down by the burden of the cross
The king of heaven
In the likeness of a servant
Has wandered over all of you, my native land,
Blessing you.

Turgenev describes how early one morning before setting off hunting he went for a stroll in a nearby wood and came upon a small wattle shed.

I glanced in through the half-open door: it was dark, quiet, dry; smelling of mint and melissa. In the corner some boards had been set up and on them, loosely covered with a blanket, was a small figure. I was about to go away when . . .

'Master, oh master! Peter Petrovich!' I caught a voice – faint, slow, soughing, like the rustle of swamp sedge. I stopped.

'Peter Petrovich' the voice repeated. 'Come nearer, please!' It was coming from the corner, from the platform I had noticed.

I approached, and was petrified in astonishment. Lying before me was a living human being – yet just what was it? The head was utterly withered, all of one hue, the hue of bronze, for all the world like an icon lined in the ancient style; the nose was narrow, like a knife blade; the lips were hardly to be seen: one could catch only the white gleam of teeth and eyes and, escaping from under a headkerchief onto the forehead, scanty wisps of yellow hair. Near the chin, where the blanket folded over, two diminutive hands, of the same bronze hue as the face, were stirring, fidgeting with fingers that were like tiny sticks. I looked closely: the face was not only not hideous but actually beautiful, yet frightening, extraordinary. And all the more frightening did this face seem to me because I saw upon it, upon its cheeks of metallic hue, a smile struggling . . . struggling, yet unable to expand.

'You don't recognize me, master?' the voice fell to whispering again; it was as though it were evaporating from the barely moving lips. 'Yes, and how should you! I'm Lukeria. . . . Remember? The girl who used to lead the round dances at your mother's, in Spasskoe. . . . I used to lead off the chorus too. Remember?'

'Lukeria?' I cried out. 'Is it really you? How can that be?'

'Yes, it's me, master, me. I'm Lukeria.'

I didn't know what to say and, as if I had been stunned, kept staring at this dark, immobile face, with its radiant and deathlike eyes fixed upon me. How could it be? This mummy – Lukeria – the leading beauty among all our household serfs, the tall, plump, fair-skinned, rosy-cheeked girl, always the great one for laughing, dancing and singing! Lukeria, whom all our young lads courted and for whom I, too, had secretly sighed, I, a sixteen year old boy!

Turgenev naturally went on to enquire as to how Lukeria had been brought to such a pass. He discovered that some six or seven years back she had become betrothed to Vasily Polyakov, 'such a fine-looking fellow with curly hair'. Then one night, just before dawn, Lukeria heard a nightingale singing wonderfully sweetly and went out to the porch to listen to it. There, thinking she heard Vasily's voice softly calling her name, 'Lushka', she turned, but too quickly. And in so doing she fell off the porch, down on to the hard ground. She was paralysed. What amazed Turgenev was that she told her story 'almost cheerfully, without moans and groans, without complaining at all, and not begging for sympathy'. And in answer to his question about Vasily she replied, 'He grieved and grieved, and then married another, a girl from Glinnoye . . . He loved me very much, but, after all, he was a young man, he could not remain single. And what sort of a helpmate could I be to him? And he found himself a good, kind wife, and they have little ones.'

In answer to her visitor's questions Lukeria recounted how

she had spent six years lying there on the boards; how people
came to her bringing flowers; how there came to her every
sort of living creature – birds and bees and butterflies; and
how she would recite some prayers, 'only I don't know many
of them, of these prayers. But also why should I bother the
Lord God? What can I ask him for? He knows better than I
do what I need. He has sent me a cross to bear, that means
he loves me. That is how we are told to understand it. I
recite the Lord's Prayer, Hail Mary, the Akathistos to All the
Sorrowing, and once again I lie without the slightest thought.'

And when Turgenev starts to pity her she stops him by
saying

> Some have it worse . . . Some haven't even a shelter . . . And
> there's some that are blind or deaf! But I, glory be to God,
> can see splendidly, and can hear everything, everything! A
> mole may be burrowing underground – well, I can hear
> even that. And I can catch every scent, even though it be
> ever so faint. When the buckwheat comes into blossom out
> in the field, or a linden in the garden, why, there's no need
> of telling me, even: I'll be the first to catch the scent right
> off. Just as long as there's a breeze blowing from there. No,
> what's the use of angering God? There's many in worse fixes
> than mine.

Indeed so little is Lukeria thinking about herself, even when
she becomes exhausted through talking to her visitor, that her
concern is for the well-being of her fellow serfs. When he
began to leave by asking her if she wanted anything, she said
with great effort but tenderly, 'I don't need anything; I am
quite satisfied, thank God. May God grant health to you all.
Just one thing, master, you should persuade your mother –
the peasants here are poor – if only she would reduce the
quit-rent a little! They have not enough land, no common
land . . . They would pray to God for you. As for me, I need
nothing, I am quite satisfied.'

A few weeks after he had bidden farewell to her Turgenev
learned that Lukeria had died 'after the fast for Saint Peter's
Day'. They said that on the actual day of her death she kept
hearing the sound of church bells although it was over five

versts from Alexeyevka to the church, and it was a weekday. However, Lukeria said that the pealing of the bells came not from the church but 'from above'. Probably she did not dare to say 'from heaven'.[8]

The deep sincerity with which Turgenev the sceptic recounts this story of Lukeria's saintly acceptance of suffering is a witness to the reality of that readiness to suffer that so many observers noted as characteristic of the Russian people, but which has few echoes in the rest of Turgenev's writing. By contrast the great body of writing produced by Nicholai Leskov, 'the most Russian of Russian writers', is suffused with an awareness of the spiritual atmosphere in which so many of the Russian people lived.

An unforgettable evocation of that atmosphere is to be found in the story of *Cathedral Folk* which he published in 1872, and which describes the life of the small cathedral town of Stargorod as seen through the eyes of the three very different characters who served in the cathedral: Archpriest Savelyi, the priest, Zakary, and the impetuous deacon, Achilla. One little vignette from the pages of *Cathedral Folk* remains in the memory as witness to the way in which traditional ceremonies can sanctify the seemingly routine moments of everyday life. Natalya Nikolaevna, the wife of Archpriest Savelyi, and herself known as 'archpriestess', had been waiting through the evening twilight for the return of her husband. 'When she heard the creaking of his footsteps on the porch' she rose, immediately lighted two candles and from beneath them cast an enquiring glance towards her husband as he entered. The archpriest himself quietly kissed his wife on her brow, quickly took off his cassock, put on his white dressing gown, tied his silk kerchief round his neck and seated himself at the little window.

A moment or two later the archpriestess invited him into the laughably small, oblong room which served as her bedroom and where Father Savelyi sat himself down at the small table, ate two soft-boiled eggs that had been cooked for him and then began to take leave of his wife for the night. The archpriestess herself never ate in the evening. As a rule she simply sat opposite her husband while he was eating and performed small services for him, at one point handing him something, at another taking a dish and removing it. Then the two of them stood up together and prayed before the icon and immediately afterwards began to make the sign of the cross over one another. They always carried out this mutual blessing of one another as preparation for sleep at the very same moment with such skill and so quickly that one could not help wondering why their hands did not clash and get entangled. After receiving this mutual blessing the husband and wife gave each other a farewell kiss, the archpriest kissing his tiny wife on her brow and she kissing him upon his heart. Then they parted. The archpriest went to his bed chamber and lay down to sleep.[9]

A very different reach of the Russian spirit is portrayed by Leskov in another of his stories, *The Enchanted Wanderer*. It is one of compassion for those who on account of one deed are refused burial in consecrated ground, namely, those guilty of suicide. The setting of the tale is a ship on Lake Ladoga bound for the island of Valaam at a moment when a discussion had arisen among the passengers concerning a young seminarian in those parts who, having fallen into despair through slavery to drink, had committed suicide. Among the passengers of every rank and occupation was a philosopher who asserted that the young man had done right because by means of suicide he had put an end to his suffering.

'How do you mean, there was an end to his suffering?' exclaimed one of the other passengers. 'What do you suppose will happen to him in the next world? Suicides, you know, are condemned to eternal torment. People are not even allowed to pray for them.'

The philosopher smiled sardonically. But now at this moment there intervened a passenger who had just joined the group. He was a man of enormous size, swarthy and of open countenance, with thick, curly hair. Though wearing the short cassock of a monastic novice he appeared to be some fifty years old.

'I do not agree with your views about the fate which is in store for suicides in the next world – that they will never be forgiven. As for there being no one to pray for them, that, too, is nonsense, for there is a man who can improve their unhappy lot quite simply.'

The speaker (whose name we later learn to be Ivan Severi-yanovich Flyagin) then told the story of a lowly village priest of the Moscow diocese, a hard drinker who himself was nearly unfrocked but who is the one who prays for suicides.

The story goes that a church official one day wrote to His Grace Archbishop Filaret of Moscow, denouncing the village priest as a terrible drunkard who drinks vodka night and day and is not good in his parish. As a result the archbishop summoned the no-good priest to Moscow for questioning, and on discovering the truth of the denunciations, he deprived the priest of his benefice. This so distressed the poor priest that he even gave up drinking and decided that the only way for him to ensure sustenance for his wife and children was to take his own life. By doing so he would oblige the archbishop to find a husband for his daughter, who would be a bread-winner for the priest's widow and orphans.

The priest even fixed a date for the terrible deed. But in the meantime the archbishop was being visited in his dreams by an old man whose face bespoke infinite goodness – none other than Saint Sergius, the most honoured of all Russian saints. Awestruck, the archbishop said to the saint, 'What dost thou, who art pure in heart, desire of me, thy unworthy servant?'

To which Sergius replied:

'I ask for mercy.'

'To whom dost thou want me to show mercy?'

So the saint named the humble priest who had been deprived of his place because of his drunkenness, and then he vanished.

When the archbishop woke up he reasoned to himself that it was incredible for so strict an advocate of the ascetic life as Saint Sergius to be interceding for such a notoriously weak character as the drunken priest. And so he dismissed the dream as of no significance.

Until the next night. When he had another dream but one which, this time, terrified him. For in it he beheld an enor-

mous band of knights, all on black horses and led by a fierce
captain wielding a black banner, who kept roaring out, 'Tear
them to pieces for they now have no one to pray for them.'
Then as the captain and his band galloped away there followed
after them a whole procession of dismal spirits, like a flock of
geese in springtime, and all of them nodded their heads sorrowfully to the archbishop and pleaded pitifully, moaning and
sobbing, 'Let him go! He alone prays for us!'

This time, of course, the archbishop could no longer ignore
the meaning of his dream, so he immediately sent for the
drunken little priest and began to question him about what
prayers he was in the habit of saying. At first the little priest
was puzzled and tried not to have to answer the archbishop's
questions. But in the end he admitted, 'I confess to being
guilty of one transgression. For, being weak in spirit myself
and in my despair thinking that it were better to take my own
life, I always during the service of Holy Communion say a
special prayer for those who die without absolution and lay
violent hands upon themselves.'

Here the storyteller paused and then continued: 'His Grace
then understood what those spirits were who in his dream had
sailed past him like lean geese. And, not wishing to give joy
to those demons who had sped before them bent on destruction, he gave his blessing to the humble priest. "Go", said His
Grace, "and sin no more, and for whomsoever thou hast been
praying, continue praying for them"; and he sent the priest
back to his parish. So he, this lowly priest, can always be
useful to people who find life's struggles too great a burden
to bear, for he isn't likely to prove untrue to his calling,
presumptuous though it may appear, but he will go on impor-
tuning the Creator for them and he will have to forgive them.'

'Why "have to?" ' one of the listeners objected.

'Because "knock and it shall be opened unto you". That
was what he himself commanded and that, sir, cannot be
altered.'[10]

Sadly something of the freshness of his early writings was
lost by Leskov over the years and a more satirical tone began
to take over. Though he tried to depict for us a series of
positive believers, the just men in these later stories are less

memorable and convincing because the satire and bitterness of
the author himself seeps into the stories.

However, during the very same years that Leskov was
attempting and failing to portray saintly characters a whole
series of them were being brought to life by a writer who had
many times indulged in savage anger and unbridled lust but
whose world for a few years now seemed to be bathed in
simple, bright goodness. For the writer in question, Leo
Tolstoy, between the years 1880 and 1887, recorded and retold
in his own fashion a succession of folk stories with moral and
spiritual lessons which will speak to the condition of Everyman
so long as human beings have eyes to see with and ears to
hear with and hearts to be moved. The title of one of these
stories, *That by which human beings live* conveys the burden of
all of them, whether the story be *Three Hermits* or *Two Old
Men*, or many others.

It is true, of course, as some critics are fond of repeating,
that Tolstoy did not copy down word for word the stories that
were current among the lowly people but shaped the stories
for a wider audience. Nevertheless we know that Tolstoy
was for ever talking with pilgrims and peasants and listening
to them in inns and monasteries, on the road and at his home.
He is among the most reliable of witnesses to that by which
the people lived – more reliable, certainly, than critics a
hundred years later who have never made a pilgrimage on foot
or spoken with peasants.

One person, for instance, from whose lips Tolstoy heard his
tale was the peasant story-teller, Vasily Petrovich Shchego-
lyonok. Tolstoy met him in 1879 or 1880 and, in his
irrepressibly direct manner, asked Shchegolynok how he
prayed. Whereupon Shchegolynok spontaneously poured forth
a prayer of epic proportions in the course of which he called
upon innumerable saints and martyrs. Tolstoy was deeply
moved, and after bidding Shchegolynok goodbye he turned
towards his aristocratic companion with the words: 'That is
how to pray, not as how the likes of you and I do.'

It was from Shchegolynok that Tolstoy heard the story of
which an outline runs as follows: One night Simon the poor
cobbler was on his way home drunk through a fierce snow-

storm when beside a chapel he noticed what he took to be a
naked frozen corpse. Fearful that robbers may have murdered
the man and were still around Simon made to hurry on, but
his conscience pricked him and he went back. On doing so
he discovered that the man still had life in him, but only just.
And so Simon stripped himself of his own coat and put it on
the stranger, whom he then led through the snowstorm to his
own home. Simon's wife was furious at first because she and
Simon and their children had insufficient food and clothing
for themselves, never mind for this stranger who hardly spoke
a word, beyond revealing that his name was Mikhail.

Mikhail, however, turned out to be a great blessing to Simon
and his wife, Matryona, because he soon became such a skilled
cobbler that all and sundry in the area, especially the high
born, came to that house for their shoes and boots. Then one
day, after six years, the identity of Mikhail was disclosed.

There came to Simon's house a well-born lady accompanied
by twin girls who were identical apart from the fact that the
left leg of one was lame and she walked with a limp. For
the twisted left foot of that twin special boots were needed
and so the making of them demanded skill such as Mikhail
alone possessed. And it was while he was making the boots
that the lady told the story of the twins.

Six years earlier on a Tuesday the father of the twins, a
forester, had been killed. A day or so later his wife had given
birth to the twins and she herself died on the Friday and, in
her death agony, had fallen upon one twin and crushed her
foot. Providentially the lady telling the story had decided to
call at the house the following day and had taken the orphaned
twins to her own bosom and cherished them as her own ever
since.

After telling her story the lady and the twins soon left. But
when Simon and Matryona turned towards Mikhail he was in
a state of bliss, the reason for which he gladly explained to
the two of them.

Mikhail was actually an angel in heaven who on one
occasion had disobeyed God. For God had sent him to bring
back to heaven the soul of a woman who had just given birth
to twins. But when Mikhail appeared to the woman she

appealed to him not to take her soul because 'little children cannot live if they have neither father nor mother'. So he did not do as God had said, as a result of which when the mother died her body rolled on to one of the twins and crushed her little foot. And as a punishment to Mikhail God sent him as a naked human being to learn that human beings are mistaken if, like the mother of the twins, they think that children cannot live without mother or father. As Mikhail said, 'My life was preserved for me not by taking thought for myself, but by the love that dwelt in a passer-by and his wife, so that they could feel for me pity and affection. Again, the two orphans were preserved alive, not by any thought that was taken for them, but by the love that dwelt in the heart of a strange woman, so that she could feel for them pity and affection. For, indeed, all men live, not by the thought that they may take for themselves, but by the love that dwells in all mankind.'

'I had known before that God gave life to men, and that he would have them live; but now I understand another thing. I understood that God would not have men live apart from one another – wherefore he had not revealed to them what was needful for each one; but that he would have them live in unity – wherefore he had revealed to them only what was needful for themselves and for their fellows *together*. Yes, at last I understood that men only *appear* to live by taking thought for themselves, but that in reality they live by Love alone.'

Then the angel (Mikhail) sang a hymn of praise to God, and the hut trembled at the sound of his voice, while the roof parted in the middle, and a pillar of fire shot up from earth to heaven. Simon and his wife and children fell down upon their faces in adoration, and as they did so wings burst forth from the angel's back, and he soared away into the sky.

When Simon opened his eyes again the hut was as it had been before, and there was no one there but his own household.[11]

It is largely owing to the famous writers of the nineteenth century, some of whom we have quoted above, that we can clearly envisage the work of the Spirit in the midst of the Russian folk. But we also have other sources in the persons of certain foreigners who spent much time in the land of

Russia and whose witness affords confirmation of the impression so vividly conveyed by the great writers.

The French scholar, Leroy-Beaulieu, for instance, travelled the length and breadth of Russia during the later years of the nineteenth century and his voluminous writings show him to have been a sharp observer. One feature of the people's religious practice that he particularly highlights was 'the very Russian custom, before going to confession, of asking pardon of all with whom they live in daily contact – relatives, friends, as well as servants. On confession days one frequently saw people, even those unacquainted with one another, bowing low to one another in silent token of mutual forgiveness.' Much to the surprise, no doubt, of his western readers he goes on to tell us that the New Testament was probably in greater demand in Russia than in any other part of Europe except the Protestant countries: 'The gospels are undoubtedly the book dearest to the Russians. The New Testament is to be found in the working man's room as well as in the peasant's cabin. Those who know how to do so read it to the others.'

Those observations are specially noteworthy since they come from the pen of a man who was himself a rationalist. They need to be supplemented by the witness of foreigners who, by virtue of themselves being quickened by the Spirit, were alive to the presence of the Spirit in others. Two such were the Englishmen Maurice Baring and Stephen Graham, both of whom during the same epoch of the early twentieth century spent many years travelling throughout the length and breadth of the Russian empire and ensconcing themselves in every section of Russian society. One sentence alone is sufficient to convey Baring's judgement upon the faith of those whom he encountered over the course of many years: 'The Russian Church has the true smell: it smells of the poor, of untanned leather, onions and human sweat.'

And if we are in need of any illustration of Baring's judgement then nothing more convincing could be provided than the heart-moving story told by Stephen Graham of his pilgrimage to Jerusalem in the company of Russian peasants, some fifteen thousand of whom used to crowd into the Holy City each year at Easter. One young lad among them came from the 'top' of the Urals, fifty versts north of Orenburg, and had walked all the way to the pilgrims' boat in Odessa, having promised God that he would eat no meat and drink no wine until he reached the Holy Sepulchre in Jerusalem. In his preface to *With the Russian Pilgrims to Jerusalem* the world traveller Graham tells of his experience as 'the most wonderful thing I ever found on the road . . . It has also been a great discovery. Jerusalem is a place of disillusion for the tourist who would like to feel himself a pilgrim, but here in the peasant world is a new road and indeed a new Jerusalem.'[12]

Of course one is not maintaining that every Russian peasant was imbued with the same intense devotion as led the peasant pilgrim to Jerusalem. How far such devotion was widespread was as impossible to determine then, as it is nowadays. But one further example of the extraordinary Christian simplicity animating many of them is to be found in the memoirs of a Prussian officer who took part in the Masurian Lakes campaign against the Russians in 1914. He tells us that a whole company of Russian peasant soldiers were once made captive without putting up serious resistance. Since they appeared to be sturdy, and in no way cowardly men, the Prussian officer asked them to explain to him why they had failed to fire at the advancing Prussian cavalry. 'Well sir', said one of them, 'We didn't mind firing when they told us to fix our sights at one thousand yards because we knew we should harm no one. But when it came to two hundred yards, then it would have been a great sin.' And the same Prussian officer goes on to tell us that he witnessed another equally striking incident. During a cavalry charge one of his fellow officers, a very young man, thrust his lance into one of the Russian peasant soldiers but found himself unable to pull the lance out. But as the young man was frustratedly trying to do so he suddenly became aware of what a terrible thing he had done to a fellow human being. At which he began to weep, only to find the Russian peasant soldier gently reaching a comforting hand towards him and saying: 'Don't weep, brother, for Christ's sake.'[13]

# A mosaic of the Spirit

'Gather up the fragments so that nothing is lost.' *St John,*
*6: 12*

The year 1917 in Russia witnessed a cataclysm of unprecedented magnitude. The Bolshevik party seized power with
the declared intention of creating a 'new man'. Everything
that had happened previously, according to them, was not
really history but simply a meaningless series of events. History
proper was to begin in 1917 with the creation of this 'new
man', who was moreover to be a man of steel, no longer *homo
sapiens* but *homo stalinensis*, a being fitted to dominate first
Russia, then the whole earth and eventually the planetary
system itself by means of a new material, the work of man
himself, steel, and a new source of energy, again devised by
man himself, that is, electricity.

The whole of Russia was to be transformed into 'one vast
office and one vast factory'. In the service of this great aim
rivers would be diverted from their normal courses in order
to make deserts fertile; forests would have to be cleared with
the same purpose; and machines would be developed that
would allow grain to be grown even in the seeming waste
permafrost regions of the Arctic. In order to achieve this, of
course, it would be necessary, as Karl Marx once predicted,
'to put an end to the idiocy of rural life'. Or as it was
eloquently stated by one intellectual enthusiast for the new
man, Boris Pilnyak,

> Peasant life is known – it is to eat in order to work, to work
> in order to eat, and, beside that, to be born, to bear and to
> die. Our Revolution is a rebellion in the name of the
> conscious, rational, purposeful and dynamic principle of life,
> against the elemental, senseless, biological automatism of life:
> that is, against the peasant roots of our old Russian history,

against its aimlessness, its non-technological character, against
the holy and idiotic philosophy of Tolstoy's Karataev in *War
and Peace*. It will take decades to burn out Karataev's philosophy but the process has begun.[14]

Sadly, the process Pilnyak had welcomed led to his own
execution at the hands of the Bolsheviks in 1937. But he had
at least put his finger on the crux of the matter: before the
new man could emerge the two cultures that had provided
Russia with continuity for a thousand years would have to be
uprooted and burnt out, that of the peasantry and that of
holiness enshrined in the Orthodox Church. These two cultures, though distinguishable one from another, had become
so meshed together that burning out one inevitably meant
burning out the other. Nor, in doing so, could the new man
afford to exhibit any of that pity for the unfortunate, that
melting of the heart so characteristic of traditional Russia.
The leader of the Bolsheviks, Lenin, once rejected any such
sentimentality when speaking about Beethoven's music: 'I
know nothing more beautiful than the *Appassionata*, I could
listen to it every day. It is marvellous, unearthly music. . . . But
I cannot listen to music often; it affects my nerves. I want to
say amiable stupidities and stroke the heads of people who can
create such beauty in a filthy hell. But today is not the time
to stroke people's heads; today hands have to descend to split
skulls open, split them open ruthlessly, although opposition to
all violence is our ultimate ideal.'

Eighty years later, as we all know, the attempt to create the
'new man' has ended in complete disaster. It has cost the lives
of tens of millions of human beings and instituted state cruelty
on a scale undreamt of eighty years ago, only to produce 'the
most dreary, the most oppressively, comprehensively dreary
society, physically and spiritually, that has ever been created for
the chastisement of mankind'.

And what makes this sad story sadder still is that the contemporary westerner, he of the shrunken heart and narrow mind
depicted by the Slavophiles, seems incapable of learning the
priceless lessons that are to be garnered from the incomparable
experience of evil and goodness during the last eighty years

in the former Soviet Union. In this respect the West's understanding of the Soviet story displays a marked contrast to its grasp of similar events precipitated by another regime for which soldiers made of steel represented the height of human aspirations; that is, the regime of the National Socialists in Germany. For instance, the names of Bonhoeffer, von Moltke and the Scholls, who perished at the hands of the Nazis, and the testimonies of Bielenberg, von Galen and Niemoller who survived, have entered into the consciousness of millions of citizens of the western countries. But how many of those same citizens could name even one of the millions who were martyred by the Soviets or is familiar with the testimonies, say, of Dmitri Likachev or Oleg Volkov or Varlam Shalamov (whose experiences were far more searing and lasted years longer than those of the one person likely to have been heard of, Alexander Solzhenitsyn)?

The explanation for the ignorance of the present generation in the West about the heroic witnesses in the Soviet Union, as compared with the receptiveness of an earlier generation to the heroes of the German resistance, may well lie in the fact that the categories and terms in which the present generation seeks to understand events are almost entirely those of economics, politics, diplomacy and military strategy, whereas their predecessors were far more alive to the crucial importance of the Spirit. And so they really listened to those Germans who were honest enough to trace their failure at an early stage to grasp the horror of what was happening as due to their 'lack of the gift for the discernment of spirits'. They eventually awakened to the realization that 'we are not contending against flesh and blood, but against the principalities, against the world rulers of this present darkness, against the spiritual hosts of wickedness in the heavenly places' (Ephesians, 6: 12).

So if we ourselves are to understand at the deepest level what was going on in the Soviet Union beneath the surface of economic, political, diplomatic and military events, we have to be open to 'the gift for the discernment of spirits' and to learn from those who 'resisted the world rulers of this present darkness'.

One of the striking differences between the story in

Germany and the story in the Soviet Union is that though there were occasional conspiracies against the regime in the Soviet Union there were no organized resistance movements rooted in Soviet society. The reason, clearly, is that Russia had never formed those networks of institutions – local councils, trade unions, philanthropic associations of every sort – which provided Germans with bases for resistance. And though the Orthodox Church in Russia did protest vigorously in the 1920s the Church itself had never become sufficiently tightly knit to be able to present a united front across the whole land. In any case, because the clerical order lived separately from ordinary society, neither had the Church elaborated a social and political teaching that might have held a resistance movement together.

As a result of this backwardness in Russian society, its haphazard character, the Bolsheviks found it easier to bring down their symbolic hammer upon the fabric of even the most ancient Russian cultures, those of the peasants and of the Church, and shatter them into fragments. That is why evidence for the triumph of the Spirit during the Soviet era is bound to be fragmentary, which in turn makes it completely apposite for anyone concerned about spiritual truth to obey Jesus' injunction in Saint John's Gospel to 'gather up the fragments that remain'. In an attempt to follow that injunction I have come to recognize that the fragments witnessing to the triumph of the Spirit in the Soviet Union could only be shaped into a monument worthy of the host of Russian martyrs by virtue of many researchers working in collaboration for several generations. Nevertheless over the years I have collected a number of fragments, which I present here as a kind of small mosaic to assure readers that the tradition of Russian spirituality contained in this book is not dead. What is more, in gathering fragments I have noticed one feature of them which I believe offers us a clue to the very deepest significance of that 'struggle against the spiritual hosts of wickedness' referred to in the letter to the Ephesians.

That feature is the predominance in the fragments of the witness of women. The easiest way to explain that predominance, of course, is to say that even the Soviet authorities allowed more scope to women than to men. But that was not the case. I believe, rather, that a clue to the true explanation is to be found in a movement of the Spirit that is to be discerned in late-nineteenth-century Russian theology whose significance has not yet been realized.

I am referring to the 'revelation' of femininity within the Godhead that a number of the most gifted Russian thinkers felt themselves to have received during that period. The most dramatic manifestations of that familiarity occurred in the life of Vladimir Solovyov, Dostoevsky's young friend, who had a vision of the feminine *Sophia*, the eternal Wisdom of God, on three separate occasions, which inspired the poem *Three Meetings* composed in 1898, not long before his death. The theological theses that Solovyov formulated on the basis of his 'revelation' did not altogether satisfy those who took up the same theme, such as Pavel Florensky and Sergei Bulgakov, whose own reformulations have not themselves satisfied further Orthodox thinkers (though Florensky could at least point to the existence of a special Divine Office to Sophia, the Wisdom of God, in Old Church Slavonic, which shows that the significance he gave to Sophia is no mere fancy).

Again, this 'revelation' in Russia needs to be set in a much wider context which includes among others, for example, the contemporary Teilhard de Chardin, for whom also the eternal feminine emerged ever more powerfully. And it includes those many appearances of Mary reported all over the earth during this period, the most celebrated of which, that in Fatima, was said to have a special message for Russia. All of which suggests that beneath the surface of economic, political, diplomatic and military events, and indeed theological formulations, a change of consciousness was taking place throughout the human family, instigated by the Spirit, more profound than anyone could grasp.

Does that suggestion not throw fresh light on why it was that the women of Russia were mainstays in the struggle against 'the world rulers of darkness' and of what nature those rulers were? Surely in the light of the awakening of the just to the femininity within the Godhead we can now see that the regime instituted by those declared enemies of God, the Bolsheviks, was at the same time driven by a violent hatred for all those blessings of the feminine that were rooted in traditional Russian culture – pity for unfortunates, tenderness, gentleness, motherliness. In vivid contrast has there ever been a more fanatically masculine regime than that of the Soviet rulers?

There is no more accurate test of the mentality of either an individual or a society than the sort of metaphors and similes that they use, and in the case of the Soviet *apparatchiki*, 'machine men', as they used to define themselves, every metaphor is derived from warfare and is concerned to assert the irresistible power of the masculine principle. And just as they rode rough shod over the sense that the earth is, in Dostoevsky's terminology, 'sacramental', so, with their steely logic, they denied the 'sacramentality' of the love between man and woman. Hence the fury of the *apparatchiki* of the Soviet literary establishment at the appearance of Pasternak's *Dr Zhivago*, which centres around a heroine who embodies all the joy and vulnerability of femininity. The novel is a sustained, lyrical celebration of human love which shows up the bankruptcy of manmade ideology without even trying to do so.

And maybe it is a sign of Sophia (the feminine spirit moving Solovyov, Florensky and Bulgakov a century ago) once more being welcomed in Russia that a series of most gifted writers have emerged in our own day who sense some sacramental relationship beteween man and nature mediated by woman. One of them, Valentin Rasputin, a Siberian writer well known for his campaign to save Lake Baikal from industrial pollution, expresses a sense of that relationship in his novel *Farewell to Matyora*. Here a chorus of wise old peasant women led by the heroine Darya refuse to give way in face of the plan of the *apparatchiki* to drown *Matyora*, their ancestral island. Perhaps, therefore, one may say that the triumph of the Spirit in Russia is the triumph of the old woman over the new man!

**Anatoli Emilianovich Levitin** was born in 1915 in the city of Baku. His father was a Jew who had been baptized into the Christian faith. His mother was an actress. Very devout from early childhood he was nevertheless drawn for a time

into the schismatic so-called Living Church before returning
to Orthodoxy in 1944. In 1949 he was arrested by the KGB
and sentenced to ten years. Through his writings and his
speeches he was a constant thorn in the side of the Soviet
authorities and eventually left for the West, where he died.

Every two or three months brought some kind of unpleasant
surprise – the arrest of a group of priests. By 1937 there were
only fifteen of them left in the whole of the Leningrad region,
whereas in 1930 they had numbered more than a thousand.
In the spring of 1937 the metropolitan was turned out of his
rooms in the Novodevichy monastery at the Moscow Gates
and found shelter for himself in the bell-tower of the Prince
Vladimir Cathedral in the cramped and gloomy accom-
modation formerly occupied by the caretakers. Metropolitan
Alexi took church services along with Archdeacon Verzilin,
the only deacon left in Leningrad. After Verzilin's death in
1938 he celebrated without a deacon. At that time the metropolitan put on his robes at the altar, not in the middle of the
church, and celebrated in a way very little different from a
priest. His Grace's whole way of life at that time was essentially
modest. I remember once, as I was walking along Nevsky
Prospect, near Morskaya Street, I noticed the metropolitan
clad in civilian garb. A threadbare light-weight overcoat,
galoshes, an ordinary grey cap – all this, in conjunction with
his aristocratic face and subtle elegance of gesture, gave him
the appearance of a bankrupt landlord. As I passed I made
him a deep bow and the metropolitan acknowledged it with
a slight nod.[15]

**Yevgeny Alexandrovich Yevtushenko** was born in 1933 in
the remote Siberian town of Zima. In his autobiography he
tells us of an incident which took place not long before the
occasion described in the following extract: his uncles discovered him weeping one night over the bodies of some roe
deer shot by them on the *taiga*. Yet though he wept for the deer
he used to rejoice when he heard of the many Germans killed

at the front. He could not see the Germans as human beings. They were enemies.

In this extract he provides us with an example of *umilenie* in the heart of one *babushka* which awakened the hearts of many others.

In '41 Mama took me back to Moscow. There I saw our enemies for the first time. If my memory is right, nearly twenty thousand German war prisoners were to be marched in a single column through the streets of Moscow. The pavements swarmed with onlookers, cordoned off by soldiers and police. The crowd were mostly women – Russian women with hands roughened by hard work, lips untouched by lipstick, and thin hunched shoulders which had borne half the burden of the war. Every one of them must have had a father or a husband, a brother or a son killed by the Germans. They gazed with hatred in the direction from which the column was to appear. At last we saw it. The generals marched at the head, massive chins stuck out, lips folded disdainfully, their whole demeanour meant to show superiority over their plebeian victors.

'They smell of eau de Cologne, the bastards', someone in the crowd said with hatred.

The women were clenching their fists. The soldiers and policemen had all they could do to hold them back. All at once something happened to them. They saw German soldiers, thin, unshaven, wearing dirty blood-stained bandages, hobbling on crutches or leaning on the shoulders of their comrades; the soldiers walked with their heads down. The street became dead silent – the only sound was the shuffling of boots and the thumping of crutches.

Then I saw an elderly woman in broken-down boots push herself forward and touch a policeman's shoulder, saying: 'Let me through.' There must have been something about her that made him step aside. She went up to the column, took from inside her coat something wrapped in a coloured handkerchief and unfolded it. It was a crust of black bread. She pushed it awkwardly into the pocket of a soldier, so exhausted that he was tottering on his feet. And now suddenly from every side women were running towards the soldiers, pushing into their hands bread, cigarettes, whatever they had. The soldiers were no longer enemies. They were people.[16]

**Evgenia Semyonovna Ginzburg** was born in 1896 and died in 1980. An ardent member of the Communist Party, she along with her husband was arrested in 1937 and sentenced to ten years imprisonment, charged with 'Trotskyist' terrorism. After almost two years of solitary confinement she was sent to a hard-labour camp in the gold fields of Kolyma, the location of the following extract. She was 'rehabilitated' in 1956.

During that mortally dangerous spring, the strength of character displayed by the semi-illiterate 'believers' from Voronezh did much to keep up our morale. Easter fell that year at the end of April and these women, who fulfilled their norm by honest work and on whose output the production of Kilometre Seven was based, asked to be dispensed from work on Easter Day. 'Cousin' (the name given by the prisoners to their overseer) refused even to listen to them, though they promised to work three times as hard to make up for the day of rest.

'We don't recognize any religious holidays here, and don't try to convert me. Get out into the forest with the rest and don't be up to any of your tricks. I've wasted too much time as it is making reports about you and bothering the high-ups. I'm capable of handling you myself. If you try any subversion you'll get a punishment you won't forget in a hurry.'

The brute then gave his orders to his underlings. The women refused to leave their quarters, saying that it was a sin to work on Easter Sunday. The guards drove them out with rifle butts, but when they reached the forest the 'believers' made a neat pile of their axes and saws, and sitting down composedly on the frozen logs started to chant their prayers. The guards, acting no doubt on Cousin's instructions, ordered them to stand barefooted on one of the ice-bound forest pools, the surface of which was covered with a thin film of water. We were witnesses of this. Masha Mino, an old Bolshevik, intervened intrepidly on behalf of the victims.

'What are you doing?' she shouted at the soldiers in a voice shaking with anger. 'These are peasant women. How dare you set them against the government! We shall protest. We shall see that you are called to account for this.'

The soldiers replied with threats and shots in the air. I don't remember how long the torture, physical for the 'believers', moral for us, lasted. Barefoot on the ice, they went on praying. We threw down our tools and went from one guard to another, weeping, beseeching.

That night the punishment-cell was so full that it was almost impossible to stand, yet the night passed quickly, for until dawn we argued about the behaviour of the women from Voronezh. Was this fanaticism, or fortitude in defence of the rights of conscience? Were we to admire them or regard them as mad? And, most troubling of all, should we have had the courage to act as they had? In the heat of the argument we forgot our hunger and exhaustion and the stinking dampness of the punishment cell. It is a remarkable fact that not one of the women who had stood for so long on the ice went sick. As for the norm, next day they reached one hundred and twenty per cent.[17]

**Osip Emileivich Mandelstam** (1891–1938), poet and essayist, was brought up in the cultural milieu of St Petersburg's bourgeois intelligentsia. Regarded by many as the greatest Russian poet of the twentieth century he was never at ease under Soviet rule and virtually signed his own death warrant when his savage depiction of Stalin in one of his poems became known to the authorities. He was arrested a second time and deported to Siberia. His death is recorded to have occurred on 27 December 1938. Very moving accounts of his life are to be found in the two books by his widow Nadezhda, *Hope against Hope* and *Hope Betrayed*.

When Mandelstam was arrested in 1934 for his poem about Stalin, he at once admitted he was its author, and accepted the NKVD's judgment of its 'counter-revolutionary character'. Four years later it made no difference that he denied the new charges brought against him or that the NKVD produced no evidence to back them up. On 2 August 1938 he was condemned to five years' corrective labour for 'counter-revolutionary activity'. That same month he was moved to Moscow's Butyrskaya prison to await transportation to Kolyma in far north-eastern Siberia, the most desperate of the zones of the *Gulag*.

The prison train was ordeal enough, taking almost a month to travel from Moscow to Vladivostok, where Mandelstam was put in hut no. 11 of transit camp 3/10 of Usvitlag, the north-eastern section of the *Gulag* empire. A twenty-four-year old Yuri Moiseyenko arrived in the camp on 14 October and found a bunk in hut 11. Made of wood planks, these ran in three tiers down both sides of the hut. He writes:

> The next morning we ate breakfast on our bunks and there was an old man sitting there in shirt and trousers, very thin, bags under the eyes. The face was rather small. A high forehead. The nose stood out. The eyes were beautiful and clear. His shirt had a pattern of spots which suited him.

Several men slept on each tier of the wood planks. Moiseyenko was one of Mandelstam's five neighbours, but the poet talked most to a geologist from Leningrad, the city where he had gone to school and published his first poems (whenever possible Mandelstam wandered about the camp searching out fellow Leningraders). Another neighbour on the bunk was a beekeeper from Blagoveshchensk called Ivan Kovalyov, whom Moiseyenko remembers as an elderly, 'humble' man. Kovalyov became Mandelstam's protector. Moiseyenko calls him his 'slave'.

> Mandelstam always wanted to be first on and off the bunk, but he moved slowly, making everyone else wait. He knew the others would grumble, but he did it all the same. Then he would pacify them with a simple smile. Kovalyov stood there, helping him climb up and down.

Since it was a transit camp, where prisoners waited to be sent to Kolyma, there was no forced labour, but as winter approached Mandelstam began to feel the cold.

He simply wasn't eating, he just pecked at his food like a

sparrow. His strength was leaving him. Kovalyov began to take food to him on the bunk. The criminals had the job of bringing round the food. 'For me and my friend', Kovalyov would say. 'Is he alive? You there, lift your head up!' Mandelstam would raise himself up weakly, 'I beg you, please . . .' He was so puny and helpless, and then suddenly he showed such spiritually, strong, quiet courage. All that time he did not complain once. Not once. And yet with typhoid you have headaches, a temperature, fever. Kovalyov would ask: 'How are you feeling, Osip Emilyevich?' He only answered, 'I'm getting weak.'

The almost uneducated Kovalyov looked after Mandelstam 'because of his helplessness', explains Moiseyenko. 'Osip Emilyevich won Kovalyov over by his helplessness, he was a kind and conscientious man. You know, when everyone was sleeping Kovalyov would surreptitiously cross himself. I saw him.'

On the morning of 27 December they were sent in groups to have their clothes fumigated. Mandelstam had for some days been lying on his bunk dressed in shirt and trousers and it took him a long time to climb down. With Kovalyov holding his arm, he made his way with the rest of them to the building which housed the fumigation room. There they undressed and handed over their clothes except for Mandelstam's leather coat, which was judged unsuitable for treatment. The following day Mandelstam died.[18]

**Lev Zinovievich Kopelev**, a distinguished scholar of German literature, was born in 1912. He became a Marxist at a young age but was arrested in 1946 and was set to work as a mathematician in the 'special prison' at Marfino on the outskirts of Moscow where he met Solzhenitsyn who depicts him as Rubin in *The First Circle*. In 1968 Kopelev was expelled from the Communist Party and thrown out of the Union of Soviet Writers in 1977. Subsequently he was allowed to leave the Soviet Union and now lives in Germany. The extract below relates to a period when he was in a 'relaxed' prison.

Aunt Dusya, our housekeeper, was a small, prematurely withered woman with big, grey, youngish eyes smiling out of a
wrinkled face. Her voice was hurried, eager, with a musical
lilt. Never did a bitter or unseemly word come from her
mouth: a reproachful 'Now, dearie', or a resigned, '*Ekh*, you
cabbage head', was the closest I heard her come to anger. She
had spent more years in labour camps than anyone else I had
met – since 1932. I liked to listen to her peasant speech.

I'm a village girl, dearie, born on a bed of straw. Tended
geese when I was just a little tyke. What time was there for
school, when Papa was taken off to be a soldier, and me the
oldest of eight children? Ten years old I was then, and what
we didn't have to do – milk the cows, and feed the pigs and
chickens, and grow the vegetables, and plant the field,
and harvest the grain. Two classes of school was all I had
when the war came to our door – the Reds and the Whites
and the Greens [the anarchist peasant bands of Nestor
Makhno and other guerilla leaders of similar persuasion],
and the taxes and the levies. Then Papa came back from
soldiering. He was wounded, and he limped and he
coughed, and he wouldn't do any work but was always in
the village arguing with the other men and drinking vodka.
Froze to death one night when he was drunk, may the Lord
have mercy on his soul.

But I was taken to wife for love. I was sixteen then. His
father was a rich man and had a farm near Kaluga. In my
family we were poor, and slept on gunnysacks or on the
stove, and ate from one bowl. At my father-in-law's they
slept on sheets in their own beds and ate from plates. And
I did not even bring a dowry. But I came pure of body and
soul, and I sang in the church choir and knew all the prayers,
and I liked to work and laugh and dance and sing. My
father-in-law would say to his own daughters, 'Dusya doesn't
have a lead kopeck, but she has a golden mind, and you have
gold earrings and heads of lead.'

When Lenin adopted the New Economic Policy, the father-
in-law became one of the 'Red merchants'. He would send
Dusya and one of his daughters, Nastya, to Moscow with
supplies of butter, cottage cheese and yogurt, which found
ready buyers in the food stores. With the end of the NEP

period, such 'speculation' became a crime again. But the father-in-law continued with this arrangement, only now the two young women disposed of their products through secret middlemen.

They were spending the night at the home of one of these 'partners' when the place was raided.

> I had time to tell Nastya: 'Remember, you don't know who I am; you met me on the train; you came to Moscow to buy clothes for your dowry.' They believed her and let her go. And me – I had the goods and the money. What could I say?
>
> At the interrogation she feigned idiocy. 'I cried, and I prayed. "Let me go", I begged. "Where I'm from I won't tell you. Whose money this is I won't tell you. I swore to God I would not tell anyone. Let me go, in the name of Christ."
>
> Two months I kept it up. Then they brought in one of our partners. They had broken him, poor soul, and he had told them everything. So they gave me five years for speculation. Then, in camp, they gave me ten more years for conversation and agitation. And this happened through one old woman who told them that I was saying all kinds of things about the collective farms and about the government.

Her father-in-law, warned by Nastya, had meantime left Kaluga with his family and escaped arrest. Her husband was with the army engineers and had sent her a parcel from Germany. Her two children, a boy and a girl, had been told that she was dead.

> It's for the best. They are being raised by my sisters-in-law. They go to school; they have their lives ahead of them. Better to be an orphan, dearie, than to have a convict for a mother.

Aunt Dusya's room was next to the kitchen. It was in the kitchen, where I could read and smoke after lights out in the wards, and which also served as the duty room for the night nurse, that my liaison with the nurse Edith began. Edith, who was from one of the ethnic German areas, was serving the last two years of a ten-year sentence.

In April Aunt Dusya invited us to a secret observance of Easter. One of the inmates tending the stoves was a priest, two of the laundresses were nuns, one of the cooks was an expert in religious services, and the four of them, together with Aunt Dusya, had made one of the women's barracks into an improvised chapel, greasing palms wherever necessary to keep it quiet. Seryozha was invited as well.

'So what if you are unbelievers?' Aunt Dusya said. 'You and Seryozha stand up for people, and whoever stands up for people stands up for God. Your Nechipor, the Baptist, is always talking about God, and I don't believe him. But you and Seryozha, and your Edith, you are people with soul. I see right into you, and what I see is good, and I pray for you as for one of my own.'

The service was held in the evening. The beds were placed alongside the walls. There was a fragrant smell of incense. A little table covered by a blanket was the altar. Several home-made candles cast their glow on an icon. The priest, wearing vestments made of sheets, held up an iron cross.

The candles flickered in the dark. We could hardly see the faces of the others in the room, but I felt sure that we were not the only unbelievers present. The priest chanted the service in an old man's quaver. Several women in white kerchiefs joined in softly, their voices ardent and pure. A choir gave harmonious responses, softly, softly, in order not to be heard outside.

There, outside, ten steps from the barracks walls, was the barbed wire, with its watchtowers, its sentries in sheepskin coats; and, further on, the houses of the guards and the camp officials; and beyond them, all around us, the dense and ancient forest; and beyond the forest, the west, the Volga, and a string of villages, grey and hungry; and finally, hundreds of kilometers away, Moscow. The ruby stars in the Kremlin towers. An old, peeling house. A narrow room, where my daughters were asleep. And beyond Moscow, toward the west, a trail of ruins, ashes and freshly dug graves.

The next day, Easter Sunday, some of us were invited to Aunt Dusya's room. Each of us had tried to contribute some-thing, and she had prepared a festive spread. There were hard-boiled eggs, painted according to Easter custom, and meat and baked potatoes; there were American canned beef and sausage, and biscuits and sweets – the yield of parcels from home. The doctors had contributed some alcohol, which Aunt Dusya had mixed with a bottle of liquid vitamins for colour and taste. She had even managed to bake a *kulich* [a traditional Easter cake] and to adorn it with coloured paper flowers. We exchanged the traditional Easter toast – 'Christ is risen!' 'Truly risen!' – and Aunt Dusya took two plates of food and two glasses of the improvised vodka to Uncle Borya and Dr Telyantz who lived in the doctors' house. Aunt Dusya also insisted that we invite the informer Stepan.

Dearie, with his poor, lost, dark, sinful soul, where will he find a ray of light if we don't show it to him? Let him see that even here, in prison, the light of Christ still shines and there is pity even for such as he. We didn't tell him about the Church service, because others would be held responsible if it became known. We invited only those we could be sure of. But here in my little room I am mistress. Around this little table we are all equal, believers and unbelievers, and for all of us this is a bright holiday, and there is only good here.

And there is another reason. Oh, dearie, don't think I haven't learned. I'm a crafty one, I am. Just think, everybody who drops in for a bite and a drink: don't you think Stepan will smell the alcohol on their breath? You'll take a little food to your friends in your ward: don't you think he'll ask: from where? His eyes, his ears, his nose are always on the job, and so he'll have to squeal on us. But if we invite him and treat him and exchange toasts with him, in Christ's holy name – for Jesus taught us to love and pity our enemies – he will see things differently, and he will not be able to repay good with evil.

Aunt Dusya did as she proposed. She called Stepan, and poured a drink for him, and exchanged the Easter toast with him. And Stepan drank and ate and beamed, 'Thank you – thank you.' He even winked, as though to say that he understood and that there was no need to worry.

We were all in a tender mood and smiled and said kind

things to each other. Someone made a speech about this being a holiday not only for Christians but for all men of goodwill. I argued compellingly that a good Christian and a good Communist not only shouldn't, but couldn't be enemies.

Two days later, Aunt Dusya, her face stained with tears, told us that Stepan had squealed. She had her own intelligence network and usually knew what was going on. She had learned that Stepan had reported the reception to the Oper. The Oper wanted to conduct an investigation, but Uncle Borya and Dr Telyantz opposed the idea, and the hospital director sided with her convict-doctors. Instead, as a compromise measure, Aunt Dusya was to be transferred to a harder post in a sewing shop.[19]

One of the most eccentric figures in Russian cultural life until her death in 1970 was the pianist **Marya Veniaminovna Yudina** (1899–1970). Her life was dominated by her religious convictions that set her against the Soviet musical establishment, a position that made her something of a cult figure among Soviet audiences. It also led to her being expelled from the Leningrad Conservatoire. Shostakovich, from whose memoirs the story below is taken, knew her for many years and, though admiring her playing, was often exasperated by her habit of giving away money that she had borrowed either to beggars or to the Church. However she retained the friendship of Pasternak and Akhmatova, reading Pasternak's poetry in public when that was a sign of dissent, and playing beside his coffin for the mourners. Also it was she who arranged the memorial service for Akhmatova.

Again, Yudina went from Moscow to Leningrad in order to give concerts during the height of the siege. Her heroism was recognized by Olga Friedenberg, Pasternak's cousin, who wrote, 'One had to have a mighty and unbending spirit to choose to come to our grim city, risk the deadly bombardments and then return to her room on the seventh floor of the Astoria Hotel in the pitch blackness of Leningrad nights.'

Stalin didn't let anyone in to see him for days at a time. He listened to the radio a lot. Once Stalin called the Radio

Committee, where the administration was, and asked if they had a record of Mozart's Piano Concerto No. 23, which had been heard on the radio the day before. 'Played by Yudina', he added. They told Stalin that of course they had. Actually, there was no record, the concert had been live. But they were afraid to say no to Stalin; no one ever knew what the consequences might be. A human life meant nothing to him. All you could do was agree, submit, be a yes-man, a yes-man to a madman.

Stalin demanded that they send the record with Yudina's performance of the Mozart to his *dacha*. The committee panicked, but they had to do something. They called in Yudina and an orchestra and recorded that night. Everyone was shaking with fright, except for Yudina, naturally. But she was a special case, that one, the ocean was only knee-deep for her.

Yudina later told me that they had to send the conductor home, he was so scared he couldn't think. They called another conductor, who trembled and got everything mixed up, confusing the orchestra. Only a third conductor was in any shape to finish the recording.

I think this is a unique event in the history of recording – I mean, changing conductors three times in one night. Anyway, the record was ready by morning. They made one single copy in record time and sent it to Stalin. Now that was a record. A record in yes-ing.

Soon after, Yudina received an envelope with twenty thousand roubles. She was told it came on the express orders of Stalin. Then she wrote him a letter. I know about this letter from her, and I know that the story seems improbable. Yudina had many quirks, but I can say this: she never lied. I'm certain that her story is true. Yudina wrote something like this in her letter: 'I thank you, Josif Vissarionovich, for your aid. I will pray for you day and night and ask the Lord to forgive your great sins before the people and the country. The Lord is merciful and he'll forgive you. I gave the money to the church that I attend.'

And Yudina sent this suicidal letter to Stalin. He read it and didn't say a word. They expected at least a twitch of the eyebrow. Naturally, the order to arrest Yudina was prepared and the slightest grimace would have been enough to wipe away the last traces of her. But Stalin was silent and set the letter aside in silence. The anticipated movement of the eyebrows didn't come.

Nothing happened to Yudina. They say that her recording of the Mozart was on the record player when the leader and teacher was found dead in his *dacha*. It was the last thing he had listened to.[20]

**Vladimir Alexeyvich Soloukhin** was born of peasant stock in the region of Vladimir in 1924. Most of his writing is centred upon the folk, the customs and the atmosphere of his native region. He began to collect icons in the early 1960s and has made himself an expert on both their content and their form.

In those days I had not seen the Pskovo–Pechorsky monastery, which lies in a deep ravine, nor had I looked down from the high bank of the Dniestr on to a certain monastery in Moldavia: so I was the more impressed by the sight of Volosovo.

We had driven to the top of a high hill, and saw below us a wide, deep valley, or rather two valleys intersecting each other. The point where they crossed was the lowest in the landscape, and there we saw the white monastery, looking like a toy. A sparkling river ran past it, and the woods on the slopes above looked like a bluish cloud. The buildings could scarcely be picked out in their setting of peaceful greenery.

How absurd and incongruous, we thought, to find such an idyll amidst the harsh reality of the present day. But we had judged too soon. When we approached closer we found signs that a fierce fight had indeed been going on here; both sides had withdrawn from the field, but it was still in disorder. There were, of course, no dead bodies; but the place was full of rubble, parts of the buildings were destroyed, battered or patched up, and the dome of the church had had its crosses knocked off. A tractor stood near by, looking like a tank that had been put out of action; motor tyres and scattered piles of firewood lay about in confusion. In short, there was every sign that a clash had taken place between two hostile forces.

We walked round the monastery building, looking for a door by which we could enter, but everything was locked and boarded up. Then we came on some narrow steps, leading down to a door which, though battered, did not look completely disused. We knocked, and a quavering voice answered us from within. We pulled the door towards us and found it unlocked – indeed it was apparently unlockable, as there was neither a key-plate nor a staple for a padlock. Groping along the basement passage, we came to a second door, which opened into a room four yards square. When our eyes got used to the gloom we found that it was something between an oratory and a monk's cell, with a lectern in the middle and a religious book lying open on it. The walls were hung with icons, some in metal frames, and there were icons on the high window-sill: the room was very lofty in proportion to its area, and as the walls were five feet thick there was plenty of room for icons in the window-embrasure. The lectern was bespattered with yellow wax-drippings from cheap candles, one of which was guttering beside the open book. A few lamps glimmered in front of the icons. The room also contained a stool and a narrow iron cot.

In front of the taper and the open book we saw a tiny, bent old woman dressed in black. Her whole body trembled feverishly: her hands, her shoulders, her head, her lower lip and her tongue as she strove to get words out. None the less, we managed to hold a conversation with this strange being in her out-of-the-way habitation.

'I live alone here, all alone. Yes, I'm a nun. They pulled everything down, and I'm the only person left. I made this little cell for myself, and I get along somehow. So far they've left me alone. What's my name? Mother Eulampia. Before I was a nun? Oh, my dears, that was a long time ago, what's the good of remembering? Katerina, my name used to be. Anyway, here I am looking after the icons. I'm still alive and I look after them. I keep the flame burning night and day.'

'Who put you in charge of the icons? Who asked you to look after them?'

'Why, God, of course. I protect them by God's order.'

'So I suppose this is your main business in life, your chief duty?'

'It's the only duty I have. As long as I'm alive, my one business is to keep the flame alight in front of the icons. When I'm gone, the candles will go out too.'

'Where are these icons from?'

'Some from the convent church, some from Annino. There used to be a beautiful old church there. When they pulled it down a lot of the icons were taken to Petrokovo, but I got them to give me the Virgin of Kazan and the Archangel Mikhail, and Saint Nicholas there as well. It's a wonder-working icon of Saint Nicholas, people for miles around used to worship it, and now it's here. The church at Petrokovo is still open, it's not been destroyed and they hold services there. I ought to go there to pray and be cleansed of my sins, but as you can see I'm in no state to go anywhere – I'll not see Petrokovo again.'

'Mother Eulampia, there's no reason for you to go to Petrokovo now. The church has been closed, and all the icons smashed to bits with axes. We've just been there and seen it. So you can set your mind at rest about going.'

She made a movement as if clapping her palms together, but her hands were so paralytic that no sound came. Her aged face quivering, she turned to the icons and began to cross herself, whispering:

'Lord, forgive them their folly, they know not what they do.'

Afterwards she allowed us to look at the icons, and I examined each one in turn. It was difficult to take down those that were hanging on the walls, and I had to be content with looking at their faces; but the ones standing in the window I was able to pick up and look at thoroughly. One of these interested me especially. It was a full-length representation of the Archangel Mikhail, measuring something over a yard high and a foot broad. The panel was coal-black and badly warped, worm-eaten in places and showing the marks of rough treatment with a scraper. The cleats were narrow and extended across its whole breadth, close to the ends. But I need not enumerate the details – it was obviously a sixteenth-century panel. The painting, on the other hand, was a commonplace piece of late-nineteenth-century realism, in light blue oils. . . . I should have asked Mother Eulampia for the icon then and there. It was, after all, not one of her principal ones, as it came from the pile in front of the window. But I was so affected by the tiny room and the old woman, by finding her in the deserted monastic building and by her strange self-imposed duty of keeping alight a flame whose feebleness matched that of her own life – all this so moved me that I could not bring myself to ask her to give me the Archangel Mikhail.[21]

The extract printed below was originally published in the *samizdat* review *Nadezhda* shortly before its enforced termination in 1983. It was one of three short narratives found in an anonymous *samizdat* manuscript. The person who recorded the story of Matrionushka explains at the beginning of the manuscript that the story was told to him by **Bishop Stefan (Nikitin)**, who at the time was a layman and a doctor.

During the thirties I was imprisoned in a concentration camp and, since I was already a doctor, they put me in charge of the camp hospital. The majority of the prisoners were in such a bad state that my heart couldn't stand it, and so I let many off from work so as to help them at least a little, and took the weakest into hospital.

Then one day, during the time we saw the sick, a nurse who was working with me and was also a prisoner said to me: 'Doctor, I have heard that someone has denounced you for being too softhearted in dealing with the prisoners. They are threatening to extend your sentence by fifteen years.' My companion was a serious person, well-acquainted with camp life, and therefore I was terrified by what she said. I had already been condemned for three years, which were now coming to an end, and I was counting the months and days that separated me from my long-awaited freedom. And suddenly – another fifteen years!

I didn't sleep the whole night, and when I went to work in the morning, the nurse shook her head sadly at the sight of my haggard face. After we had seen the sick, she said in a hesitant manner: 'Doctor, I would like to give you some advice, but I'm afraid that you will laugh at me.' 'Please, tell me.' I replied. 'In Penza, the town where I was born, lives a woman called Matrionushka. The Lord has given her a special power of prayer, and once she begins to pray for someone, her prayer is answered without fail. Many people call upon her, and she refuses no one's request. You, too, should ask for her help.' I smiled sadly: 'While my letter is getting to her, they'll have time to give me fifteen more years.'

With some embarrassment the nurse replied: 'There's no need to write, in fact. You just call her.' 'Call her?' I said. 'From here? But she lives hundreds of kilometres away from us!' 'I knew you would laugh at me', she said, 'but it's true that she does hear people from everywhere. Do this: when you go out for a stroll in the evening, lag a little behind everyone else and cry out three times: "Matrionushka, help me! I am in trouble!" She will hear you and help you.'

Although all this seemed strange to me and a bit like magic, nevertheless, when I went out for my evening walk, I did what my assistant said. One day passed, a week, a month . . . They didn't send for me. Meanwhile, certain changes took place in the administration of the camp: one person was dismissed, another appointed . . . Finally, six months went by, and the day of my departure from camp arrived. When they issued me my papers at the commandant's office, I asked them to give me a warrant to stay in the town where Matrionushka lived, since before I cried out to her I had promised myself that, if she helped me, I would remember her each day in my prayers and make my first task on leaving the camp to go and thank her.

Having obtained my papers, I heard that two young men, who were also being set free, were going to the town to which I had been given permission to go. I joined up with them and we set off together. On the way I began to question my companions to see if they knew about Matrionushka. 'We know her very well', they replied. 'But then everyone knows her – both in town and throughout the district. We could take you to her if you really needed it, but we live in the country, not in town, and very much want to get home. This is what you should do. When you get there, just ask the first person you meet where Matrionushka lives, and they will point it out to you.'

On arrival I did as my companions had said and made enquiries of a young boy, who was the first person I met. 'Go down this street', he told me, 'and then, by the post office, turn down the lane. Matrionushka lives there, in the third house.' With trepidation I approached the house, intending to knock on the door. But it was not shut and opened easily. Standing on the threshold, I looked around the almost empty room. In the middle stood a table, and on the table was a large box.

'May I come in?' I asked in a fairly loud voice. 'Come in, Seriozhenka', replied a voice from the box. I gasped with surprise, and then hesitantly moved forward towards the voice. Looking into the box, I saw inside it a tiny woman, lying there motionless on the table. She was blind and had undeveloped rudimentary arms and legs. But her face was astonishingly radiant and gentle. After greeting her, I asked, 'How did you know my name?' 'How could I not know it?' came her faint but clear, pure voice. 'You called me, and I prayed to God for you. That is how I know you. Sit down, be my guest.'

I sat for a long time with Matrionushka. She told me that she had been taken ill in childhood with some sort of disease and had stopped growing or being able to move about. At birth she was able to see, but she caught smallpox when she was two years old and lost her sight. Her family was poor, and her mother packed her into a little tub when she went to work and took her to the church. There she would put the tub with the little girl in it on a bench, and would leave her until the evening. Lying there in the tub Matrionushka would hear all of the church services and all the sermons. The priest felt sorry for her, and would spend time with her. The parishioners also felt sorry for the child and would bring her things, now a little bite to eat, now a piece of clothing, while others simply caressed her and made her comfortable.

And so in this way she grew up in a deeply spiritual atmosphere of prayer.

Then the two of us talked about other things – about the purpose of life, about faith, about God. And as I listened, I was staggered by the wisdom of her judgement and by her spiritual discernment. As I was saying goodbye, she said: 'When you stand before the altar of God, remember the servant of God, Matrona.' At that time the idea of episcopacy had never occurred to me, and I was not yet even a priest. Of herself, however, she said that she would die in prison. Sitting beside her, I realized that in front of me lay not simply a sick woman, but someone who was great in the eyes of God. I found it hard to tear myself away, it was so good and comforting to be with her, and I promised myself that I would visit her again as soon as possible.

But it didn't happen. Soon they took Matrionushka off to prison, in Moscow, where she died.[22]

The poem below was written on 27 November 1948 in a Soviet labour camp by a prisoner, **Peter Savitsky** (1895–1968). It is addressed to Bishop Athanasius Sakharov (1887–1962), who was consecrated a bishop in the perilous year 1921. Within a few months – March 1922 – he was arrested, and of the remaining forty years of his life he spent over thirty either in prison, or in exile or in a labour camp. Throughout it all he maintained an amazing tranquillity of spirit.

## Snowy Russia

How very much your friendship gave me:
The evenings were miraculously transformed,
You made them rich with tales of duties, service,
Of cities, centuries, heroic deeds.

Your store of knowledge is incredible:
Through your mild words you bring to life again

The many featured scenes of Holy Russia,
Each ancient structure with its age and stones.

I listen; and it seems to me that now
The vision of my mind grows sharp and deep,
In minutes I have lived through centuries,
And snowy Russia spreads before my eyes.

# Endnotes

Every effort has been made to trace the copyright holder of material used. Darton, Longman and Todd would be glad to hear from any it has not been able to trace, so that due acknowledgement can be given in future editions of the book.

1 Robert Llewelyn: *With Pity not with Blame: reflections on the writings of Julian of Norwich and the Cloud of Unknowing* (London, 1982), pp.1f

2 Julia de Beausobre: *Flame in the Snow* (London, 1945), pp.116f

3 'A hermit of the nineteenth century' Moscow Journal (1903), quoted in Valentine Zander: *St Seraphim of Sarov*, English translation by Sister Gabriel Anne ssc of unpublished French original (New York, 1975)

4 Throughout this passage there is a play on the Russian word *mir*, which means both world and peace (the latter in the sense of the Hebrew *shalom*)

5 Fyodor Dostoevsky: *The Brothers Karamazov*, English translation by Richard Pevear and Larissa Volokhonsky (Vintage Books, London and New York, 1992), p.xi

6 This chapter previously appeared in much the same form as 'One of a great cloud of witnesses: Father Pavel Florensky', *Sourozh: a journal of Orthodox life and thought*, viii, (1994), pp.28–38

7 See *Rodina* (Moscow, June 1944), pp.44–9

8 From Ivan Turgenev: 'A living relic', in Gleb Struve, ed.: *Russian Stories* (London, 1961)

9 See *Soboryanye* (Moscow, 1960)

10 David Magarshak, trans.: *Nicholai Leskov: selected tales* (London, 1961)

11 Leo Tolstoy: *Master and Man, and other tales*, Everyman Library (London, 1963), pp.84–112

12 Stephen Graham: *With the Russian Pilgrims to Jerusalem* (London, 1914)

13 *The Tablet* (16 August 1975)

14 Quoted by John Maynard in *The Russian Peasant and other studies* (New York, 1962), p.265

15 Anatoli Levitin quoted in Mikhail Bordeaux: *Patriarch and Prophets*, Keston Book no.2 (Oxford, 1975), p.291

16 Yevgeny Yevtushenko: *A Precocious Autobiography* (London, 1965), pp.24f

17 Evgenia Ginzburg: *Into the Whirlwind* (London, 1967), pp.312f. Reproduced with permission, Harper Collins Publishers Ltd

18 'Osip Mendelstam, 1891–1938: how the *gulag* killed a genius', *Observer Review* (2 August 1992). Reproduced with permission

19 Lev Kopelev: *No Jail for Thought* (London, 1977), pp.152–6

20 From *Testimony: the memoirs of Dmitri Shostakovich* pp.148f, edited by Solomon Volkov, translated by Antonia W. Bouis (Hamish Hamilton, 1979) © 1979 by S. Volkov, British language translation © 1979 by Hamish Hamilton Ltd, English language translation © 1979 by Harper and Row Publishers. Reproduced by permission, Penguin Books Ltd

21 Vladimir Soloukhin: *Searching for icons in Russia* (London, 1967), pp.107–11. Reproduced by permission of The Harvill Press

22 *Sourozh: a journal of Orthodox life and thought*, xv, (1984/1), pp. 19–22. Reproduced with permission

# Source texts and further reading

The following source texts, from each of which in their relevant chapters material is quoted, are gratefully acknowledged. Italics in such quotations have been added by the author to highlight phrases or expressions that are key to the meaning of the passage.

Chapter 1:
Valentine Zander: *St Seraphim of Sarov*, English translation by Sister Gabriel Anne ssc of unpublished French original (New York, 1975)

Chapter 2:
Nikolai F. Feodorov: *What was man created for? The philosophy of the common task* (Lausanne, 1990)
G. M. Young: *Nikolai F. Fedorov: an introduction* (Belmont, MA, 1979)

Chapter 3:
Fyodor Dostoevsky: *The Brothers Karamazov*, translated by Richard Pevear and Larissa Volokhonsky (Quartet Books Ltd, London, 1990).
Joseph Frank: *Dostoevsky* (Princeton, 1995)
Leonid Grossman: *Dostoevsky: a critical biography* (London, 1974)
Konstantin Mochulsky: *Dostoevsky: his life and work* (Princeton, 1967)

The following additional references are given for those who wish to pursue some of the themes in this book, but who do not know Russian.

Introduction:
Nicholas Arseniev: *Russian Piety* (London, 1964)
G. P. Fedotov: *The Russian Religious Mind*, in 2 volumes (Cambridge, MA, 1946)
Georges Florovsky: *The Ways of Russian Theology*, Collected Works, vols 5 and 6 (Belmont, MA, 1974)
Pierre Pascal: *The Religion of the Russian People* (New York, 1976)

Chapter 1:
Vsevolod Rochau: *Saint Séraphim: Sarov et Divéyevo* (Bellefontaine, 1987)

Chapter 4:
Victor Bychov: *The Aesthetic Face of Being: Art in the theology of Pavel Florensky* (New York, 1993)
Robert Slensinski: *Pavel Florensky: a metaphysics of love* (New York, 1984)

# Short word-list of Russian terms

Transliterated Russian tends to be spelled differently following a range of publishing conventions. This list of words with brief definitions is given as they are usually spelled in this book, though exceptions may be found according to sources quoted.

| | |
|---|---|
| *apparatchiki* | functionary of the Communist Party |
| *babushka* | grandmother, older woman in the community |
| *barin* | nobleman |
| *batiouchka* | 'little' father, a term of endearment |
| *boyarin* | a member of the old Russian aristocracy next in rank to the ruling princes, before the reforms of Peter the Great |
| *dacha* | summer cottage |
| *iurodivi* | fool for Christ |
| *katorga* | hard-labour camp |
| *katorzhinik* | convict |
| *khristianin* | Christian |
| *klobouk* | monastic head-dress |
| *krestianin* | peasant |
| *kulich* | a traditional Russian Easter cake |
| *lapti* | sandals made of wood |
| *matouchka* | 'little' mother |
| *mir* | world, also peace |
| *narod* | people |
| *neschastyi* | unfortunate, unhappy |
| *nyanya* | nanny or nanna: a close familiar carer |
| *nyerodstvo* | unrelatedness, alienation |
| *podvig* | ascetic exploit; heroic deed done for Christ's sake |
| *prozorlivost* | spiritual discernment |
| *rasputitsa* | season of bad roads |
| *rod* | clan, line of ancestry, kinship |
| *rodina* | native land |
| *rodno* | dear, close to the heart |
| *rodstvo* | kinship |

| | |
|---|---|
| *rozhdenie* | a common ancestor to those in a *rod* |
| *rozhdestvo* | Christmas |
| *samizdat* | underground press |
| *sobirat* | to gather together |
| *sobor* | a cathedral (of which there may be several in a diocese) or the central church of a monastery in which the Sunday Liturgy is celebrated |
| *sobornost* | organic catholicity or gathered fellowship of the Church whereby the many members while retaining full personal freedom experience the living unity of the Body of Christ; Greek equivalent: *koinonia* |
| *starets* | spiritual elder; spiritual guide recognized by the people because of a closeness to God; not a position of hierarchy or status |
| *strastotpertsi* | passion-bearers |
| *umilenie* | compunction, tender loving-kindness of heart; Greek equivalent *katanyxis* |
| *zabyt* | to forget |
| *zhalost* | pity |

With thanks to Wendy Robinson, Bishop Kallistos, Bishop Vasily, and the Reverend Dr Ann Shukman, for the compilation of this list.